BONDS & THE MONEY MARKET SIMPLIFIED

Martin Torosian

MTA Financial Services Corporation

Library of Congress Cataloging-in-Publication Data

Torosian, Martin
Bonds, money market instruments
Includes index.
Securities -- United States
ISBN 0-9603592-5-7

TOROSIAN, MARTIN
Bonds & the Money Market Simplified
MTA Financial Services Corporation

This publication is designed to provide accurate and authoritative information in regard to the subject matter covered. It is sold with the understanding that the publisher is not engaged in rendering legal, accounting, and other professional services. If legal advice or other expert assistance is required, the services of a competent professional person should be sought.

From a Declaration of Principles jointly adopted by a committee of the American Bar Association and a Committee of Publishers and Associations.

Other books by Martin Torosian:
Legal Transfer Guide
Securities Transfer -- Principles and Procedures
Modern Stock Market Handbook - 2nd Edition
The Margin Book
Dynamics of the Options Market
Series 7 Made Ridiculously Simple
What Every Banker Should Know About Broker-Dealers
The Securities Handbook
Foreign Securities Handbook
The Foreign Securities Transfer
How to Save Money on Insurance

Printed in the United States of America
10 9 8 7 6 5 4

MTA Financial Services Corporation
670 Newcastle Drive
Lake Forest, Illinois 60045
(847)234-9050 (847)234-9051

CONTENTS

CHAPTER TEN
THE SECURITIES OF THE UNITED STATES GOVERNMENT, 141

CHAPTER ELEVEN
FEDERAL AGENCY OBLIGATIONS, 160

CHAPTER TWELVE
THE MONEY MARKET INSTRUMENTS, 178

CHAPTER THIRTEEN
MORTGAGE-BACKED SECURITIES, 207

PREFACE

The explosive and unprecedented growth in the bond and the money market has necessitated the publication of this book. The so-called fixed-income securities have acquired different meaning with esoteric products and opportunities for professionals and investors. What used to be a simple investment activity in which customers used to invest a sum of money in a debt obligation with the promise to get it back at maturity has become an extremely complex and sophisticated experience. The market proliferates with products that were unknown a decade ago. The products are numerous with new ones being created practically overnight. The investor is often confused and frustrated in his attempt to satisfy his investment objectives.

The purpose of this book is to provide an up-to-date description of all the securities in the bond and the money market. The objective is to shed new light on the full range of investment possibilities that are now open to investors. The book provides information on how to purchase, sell, and process corporate and municipal bonds, U.S. government and federal agency securities, mortgage-backed securities, and short-term money market instruments, with the latest information on the procedures in the organized stock exchanges as well as the over-the-counter trading operation.

In the last several years, changes in the interest rate levels have occurred much more frequently than ever before. It has become increasingly difficult for the professional and the investor to forecast the direction of interest rates. Unlike the market for equity securities, the prices of bonds and the money market instruments are affected and influenced by current interest rates in the U.S. economy. To aid the investor in his attempt to understand the volatility of interest rates, we have included a chapter that discusses the activities of the Federal Reserve System which has played a dominant role in formulating and implementing the monetary policies of the United States.

Throughout the book the investor or the professional is referred to by the pronoun *he*. This is used for the sake of brevity and not as a gender preference.

Martin Torosian

CHAPTER ONE

CORPORATE BONDS

Corporate bonds are debt securities that represent a contractual obligation of the corporation to the bondholder. Bonds are not ownership securities. The bondholder does not have the right to participate in the affairs or the earnings of the corporation and he has no voting privileges. By lending a sum of money to the corporation, he receives a contractual promise that he will be paid interest at definite intervals specified in the agreement and that the corporation will repay the debt at the maturity of the contract. This promise to pay is not contingent on the earnings of the corporation. When purchasing a bond, the bondholder receives prior claims over all other types of securities of the corporation. In the event of a dissolution, the bondholder's claims will be satisfied first.

Bonds may constitute long-term or short-term borrowings of the corporation. If the life of the funded debt is less than five years, it is generally called a *note*. If it exceeds five years, then it is a *bond*. Bonds may be issued with certain covenants that are indicated in the bond indenture. There are two types of indentures: open-end and closed-end. Through an open-end indenture, a corporation may issue new bonds on the same property. The new bond will have the same claims as the bonds issued previously with no priority of claims. Through the closed-end indenture, a corporation may issue new bonds on the same property but the second bond will be junior to the one issued previously. In both cases, the face value of the bond may not exceed the value of the property pledged.

TYPES OF CORPORATE BONDS

Bonds are difficult to classify. There are many factors that enter into their classification—their legal nature, maturity, method of payments, transferability, and so on. Because of their varying characteristics, the method of grouping them into classes is substantially different from that of stocks. The principal factors used in classifying stocks are the rights of the stockholder, his voting privileges, and his claims over the assets of the corporation or the degree of control in the management. Bonds, on the other hand, have different purposes as basis for their creation and classification. A minor change in the contract provision of the security places the bond in a different category.

There are five general ways of classifying bonds:

1. *Purpose*. Classified according to their purpose: construction bonds, school bonds, etc.
2. *Character*. Classified according to their character: secured bonds and unsecured bonds.
3. *Obligor*. Classified as to the issuer: municipal bonds, corporate bonds, foreign government bonds, etc.
4. *Payment*. Classified as to the method of payment of the principal: redeemable bonds, serial bonds, sinking fund bonds, etc.
5. *Transferability*. Classified as to the transferability of the issue: registered bonds, coupon-bearer bonds.

Bonds also are classified according to maturity dates or dates of issuance.

Term Bonds

The term bond will have only one date of maturity.

Serial Bond

The serial bond will have different dates of maturity.

Series Bond

The series bond has different dates of issuance. The series bonds may or may not have the same maturity date.

Refunding

This is the process through which the corporation redeems an old bond by using the proceeds of the sale of a new bond.

Refinancing

This is the process through which the corporation redeems an old bond by using the proceeds of the sale of an equity security.

Ballooning

Ballooning is a technique through which a corporation will reduce the debt at various intervals. This will give an added protection to the bondholder. Ballooning may be at different maturity dates or at different interest rates.

EXAMPLE

Principal Amount	*Maturity*	*Interest Rates*
$400,000	1995	6¼ %
$395,000	1997	6¾ %

Amortization

Through the process of amortization, the debt on the bond instrument is set aside during the life of the security. This may be accomplished through a serial bond or a sinking fund bond.

The following is a discussion of different types of corporate bonds:

INCOME BONDS

Income bonds carry maturity dates between 150 to 200 years. There is no commitment on the part of the corporation to pay the principal or the interest. The interest is paid only if the corporation earns income. Income bonds are generally issued after a corporation files bankruptcy and the trustee in receivership attempts to reorganize the corporation by offering Income Bonds to the previous bondholders. Income Bonds are also called Adjustment Bonds. They are traded with no accrued interest.

EXAMPLE

The trustee may offer an Income Bond of $1,300 at 10 percent interest to the holder of a previous bond of $1,000 at 6 percent. If the reorganized corporation succeeds in its recovery and becomes profitable, the holder of the Income Bond will have more of the principal at a higher interest rate.

SINKING FUND BONDS

In issuing a Sinking Fund Bond the corporation sets aside an annual reserve of capital to retire the bond. Annual reserves are scheduled in such a way that over the years sufficient funds will be accumulated to retire the bond at maturity. This can be a regularly scheduled payment or payments made on a periodic basis. The funds will be deposited at a trustee bank. The funds may be invested in money market instruments earning interest.

CALLABLE BONDS

A callable bond may be called or redeemed by the corporation at any time before the maturity date.

A corporation may also purchase its bonds in the open market to reduce its debt obligation, especially when the bonds are traded at prices below the redemption value. The call may be partial or total, depending on the corporation's financial requirements. The terms of the bond indenture must indicate, however, that the corporation has the right to call the bond.

This callable privilege is important for corporate finance. At the time of the issuance of the bonds, the directors of a corporation are inclined to offer attractive high interest rates to the bondholders during the life of the bond. Interest rates may decline, and the corporation with an improved credit position finds it advantageous to retire the bond with high interest rates by utilizing funds raised through the issuance of a new bond with lower interest rates.

If the bond is in registered form, the holder will receive a notice of the call from the corporation. If it is in bearer form, the corporation utilizes the facilities of a newspaper in announcing the call.

DISCOUNT BONDS

The discount bonds are bonds with a market value lower than the face value of the security. For discount bonds, the nominal rate is lower than the current yield, which is lower than the yield to maturity, which is lower than the yield to call. This is true for both corporate and municipal bonds.

PREMIUM BONDS

Premium bonds are bonds with a market value higher than the face value. For premium bonds, the nominal yield is higher than the current yield, which is higher than the yield to maturity, which is higher than the yield to call. This is true for both corporate and municipal bonds.

BONDS WITH WARRANTS ATTACHED

The corporation may issue bonds with warrants attached. The warrant will grant a privilege to the holder to purchase shares at a specified price during a specified period of time. Bonds with warrants attached will have low interest rates and less restrictive indenture provisions.

SECURED BONDS

A secured bond has a specific lien on the issuer's assets and property with respect to the bond obligation.

UNSECURED BONDS OR DEBENTURES

Debentures are not secured by any property or asset of the issuer. It is only secured by the good faith of the corporation.

SUBORDINATED DEBENTURES

Subordinated debentures are unsecured bonds but junior in ranking. At the time of the dissolution of the corporation, the bondholder of a subordinated debenture is satisfied only after all creditors have been satisfied. Subordinated debentures usually pay high interest rates and may be convertible into common shares.

EQUIPMENT TRUST BONDS

An Equipment Trust Bond is a type of bond generally issued by airline companies or railroad corporations. In issuing these bonds, the issuer secures a specific piece of equipment—railroad car or an aircraft. The trustee bank will lease the equipment to the corporation at a rental fee that will coincide with the scheduled payments of interest at different series of maturities. When the debt has matured and the equipment is paid for, the ownership will be transferred to the corporation. There are certain requirements as to the proper maintenance of the equipment and the identification as to its ownership. Equipment Trust is also known as Philadelphia Plan.

A company will issue equipment trust bonds if it has difficulty in purchasing the equipment outright. The financing is facilitated, therefore, by mortgaging the cars or the aircrafts and selling bonds secured by the mortgage.

COMPOUND COUPON BONDS

The compound coupon bond pays interest at the time of maturity. Interest is not paid during the life of the bond. The issuer will pay the interest compounded at maturity with the payment of the principal amount.

ZERO BONDS

In issuing a zero bond, the issuer sells the bond at a discount price from the face value but pays no interest during the life of the bond. The difference between the cost of the purchase and redemption value will be the bondholder's profit. Example: The bondholder purchases a zero bond of $1,000 face value for $200. He will receive $1,000 at maturity. His profit will be $800 with no interest accrued during the term of the bond.

Tax laws narrow the advantages available to corporate issuers of zero bonds. Corporations are entitled to accrete annual interest deductions for a zero bond originally issued below face value, even though some or all of the interest is not actually paid until maturity. Regulations, however, require a compounding computation over the life of the bond. As a result, the discount would not be amortized on a straight-line basis. Instead, the issuer's first year tax deduction would be based on the issue price of the security, with each successive year's expense increasing to reflect the compounded interest.

EXAMPLE

$1,000 eight-year zero coupon bond issued at $304 to yield 15% to maturity. The interest deductions would be calculated as follows (based on monthly compounding):

Year	*Old Tax Rules*	*New Tax Rules*
1	87	49
2	87	57
3	87	65
4	87	77
5	87	89
6	87	103
7	87	119
8	87	137
	$696	$696
	(1,000 − 304 = 696)	(1,000 − 304 = 696)

When purchasing zero corporate bonds, the investor must pay income tax on an accrued basis even though interest payments are not received. To avoid paying income tax, the investor can use zero corporate bonds as investment vehicles for tax-deferred accounts, such as IRA, Keogh, and pension funds.

There are two types of zero bonds: *original issue zero bond* and *synthetic zero bond*. The original issue zero bond is a bond sold at a discount from the face value. The investor receives no interest during the life of the bond. At maturity, he will receive the full face value. The discount price is established to provide a certain return at maturity. The issuer will benefit because, through the zero bond, the issuer borrows money without having to pay interest until maturity.

The synthetic zero bond is created by a dealer. The dealer will take a U.S. Treasury bond and strip the interest coupon payment from the principal. The principal portion is placed at a bank for the account of the holder. The U.S. Treasury will issue interest on the Treasury bond semi-annually. Each semi-annual interest payment becomes a zero bond for specific dates in the future. These are zero bonds because the customer receives no interest payments. His gain will be the difference in money between the discounted selling price and the value of the bond at maturity.

EUROBONDS

Eurobonds are bonds issued by American corporations but sold and distributed exclusively in foreign jurisdictions.

OPTION BONDS OR PUT BONDS

Option bonds are long-term bonds allowing flexibility to the bondholder to redeem the bond at its face value at the first anniversary of the issuance of the bond or every anniversary thereafter. The schedule for redemption may vary. Some corporations offer a redemption privilege a year later, some six months, some two years later, and so on.

TIGRS AND CATS

TIGRS and CATS are unusual names with unusual features. These instruments, created and issued by various investment firms, represent investments in long-term U.S. Treasury bonds. TIGRS and CATS are acronyms. They stand for:

TIGR = Treasury Investment Growth Receipt

CATS = Certificate of Accrual of Treasury Securities

Instead of the investor purchasing the U.S. Treasury bonds and receiving semi-annual interest on them, the securities firm will purchase the bonds for the investor.

The procedure is as follows:

1. The securities firm will turn the U.S. Treasury bonds into a series of zero coupon investments by "stripping" the coupons from the bonds and selling the coupons and the stripped bonds separately.
2. The coupon and the Treasury bond thus become separate securities sold at a discount price, similar to a discounted U.S. Treasury bill.
3. Both the coupon and the stripped bond pay no interest until the maturity dates.
4. This technique transforms a long-term bond with reinvestment risk into a series of securities with no reinvestment risk.
5. The securities firm will pool the stripped coupons and bonds according to their dates of maturity. The maturity is every six months over the life of the bond.

6. The securities firm will then offer investors receipts for a portion of each pool for each maturity date.

7. The receipt is only a promise to pay a specific yield at a specific date in the future, just like a futures contract.

8. The securities firm has no obligations to provide a secondary market for these receipts.

9. The IRS expects the customer to pay interest on accrued income earned through the life of the instrument, even though the customer has not received any income on the investment. These securities are ideal investment vehicles for tax-deferred accounts, such as IRAs or pension accounts, because they enable the investor to defer paying income tax on unrealized interest income.

Advantages of TIGRS and CATS

1. Fixed interest paid at maturity.
2. Interest payments may be reinvested during the life of the security.
3. The securities are backed by U.S. Treasury bonds.

Disadvantages

1. If interest rates climb during the life of the security, fixed rates may be undesirable.
2. Selling the security before the maturity date may be difficult.
3. Income taxes on interest must be paid annually (except for tax-deferred accounts), even though interest is not received.
4. The customer gets a receipt for the U.S. Treasury bond or the coupon but not the actual security itself. These receipts are not secured by the good faith of the U.S. Treasury.
5. Brokerage commissions are computed into the yield.

REGISTERED AS TO PRINCIPAL ONLY

Registered as to principal applies to registered coupon bonds in which the principal portion of the bond is registered in the name of the bondholder, but the attached coupon is in bearer form. The coupon is negotiable and payable to the bearer, and the registered portion is transferable only by the holder of record.

REGISTERED AS TO PRINCIPAL AND INTEREST

Registered as to principal and interest refers to registered bonds with no coupons attached. Both the principal and interest are payable to the bondholder at specified dates. The transferable aspect of a registered bond makes its market price slightly lower than the corresponding coupon bond of the same issue.

COUPON BONDS

Coupon bonds are bearer instruments similar to a monetary unit. The coupon bond is payable to the bearer, and the interest is payable upon presentation of the coupon. Coupon bond titles are passed by the delivery of the instruments to the buyer. Coupons attached to the bond bear definite identifications, such as the name of the issuer, the serial number, and the bond number.

CONVERTIBLE BONDS

The convertible bond provides an opportunity for the bondholder to convert the bond certificate into another class of stock of the same corporation. These bonds are generally convertible into the common stock and occasionally into the preferred stock of the company.

A corporation creates a convertible bond to enhance the bond's marketability. A holder of a convertible bond is in an advantageous position to convert his bond into common shares when the market price of the common share exceeds the value of the bond. This is an important privilege for the investor. He has a contractual commitment by the company in holding the bond and yet may participate in the affairs of the corporation if he so desires. This dual privilege is terminated, however, at the time of the conversion. Due to the fact that interest on bonds are "before income tax" expense to the corporation and dividends on stocks are "after income tax payment," the corporation will increase its income tax liability after the convertible bonds are converted.

The convertible feature of the bond makes it possible to have price fluctuations parallel with the price of the stock into which the bond may be converted. Parity exists when the market value of the convertible bond is equal to the market value of the converted shares.

The following formula may be used to determine the parity of the common stock with the market value of the bond.

$$\begin{pmatrix}\text{Price per}\\ \text{share of}\\ \text{common}\\ \text{at parity}\end{pmatrix} = \frac{\begin{pmatrix}\text{Market value}\\ \text{of the bond}\end{pmatrix} \times \begin{pmatrix}\text{Conversion price}\\ \text{of common}\end{pmatrix}}{\text{Face value of the bond}}$$

EXAMPLE:

A convertible bond of Bee Corp. has a conversion price of \$30. The market value of the bond is \$110. The price per share of common at parity will be:

$$\frac{1{,}100 \times 30}{1{,}000} = 33$$

The bond instrument indicates the conversion ratio, various limits for conversion, the time period for conversion, and the class of security with which the bonds may be converted.

Convertible bonds may not be issued until the security into which they may be converted is legally created. They usually pay a lower rate of interest than debenture bonds; therefore, it will cost the corporation less to finance the issuance of these bonds.

The logic in purchasing convertible bonds is simple: When interest rates decline, and the prospects for stocks continue to be good, the convertible bonds will offer high yields with the opportunity to participate in the appreciation of the underlying security. If the stock goes down, the price of the convertible bond will not fall below the price of an ordinary bond. With convertible bonds, there is, therefore, a double protection. Because of this feature, however, the convertible bonds are often sold at prices higher than the conversion value.

The convertible bonds may be called by the corporation. A decline in interest rates will increase the risk of a call as the corporation seeks to refinance its debt at more favorable rates.

Convertible bonds have the following classifications:

1. Callable convertible bonds as discussed above.

2. Convertible bonds with a sinking fund provision. This permits the corporation to redeem a certain number of bonds each year.

3. Convertible bonds with a variable conversion ratio. The number of common shares that a convertible bond can be exchanged for varies at different times over the life of the bond.

4. Convertible bonds with an interest rate linked to the dividend rate on the common. While the interest rate is adjustable, it will always be higher on an annual basis than the dividend on the stock.

REAL ESTATE BONDS

Real estate bonds offer regular coupon interests plus part of any appreciation on real estate properties.

STABILIZED BONDS

Stabilized bonds are a type of bond financing in which the method of payment of the obligation depends upon the purchasing power of the dollar. When borrowing funds, a corporation promises to pay the obligation off in amounts equal to the purchasing power of the dollar at the time of maturity. The objective of these bonds is to stabilize the debt obligation by taking all the elements of economics into consideration, so that at the time of maturity the purchasing value of the dollar will remain the same as it was at the time of the issuance of the bond.

Because this type of financing is extremely difficult to administer, it has not achieved much popularity over the years.

GOLD BONDS

Gold bond is a class of bonds where payment is made in gold coins. Before 1933, most bonds were payable in gold as the lawful money of the United States. Congress repealed this, as it did other "currency" bonds. At present, all bonds are payable in the legal tender of the country.

PERPETUAL BONDS

Perpetual bonds are bonds without any maturity dates. They run perpetually and resemble annuity bonds. This type of bond is generally callable at the option of the issuing organization. Examples of this class are rare in the United States, but some prominent foreign examples are the English "Consols" and French "Rentes."

COLLATERAL TRUST BONDS

Collateral trust bonds are secured by a lien on a pool of securities that are held by a trustee or a trust company as collateral. This type of bond is largely found in holding companies where the securities of a subsidiary company are used as collateral in the creation of a bond by the parent corporation.

RECEIVERS' CERTIFICATES

The receivers' certificates are created to provide funds for the operation of a company under receivership. These are short-term notes authorized by the court. They are largely unsecured bonds and rely on the general credit of the company.

PURCHASE MONEY BONDS

Purchase money bonds generally are used for real estate purposes although their utilization in corporate finance is not uncommon. Purchase money mortgage is established between a purchaser of real estate and its seller to secure the unpaid balance of the property. The bonds are secured by the mortgage. The funds derived from the sale of the bonds are used to purchase the property. In the case of corporate finance, mortgage money bonds are used by a company about to be acquired by another company. They will be secured by the stock of the company being acquired.

INTERIM BONDS

Interim bonds are temporary bond certificates exchangeable into definitive ones after they are engraved by the bank note company. If at the time of the underwriting, the company does not have the permanent bond certificates available, it will issue temporary certificates.

EXTENDED BONDS

In the event that the company does not have the necessary funds to redeem the bonds at the time of maturity, it may elect to postpone the maturity of the bonds without changing the security or other provisions of the bonds by using extended bonds. The bond certificate will bear a statement indicating this extension privilege of the corporation.

DIVISIONAL BONDS

Divisional bonds are common in the railroad industry, where they are taken as the obligations of a division or branch of the railroad system. In their original form, they may have been the bonds of a company later acquired by another company. The parent company leaves the bonds of the subsidiary company undisturbed calling them divisional or sometimes sectional bonds.

ASSUMED BONDS

In acquiring another company through an exchange of stocks, a company sometimes prefers to assume the obligations and the liabilities of the company being acquired. The bonds of the latter, therefore, are assumed by the parent company and are called assumed bonds.

JOINT BONDS

Joint bonds are the joint obligations of two or more companies. They are largely secured by different assets of the debtor companies. These are popular in railroad financing in which the proceeds of the sale of the bonds have been utilized to provide joint facilities, such as terminals and bridges, for several companies.

GUARANTEED BONDS OR INDORSED BONDS

The payment and interest of these bonds are guaranteed by another company. This type of bond is popular in both industrial and railroad financing where a company, having a financial interest in another company, guarantees the payment of the obligation of the debtor company.

PARTICIPATING BONDS

Participating bonds offer the bondholder an opportunity to share the profits of the company.

CONSOLIDATED BONDS

Consolidated bonds are secured by a combined mortgage of a group of properties. They also may indicate the consolidation of a group of a corporation's debt obligation into one.

CORPORATE BOND FUNDS

Corporate bond funds are mutual funds organized to invest in corporate bonds.

CURRENT COUPON BONDS

Current coupon bonds refer to bonds with coupon rates close to current interest bonds. They generally trade a few points above or below the face value of the bond.

CORPORATE NOTES

Corporate notes are securities with an initial maturity of five years or less. They may be secured or unsecured.

DOLLAR-DENOMINATED FOREIGN BONDS

Dollar-denominated foreign bonds are offered in the United States by non-American corporations. Trading practices are the same as those employed for American corporate bonds. The interest received is fully taxable at the federal, state, and local level.

COMMODITY-BACKED BONDS

Commodity backed bonds are corporate issues with a face value indexed to the prices of certain commodities.

STOCK-INDEXED BONDS

Stock-indexed bonds are corporate bonds with interest rates indexed to the trading volume of the New York Stock Exchange.

FLOATING RATE OR VARIABLE RATE BONDS

Variable rate bonds do not offer a set rate of interest. The interest rate is adjusted at regular intervals.

CHAPTER TWO

DISTRIBUTION OF CORPORATE BONDS TO THE PUBLIC

Unlike municipal general obligation bonds, corporate bonds are usually created through a negotiated underwriting method, although competitive underwriting is done occasionally.

TYPES OF UNDERWRITING

There are three types of offerings used to distribute the security to the public: A *Primary Offering* is when the proceeds of the sale go to the issuer; a *Secondary Offering* is when the proceeds go to a person other than the issuer; and a *Split Offering* is when the proceeds are divided between the issuer and another person.

The following are different types of procedures used to underwrite a corporate bond:

- ***Firm Commitment.*** "Firm commitment" underwriting is a type of underwriting in which the investment banker commits to purchase the entire issue at a set price from the issuer.

- ***Best Efforts.*** In a "best efforts" offering, the underwriter agrees to act as agent for the issuing entity. There is no commitment on the part of the underwriter to sell the entire issue, however. He will do his best to sell the bonds to the public, but the unsold portion will be returned to the issuer.

• ***All or Nothing.*** In an "all or nothing" underwriting, the corporation advises the underwriter to cancel the issue if all the bonds are not sold to the public. The customers' funds are held in escrow until the underwriting is completed.

• ***Competitive Underwriting.*** In a competitive underwriting method, the issuer accepts competitive bids from various underwriters and chooses the one with the most favorable price.

The procedure is as follows:

1. The issuer announces the creation of the security and invites investment bankers to submit their bids.
2. For a bond issue, a bid may cover the price of the issue and the interest rate.
3. The issuing entity will decide the winning bid, and the investment banker will then proceed to accept the security and offer it to the public, hopefully at a price higher than the bid price.

• ***Negotiated Underwriting.*** In a negotiated underwriting, the term of the offering is negotiated between the issuer and the investment banker.

THE UNDERWRITING PROCESS

The underwriting process starts when the corporation approaches an investment banking firm and offers to sell the bonds wholesale.

When deciding to underwrite the bonds, the investment banker will consider the following factors:

- The corporation's financial needs and the amount of money needed
- The type of business and the industry
- The quality of management and the purpose of issuing the security

The Procedure to Underwrite a Corporate Bond

1. After the agreement is made to underwrite the issue, the underwriter, with the help of the corporation, will file a Registration Statement with the Securities and Exchange Commission (SEC) under the Securities Act of 1933. If the bond is exempt from the registration requirement, the corporation must file an Indenture Qualification statement with the SEC.

2. If the total principal amount of the bond is in excess of $2 million, the corporation must also file a statement with the SEC under the Trust Indenture Act of 1939. Under this Act, the corporation is required to appoint a bank to act as trustee to assure the terms of the bond indenture and safeguard the interests of the bondholders. The trustee bank is required to file an annual report with the SEC, indicating its continued qualification to serve as trustee.

3. The SEC staff will examine the Registration Statement for at least 20 days. This 20-day period is called the "Cooling Off" period. If the staff at the SEC finds any omissions or misrepresentations in the Registration Statement, it will send a Deficiency Letter to the issuer. The effective date of the registration will be postponed until all the deficiencies are corrected. The SEC may issue a "stop order" to stop the registration process indefinitely.

4. If there are no deficiencies, the effective date will be the 20th calendar day after the Registration Statement has been filed.

5. The SEC may delay the effective date beyond the 20th calendar day if it has not completed the examination of the statement.

6. The SEC, in examining the Registration Statement, does not guarantee the adequacy or the accuracy of the Registration Statement or pass judgment on the quality or the merit of the security being offered. If there are any misrepresentations or inaccuracies in the Registration Statement, the purchasers have the right to sue the officers, the underwriters, the directors, and the potential insiders of the corporation for reimbursement of financial losses.

7. During the "Cooling Off" period, the corporation, with the help of the underwriter, will prepare a preliminary prospectus known as a *Red Herring*. This document will be an excerpt of the Registration Statement and will include a full disclosure as to the purpose of the underwriting, as well as the financial and operational conditions of the corporation. The preliminary prospectus will have all pertinent data, with the exception of the public offering price of the bond and the effective date. Both the preliminary and the final prospectus must have an SEC Disclaimer Statement. The Red Herring may be used to solicit indications of interest from prospective investors. It may not be used, however, to solicit purchase orders. The indication of interest may be used to establish the public offering price of the bond. The security may not be sold, and the customer is not allowed to make any commitments to purchase the bond, however. These are only indications that the customer *may* be interested in purchasing the security. The indication of interest is often called "circle."

8. During the "Cooling Off" period, a Purchase Agreement is signed between the issuer and the underwriter.

9. The underwriter will file the offering documents

with the Committee of Corporate Financing of the NASD. The Committee will review the underwriting spread and the compensation to the underwriters.

10. In addition to the registration requirements of the SEC, the issuer must also comply with state securities laws before the bonds are sold to the residents of those states. The filing with the securities commission of the state is usually done by the managing underwriter on behalf of the corporation. This procedure is known as the "Blue Sky" requirement.

11. The underwriter may either take the entire security position for himself or invite other investment bankers to form a syndicate. The first underwriter will be the managing underwriter and the others will be co-underwriters. The selection of the co-underwriters is made on the basis of traditional ties within the financial community. Each underwriter is allocated a number of bonds by the managing underwriter. The allocation is based on the distribution capabilities of the securities firm.

12. The managing underwriter will prepare the underwriting agreement or the syndicate letter to be signed by all the underwriters. The agreement will be signed on the effective date of the Registration Statement and must state the type of account on which the syndicate is formed. There are two types of underwriting accounts: an Eastern or United Account, and a Western or Divided Account. If the syndicate is formed in an Eastern account, the underwriters will be responsible for selling not only their allocated portion, but also the unsold portion of the other underwriters. In a Western account, each party will be responsible for his own portion of the commitment. In a Western account, an underwriter is not held responsible if another underwriter is unable to distribute his allocated amount. When the syndicate is broken in an Eastern account, the unsold portion is divided among the underwriters, based on their percentage of participation in the underwriting.

The syndicate letter may have a "market out" or a "drop out" provision that allows an underwriter to get out of the syndicate in the event the conditions become adverse and the underwriter would be unable to sell the bonds.

The syndicate letter will state the specific duties and responsibilities of the managing underwriter. The responsibilities include:

a. Choosing the co-underwriters
b. Selecting the selling group members
c. Stabilizing the market price of the security
d. Conducting sales meetings to ensure success of distributing the bonds to the public
e. Preparing the "Selected Dealer Agreement" that will disclose the amount of the dealer's concession

13. Before the effective date of the Registration Statement, the managing underwriter will arrange a meeting between the officers of the corporation and the members of the syndicate. This is called the "due diligence" meeting. At this meeting, the underwriter will prepare the final prospectus, discuss the terms of the Underwriting Agreement, and determine the public offering price of the security.

14. On the effective date, the security will be offered to the public. A final prospectus must be presented to all customers purchasing the bond. If the customer has not received a final prospectus, he will have the right to cancel the order. The customer may not purchase the bond on margin. The Federal Reserve does not allow margin transactions in a primary distribution until up to 30 days after the distribution of the security is completed.

15. The effective period of the Registration Statement is 90 days after the effective date for original primary issues and 40 days for additional distribution of registered securities. During this period, the broker is required to send a copy of the final prospectus within 48 hours after the trade is executed to customers purchasing the bond. This period is known as the "Quiet Period."

16. The managing underwriter may advertise the security in a newspaper or a periodical. This advertisement

is called the "tombstone." The tombstone is not a solicitation to sell nor an offer to buy the security.

17. On a given day, the managing underwriter will hold a meeting with the officers of the corporation. This is the "closing date." At this meeting, the underwriter will present a check to the corporation in exchange for securities. The difference between the public offering price and the proceeds to the corporation will be the *underwriting spread*. During the primary distribution, the underwriters and the selling group members must sell the bonds at the predetermined public offering price as principals with no commission charged to customers.

CHAPTER THREE

THE SECONDARY MARKET FOR CORPORATE BONDS

The secondary market for corporate bonds is the organized stock exchanges and the over-the-counter market. Securities firms will maintain inventory of bonds and the bond department may be divided into several specialized groups—utility bonds, industrial bonds, convertible bonds, etc.

In the process of selling a bond, the broker may act as agent and charge a commission, or he may act as the dealer and sell the bond from his inventory, charging no commissions. The difference between his cost of purchase and the sale price will be his profit or loss. The rule requires the broker–dealer to indicate whether he is acting as a broker or as a dealer on the trade confirmation ticket to the customer.

Corporate bonds are traded on a dollar basis rather than a yield basis. A point is equal to $10, and the fractions of a point are:

1/8 = $1.25

1/4 = $2.50

3/8 = $3.75

1/2 = \$5.00

5/8 = \$6.25

3/4 = \$7.50

7/8 = \$8.75

1 bond means \$1,000 face value or principal value or par value. The prices of bonds are quoted in two digits or in three digits.

The price 95 means it takes \$950 to purchase \$1,000 face value of bonds. The price 105 means it will cost the customer \$1,050 to purchase \$1,000 face value of bonds. When the market price is lower than the face value, that means the investor is purchasing the bond on *discount*; when the market value is higher than the face value, he is purchasing the bonds on *premium*.

95⅛ means

950 + 1.25 = \$951.25 to purchase \$1,000 face value of bond.

105⅞ means

1,050 + 8.75 = \$1,058.75 to purchase \$1,000 face value of bond.

When determining the market value of the bond, the investor must consider the short-term and long-term interest rates in the economy. The short-term interest rates tend to fluctuate more than long-term interest rates, and the market value of long-term bonds fluctuate more than the market value of the short-term bonds. The market price of a long-term discount bond fluctuates more than the market price of a premium bond.

If the corporate bond is listed on the New York Stock Exchange, it will be traded in the Bond Room. The procedure for trading is different from the trading of equity securities. There are no Specialists in the Bond Room, and bonds are divided into two groups: Active and Inactive. Active Bonds are traded in a Free Crowd where the broker is free to trade—that means he may withdraw from the Bond Ring if he is not interested in trading.

The Inactive Bonds are traded in the Cabinet or Can Crowd. Cards indicate the securities that are filed in cabinets. The color of the cards will indicate the type of order; e.g., Day order, 1 week order, 1 month order, GTC order, etc. When the broker in the Bond Crowd receives an order from the Order Room, he will go to the cabinet and try to match the order with a card in the cabinet. When he locates a card, he will call the broker whose name is on the card to go with him to the Bond Ring and make the transaction. If he does not find any card, he will file his own card in the cabinet.

If the broker is unable to make the transaction on the exchange floor, he may go to the over-the-counter market to make the trade. CRT terminals in the Order Room link various dealers in corporate bonds as market makers. The market maker will maintain an inventory of a group of bonds and offer the securities in the over-the-counter market. The broker's order room clerk will punch the keys on the CRT machine to see which market makers are interested in buying and selling a particular issue. He then will simply call the market maker, negotiate the price, and purchase the security.

THE CORPORATE BOND TABLES—BONDS LISTED ON THE STOCK EXCHANGE

The market quotations of bonds listed on the stock exchanges are reported in the following manner:

Bonds	*Cur Yld.*	*Vol.*	*High*	*Low*	*Net Close*	*Net Chg*
Att 8¾s 00	11	375	82¾	82¼	82½	+⅛
1	2	3	4	5	6	7

There are seven columns used for reporting:

Column 1. *The name of the bond, the year it matures, and the nominal interest rate.* These are American Tel & Tel bonds maturing in the year 2000. Only the last 2 digits of the year are printed. 1997 will appear as 97. 8¾ percent is the (nominal) interest rate. This means the corporation pays an annual interest of 8¾ % per each $1,000 face value of a bond.

Column 2. *The current yield* is the investor's percentage of return on his investment. It is computed by:

$$\frac{\text{Annual interest on 1 bond}}{\text{Current market value of 1 bond}} = \text{Current yield}$$

If the bond is a convertible bond, the current yield is not calculated.

Column 3. *Number of bonds traded.* This is expressed in $1,000. In the above example, there were $375,000 bonds traded.

Column 4. *High.* This is the highest execution price on that day. It is reported in two digits or in three digits. 82 means one has to pay $820 to purchase a bond with a face value of $1,000.

Column 5. *Low.* The lowest price for the day.

Column 6. *The closing price* of the day.

Column 7. *The net change* is the difference between yesterday's closing price and today's closing price. It is expressed as a percentage of the bond's $1,000 face value. In this example, the net change is +1/8. This means the bond's price has gone up $1.25 per $1,000 bond.

DETERMINATION OF THE MARKET PRICE

Nominal Rate

The nominal rate or yield is the rate specified on the face of the bond at the time of issuance:

EXAMPLE

$1,000 Bee Corp. 6% 1 – 1 – 2011

This means the bond with a face value of $1,000 will pay $60 in interest every year. The bondholder will receive the $60 in two installments—$30 and $30, with the last interest payment made at maturity. By looking at the maturity date, we can determine the dates when the holder expects to receive the interest checks. Since the bonds will mature on January 1, 2011, the interest payment dates will be on January 1 and on July 1.

The nominal interest rate will never change. But the interest rate in the general economy will change constantly. The market price of the bond in the secondary market will rise or decline based on current interest rates. When interest rates rise, the market price will go down and vice versa. To calculate the current market price, the bondholder will use the following formula:

$$\frac{\text{Nominal rate}}{\text{Current rate}} = \frac{X}{1{,}000}$$

X is the current market price of the bond.

EXAMPLE

$1,000 4¼%. Let us assume the current interest rate is 6½%, then the market value per $1,000 bond will be:

$$\frac{0.045}{0.065} = \frac{X}{1{,}000}\; X = \$692.31 \;.$$

It will cost the bondholder $692.31 to purchase a $1,000 bond in the secondary market when the current interest rate is 6½ %.

Calculation of Accrued Interest

For corporate and municipal bonds, the accrued interest is calculated on the basis of 30 calendar days in each month. The seller of the bond will receive accrued interest from the buyer that is calculated from the last interest payment day until the settlement date of the trade, but not including the day of settlement.

EXAMPLE

1. The customer sells $1,000 Bee Corp. 6% 1/1/2000 on Oct. 19, the settlement date.
2. Bee Corp. pays 6% interest on January 1 and July 1 as indicated by the maturity date of the bond.
3. The bondholder will, therefore, receive 6% of $1,000 every year in two installments—$30 in January and $30 in July.
4. On January 1, following this trade, the new buyer will receive $30 in interest from the issuing corporation.
5. $30 covers the last six-month period, but due to the fact that he was not the owner of the bond during the entire period of time, part of the $30 interest belongs to the seller in proportion to the period of his ownership of the security.
6. The buyer, therefore, must give the seller a portion of the interest payment. This portion is called the accrued interest.

7. To calculate the accrued interest for the above example:

a. the last interest payment date was July 1
b. July has 30 days
c. August has 30 days
d. September has 30 days
e. October, in this case, has 18 days, up to but not including the day of settlement.
f. Altogether, therefore, the seller must receive from the buyer accrued interest on the basis of 108 days.
g. The formula for calculating interest is:

$$\text{Interest} = \text{Principal} \times \frac{\text{Rate}}{100} \times \frac{\text{Time}}{360}$$

In this example:

$$\text{Interest} = 1{,}000 \times \frac{6}{100} \times \frac{108}{360} = \$18.00$$

$18.00 is due the seller, and will be charged to the buyer as part of his cost.

If the transaction was for a cash trade, the accrued interest will again be calculated in the same way. In this case, the settlement day of the trade will be the day of the trade. Therefore, the calculation will be from the last payment day until the day of the settlement (which is the trade day), but not including the day of settlement.

The following bond transactions will not carry accrued interests:

1. Income bonds
2. Bonds in a default status
3. Transactions in bonds executed five business days prior to an interest record day

EXAMPLE

The customer sells $1,000 Bee Corp. 6% 1/1/2000 on June 24. The settlement date will be July 1, which is also the interest payment date. Using the above formula, the accrued interest calculation will be:

January	30 days
February	30 days
March	30 days
April	30 days
May	30 days
June	30 days (up to the settlement day)
	180 days of interest

This is the full six months. No accrued interest will be given to the seller. He will receive his full interest check directly from the issuer.

If the maturity date of the bond is 1/15/2000, the month of January will have 16 days for accrued interest calculation purposes. In this example, if the customer sells the bond on March 20, the settlement date, he will receive accrued interest from the buyer calculated on the basis of 65 days—January has 16 days, February has 30, and March has 19.

CALCULATION OF YIELDS

Current Yield

To calculate the current yield of the bond, the bondholder will divide the annual interest by the current market price of the security.

EXAMPLE

$1,000 at 6%.

The market price per \$1,000 bond is \$892. This bond earns \$60 a year interest at the nominal rate of 6%.

$$\frac{\$60}{\$892} = 0.0672$$

The current yield is 6.72%.

Yield to Maturity

The yield to maturity determines the return on investment based on the nominal interest rate, the current market price of the bond, and the number of years to maturity. The bondholder will use a Yield Table to get the yield to maturity of a bond. If Yield Tables are not available, he may use the following formulas:

Bonds Sold at Discount from the Face Value

$$\text{Yield to maturity} = \frac{\left(\begin{array}{c}\text{Total dollar}\\ \text{amount of}\\ \text{annual interest}\\ \text{per one bond}\end{array}\right) + \left(\begin{array}{c}\text{Total discount}\\ \text{divided by the}\\ \text{number of years}\\ \text{to maturity}\end{array}\right)}{(\text{Discount bond cost} + \text{par value}) \div 2}$$

EXAMPLE

The yield to maturity of \$1,000 bond 7% maturing in 12 years purchased at \$95.

$$\frac{\$70 + (\$50 \div 12 \text{ years})}{(\$950 + \$1{,}000) \div 2} = .076\ (7.6\%)$$

Bonds Sold at a Premium

$$\text{Yield to maturity} = \frac{\left(\begin{array}{c}\text{Total dollar}\\ \text{amount of}\\ \text{annual interest}\\ \text{per one bond}\end{array}\right) - \left(\begin{array}{c}\text{Total premium}\\ \text{divided by the}\\ \text{number of years}\\ \text{to maturity}\end{array}\right)}{(\text{Premium bond cost} + \text{par value}) \div 2}$$

EXAMPLE

The yield to maturity of $1,000 bond 7% maturing in 12 years purchased at $108.

$$\frac{\$70 - (\$80 \div 12\ \text{years})}{(\$1{,}080 + \$1{,}000) \div 2} = .06\ (6\%)$$

DELIVERY REQUIREMENTS FOR CORPORATE BONDS

If the unit of trading is $1,000 or $5,000, the denomination of the bonds must be either $1,000 or $5,000. If the unit of trading is more than $5,000, the delivery must be made in the denominations of the trading unit. Bonds in larger denominations are acceptable if they can be exchangeable without charge for bonds in the unit of trading.

Contracts in bonds may be settled by delivering bonds in coupon or registered form, provided that these bonds are interchangeable without charge.

In all cases, the buyer must accept partial deliveries from the seller if delivered in lots of one trading unit or multiples of the unit.

THE ROLE OF THE BOND TRUSTEE

Under the Trust Indenture Act of 1939, the corporation must appoint a bank to act as the trustee for the bonds. The bank must meet established eligibility and qualification standards. The bank's role as trustee is to protect the bondholder under the Trust Indenture Act of 1939. The trustee will protect the rights of the bondholder in the event the corporation defaults on its debt obligation. The trustee acts in the capacity of a supervisor in administering the trust indenture, the terms of interest payments, etc. The trustee must maintain accurate records of bonds outstanding, and once a year it must send a report to the company's independent auditors, indicating the amount of principal that is still outstanding and the amount of debt that has been retired through conversion or redemption. Once a year the trustee must also report to the bondholders with respect to its continuing eligibility to act as trustee.

The trustee must maintain separate records for the corporation's senior debt and subordinated debt. Senior debt has a priority call on the company's assets in the event of bankruptcy. The bank cannot act as trustee for both senior and subordinated debt issues.

THE ROLE OF THE AUTHENTICATING AGENT

During the underwriting process, the authenticating agent must validate each bond before delivery to the managing underwriter. The agent will sign each certificate of bond and certify that the bond is a valid obligation of the issuer.

THE ROLE OF THE REGISTRAR

As registrars of the bond, the bank will maintain the official register of the bondholders and handle the physical transfer of bonds. The registrar acting as transfer agents for the bond must maintain the bondholder records and on request register new bonds in the name of new purchasers.

THE ROLE OF THE PAYING AGENT

Acting as paying agent, the bank will send interest checks to the bondholders on interest payment day. If the registrar is also the paying agent, it will close the books on the record date, prepare checks, and mail them to the bondholders whose names are recorded with the registrar. This applies only for registered bonds. For bonds in coupon or bearer form, it will be the obligation of the bondholder to clip the coupon on the due date and present it to the paying agent for collection.

If the paying agent is a bank other than the registrar, it will be the obligation of the registrar to submit the list of the registered bondholders to the paying agent for issuance of interest checks.

THE ROLE OF THE CONVERSION AGENT

The issuing corporation may choose to issue a convertible bond. The bondholder may request the conversion of the bond into common shares. This conversion may be either at the option of the bondholder or at the option of the corporation.

The corporation will appoint a bank to act as the conversion agent. The bondholder will present his bond to the conversion agent who will cancel the bond and issue an appropriate number of shares of common stock if the bank is also the transfer agent of the stock. If another bank is appointed as the transfer agent, the conversion agent will cancel the convertible bond and advise the transfer agent to issue the appropriate shares of common.

CHAPTER FOUR

MUNICIPAL BONDS

Municipal bonds are securities issued by political entities. The word "municipal" is a generic term. It applies to all securities issued by states, municipalities, counties, villages, school districts, public authorities, and special districts. Even though state governments and school districts are not municipalities in the lexicon of municipal bond operation, the securities issued by these entities are called municipal securities.

A township or a municipality is a nonprofit entity. It operates under statutory, legislative, and constitutional authority to provide services to the residents of the community. Its revenues come largely from taxes, grants, appropriations and public facilities. Municipal securities are issued to finance the operation of the governmental entity and the functioning of various public authorities and agencies.

Municipal securities are purchased for investment purposes. The largest purchasers are commercial banks, savings and loan associations, life insurance companies, endowment funds, and investment companies. The most important characteristic of these securities is their tax-exempt status. This tax exemption was established by the Mutual Reciprocity Doctrine of the Supreme Court in the latter part of the 19th century. The Doctrine states that interest on municipal securities is tax-exempt under the federal taxation law and interest on U.S. Treasury securities is tax-exempt under state taxation laws. Interest on bonds issued by territories or possessions of the U.S. government are triple exempt. They are exempt under the federal, state, and local tax laws. These bonds are called territorial or triple-exempt bonds.

This tax-exempt status has helped the municipalities and state governments to issue their bonds at a lower interest rate than the prevailing corporate bond rate.

When purchasing a municipal bond, the investor's most important consideration is the tax equivalency yield of the bond. This is a measuring device that will compare the yield on a tax-exempt municipal bond with the yield of a taxable security. This tax equivalency yield is determined by the following formula:

$$\frac{\text{Yield on the municipal security}}{100 - \text{Investor's tax bracket}} \times 100$$

If the yield on the municipal bond is 6 percent and the investor's tax bracket is 28 percent, the tax equivalency yield will be:

$$\frac{6}{100 - 28} \times 100 = 8.3\%$$

GENERAL CHARACTERISTICS OF MUNICIPAL BONDS

Municipal bonds represent the debt of local governments. They are highly liquid and marketable, and usually traded on the over-the-counter market.

A great majority of them have serial maturities. They are usually quoted in yield rather than in dollars. Prices of municipal bonds tend to fluctuate in conjunction with the U.S. government securities.

There are basically two types of municipal bonds: general obligation bonds and revenue bonds. The general obligation bonds, popularly known as GO bonds, are secured by the good faith and credit of the municipality based on its taxing power. They are considered as "legal" investments by banks, savings and loan associations, and insurance companies. The revenue bonds are issued to fund a revenue-producing project. These bonds are secured by the revenue of a particular project and payable solely from the revenue of the facility. The municipality will set the maturity date of the revenue bond usually to coincide with the life of the project.

Municipal bonds are issued either in bearer form with coupons attached or in a registered form, which means the bonds are issued in the name of the bondholder. They may also be registered in the name of the principal with coupons attached. This means that the certificate is in the name of the bondholder; but in order to collect his interest, the bondholder must clip the coupon and present it to the paying agent. The Tax Equity and Fiscal Responsibility Act enacted in 1982 requires corporations and municipalities to issue their bonds in registered form.

GENERAL OBLIGATION BONDS

The general obligation bonds are usually issued in serial form. Serial bonds are bonds that have different dates of maturity. They are secured by the full faith, credit, and the taxing power of the issuing entity. In the case of a state, general obligation bonds are secured by franchise taxes, income taxes, personal property taxes, motor vehicle taxes, gasoline taxes, liquor and tobacco taxes, and other sources of state revenue. In the case of a municipality, county or a school district, the general obligation bonds are secured by property taxes, sales, income, and business taxes.

Governments issue general obligation bonds to raise

funds for capital improvements and for construction of public works, such as streets, roads, and public buildings. They also are issued to meet the debt service requirement of certain facilities.

General obligation bonds are considered to be safe investments because there has never been any question as to the constitutional right of a political entity to levy taxes.

Some political divisions issue general obligation bonds with double guarantees. These are called "double-barreled bonds." A general obligation transportation bond, for instance, will have the guarantee of the state's full faith and credit, with an added security backed by the gasoline taxes in the state's transportation fund. Special tax bonds and special assessment revenue bonds may also be classified as doubled-barreled bonds.

Before issuing a general obligation and a double-barreled revenue bond, a municipality must receive a voter referendum and approval of the debt ceiling.

In analyzing the credit standing of general obligation bonds, one must consider the following factors:

1. the issuer's economic condition
2. legal considerations
3. the debt structure
4. operating procedures

The Issuer's Economic Condition

The economic condition of the community depends on its industrial growth and the population mix. These factors will reflect the strengths and the weaknesses of the community. If the analysis shows that the community is dependent upon a single industry, this will be considered a point of economic weakness.

Legal Considerations

The legal factors include: the type of government, its powers to levy taxes, political history, and the issuer's willingness to pay its debts. Points of strength will be a stable political system, well-developed fiscal policies, and adequate annual revenues to meet expenses. Points of weakness will be an unstable political system, overlapping governmental units, and limitations upon the issuer to levy taxes.

The Debt Structure

This is an important factor in determining the credit worthiness of a political entity. The analyst will consider the ratio between the debt service and the annual revenue and the city's share of the debt of its overlapping units. These overlapping units may be governmental subdivisions, such as school districts, counties, fire districts, etc.

A rule of thumb is that the municipality's overall debt should not exceed 25 percent of the assessed valuation.

The Operating Procedures

The analyst will consider the municipality's operating procedures and the method in which the municipality prepares its financial statements. Most major municipalities prepare their financial statements under the generally accepted accounting principles (GAAP).

In addition, the analyst will consider the schedule for tax collection, tax per capita, the uncollected tax per capita, debt per capita, budget trends, the municipality's auditing procedures, and the rate of unemployment in the community.

Most general obligation bonds are secured by "unlimited" taxes. This means that the municipality has unlimited power to levy taxes to pay its debt. In certain states, however, notably California, the state's legislation prescribes limits on the municipality's power to levy taxes. General obligation bonds issued by these governments are called Limited Tax Bonds. Limited Tax Bonds have a limited market, and, in some cases, they are ineligible as legal investment vehicles for certain institutions.

TYPES OF MUNICIPAL BONDS

State Bonds

States having sovereign power have the right to engage in public borrowing for the operation of the government. A state borrows funds from the public to construct highways, hospitals, penal institutions, schools, etc.

Most states allow mandamus proceedings, in which the taxation officer of the state government is authorized to levy enough taxes to satisfy the bond obligation.

Callable Bonds

In issuing a callable bond, the state or the municipality will have the authority to call the bond before maturity. This call feature makes the security less marketable.

Term Bonds

Term bonds will have one date of maturity. Revenue bonds are typically term bonds. They are quoted in dollar basis.

Serial Bonds

Serial bonds have many dates of maturity. It will be described as maturity 1/1/1995–2010. This means the bonds may mature on January 1, 1995, January 1, 1996, January 1, 1997, and so on. The final date of maturity is January 1, 2010. General obligation bonds are typically serial bonds. They are quoted on the basis of yield to maturity.

Series Bonds

Series bonds are issued at different time periods. They have different dates of issuance.

Premium Bonds

Premium bonds are sold at a price higher than par. When purchasing a premium bond, the investor must amortize the bond. He will determine the annual amortization by dividing the premium by the number of years to maturity. This amount will then be deducted from the cost of purchasing the bond to determine the ***adjusted cost basis***. For example: the customer buys a $10,000 bond for $11,000. The bonds mature in five years. To determine the annual amortization amount, the customer will divide the amount of the premium, in this case $1,000, by 5, the number of years to maturity. The result is $200. This is the amount of amortization on an annual basis. If he holds the bonds two years, the total amortization amount will be $400 (2 × 200). Two years later, if he wants to sell the bonds, his adjusted cost basis will be $10,600 (11,000 – 400).

Discount Bonds

Discount bonds are sold at a price below par. If the bond is being sold in a public offering at a discount, then the amount is the Original Issue Discount (OID). For tax purposes the Original Issue Discount must be accreted. The annual accretion is determined by dividing the OID by the number of years to maturity. The amount is then added to the purchase price each year to arrive at the *adjusted cost basis*. At maturity, the adjusted cost basis becomes par.

EXAMPLE

The customer buys a $10,000 bond for $9,000 at original issue. The bond matures in five years. To determine the annual accretion, the customer divides the original issue discount, in this case $1,000, by 5, or $200. Two years later if he wants to sell the bond, his total accretion amount will be $400 (2 × 200). He will then add $400 to the cost of purchasing the bond, $9,000. His adjusted cost basis will be $9,400.

Ballooning

Ballooning is a procedure through which a municipality may reduce its debt at various intervals. This gives added protection to the bondholder. Ballooning may be accomplished at different maturity dates or at different interest rates.

EXAMPLE

Principal Amount	*Maturity*	*Interest Rates*
$11,500,000	1995	6¼%
$8,000,000	2000	6¾%

Sinking Fund Bonds

When issuing a sinking fund bond, the municipality sets aside an annual reserve to retire the bond. The annual reserves are scheduled in such a way that over the years sufficient funds will be accumulated. This can be regularly scheduled payments to a trustee bank or payments made on a periodic basis. The funds deposited at the trustee bank may earn interest for the municipality.

Put Option Municipal Bonds

In order to induce investors to purchase municipal bonds, some municipalities issue bonds with a put or a tender provision. This will give the bondholder the option to surrender the bond to the issuer and receive the face value plus the accrued interest at some future date. The investor will decide to redeem the bond when interest rates in the economy go up.

There are basically two types of put option bonds—one is the *Window put* or the European put, and the other is the *Anniversary put*. The Window put can only be exercised once at a specific date in the future. The Anniversary put allows the investor to redeem the bond periodically, on a given date once every year. In both cases, the put provision will protect the bondholder against rising interest rates and falling bond prices.

To ensure that the municipality will have sufficient funds to honor the redemption of the put option, a bank will issue an irrevocable letter of credit, or the municipality will make an arrangement with an underwriter to resell the bonds when the puts are exercised. The proceeds of the resale will be used to redeem the bond. The rating agencies assign two different ratings for put option bonds. One will be based on the long-term creditworthiness of the issue. The other will reflect the short-term ability of the issuer to repay the principal and interest when the put options are exercised. If the put bond is supported by a bank letter of credit, it will generally carry the same rating as the bank that has issued the letter of credit (LC).

Put bonds offer advantages to both the issuer and the investor. The issuer will reduce the cost of issuing the bond, and the investor will have a protection from a major drop in the value of the bond.

Some put bonds are issued with a "one shot" put, in which the holder has only a one time option to redeem the bond before maturity. Most put bonds, however, are issued with an option feature, allowing the bondholder to redeem the bond a year after the date of issuance and every five or six years thereafter.

The yield spread between a put bond and a similar traditional bond is between 1/4 to 2 percent. The yield is lower for put bonds. Another negative point for the put bond: It does not offer any appreciable potential for capital gain.

Original Issue Discount Municipal Bonds

An Original Issue Discount municipal bond is a bond that pays interest to the bondholder. It is sold at a discount price from the face value. The return to the bondholder occurs through a gradual accretion in the value of the bond until maturity. The difference in money between the cost of purchasing the bond and its face value is the Original Issue Discount (OID). This is considered as interest income, and for municipal bonds it is tax-exempt. The Original Issue Discount will determine the yield to maturity. On a 20-year $100 par bond sold at $95 with a 10 percent coupon, the yield to maturity will be 10.60 percent. For a similar bond sold at $80 with an 8.25 percent coupon, the yield to maturity will be 10.72 percent. The yield is usually less than the rates for traditional bonds.

These bonds are attractive instruments to investors who anticipate that future interest rates will be lower than the present rate. The bondholder does not have to be concerned about reinvesting the coupon payments. This reinvestment risk is born by the issuing municipality.

Zero Coupon Municipal Bonds

The zero coupon bonds are sold at a discount price from the face value but offer no interest income during the life of the bond. The bondholder receives the face value at the time of maturity. As in Original Issue Discount bonds, the difference in money between the cost and the face value will be the OID and is considered as tax-exempt interest income for municipal bonds. In purchasing the zero-coupon bond, the bondholder will be able to lock in a fixed reinvestment rate, thus maximizing the long-term gain with a minimum risk.

Some zero bonds are issued with a callable feature. The issuer may be able to call the bonds at any time before maturity. The bondholder, however, will be compensated for a call premium, which is usually par plus 4 percent. The investor will be entitled to a yield equal to the expected bond yield on the original sale date.

When issuing the zero bonds, it is customary for the issuer to provide for a sinking fund or a debt service reserve fund to assure the bondholder that he will receive the face value at the time of maturity. The municipality will also consider its debt limitations, since the face value of the bond is much greater than the proceeds of the sale. For legal purposes, it is the face amount of the bond that the municipality is responsible to pay.

The legislation of certain states does not allow municipalities to issue deep-discount zero bonds.

Compound Coupon Municipal Bonds

Unlike the zero bonds, the compound coupon bonds are sold at par at the time of issuance. These bonds do not pay interest during the life of the bond; but, at the time of maturity, they pay the principal amount plus the amount of interest that has been accumulated during the life of the bond at a semi-annually compounded rate. The investor is assured a definite yield to maturity.

Compound coupon bonds are also known as Municipal Multipliers or Capital Appreciation bonds.

Variable Rate or Floating Rate Bonds

The variable rate or a floating rate bond is a bond on which the interest rate is changed and adjusted periodically. These bonds do not have a fixed rate of interest. Their yield is adjusted to the prevailing market rates. These are attractive investment vehicles for investors who believe interest rates will continue to rise. The investor must consider, however, two important elements before purchasing these bonds: the formula to which the interest rate is adjusted and the frequency of the interest rate adjustments. The bonds usually have an interest floor and a ceiling. This will protect the issuer from extreme fluctuations in interest rates. The formula for most bonds is the weekly offering of the U.S. Treasury bill rate. These rates are determined weekly through an auction process. The weekly bills are sold on a discount basis. The amount of the discount is the difference in money between the cost of purchasing the bill and the face value. The interest rate of the Treasury bill will be the percentage obtained by dividing the amount of the discount by the purchase price, which is the difference between the face value and the amount of the discount. It is this interest rate that is generally used by issuers in adjusting the interest rates on variable rate bonds.

The interest rate adjustments can be weekly, monthly, or semi-annually. The adjustment schedule is based on the life of the bond. The issuers adjust the rates every week for short-term bonds and every month or every six months for long-term issues.

Most variable rate bonds are issued with an option provision. That means the bondholder may redeem the bond at any time before maturity. This will protect the investor against sharp drops in interest rates. This option feature has made these bonds attractive instruments particularly for managers of money market mutual funds. To meet the bondholder's demand to receive the principal and interest at the time of redemption, the issuer is required to have a letter of credit issued by a bank.

Similar to variable rate bonds are the Flexible Rate Notes, also known as *rolling notes*. Here the interest rates are changed monthly based on a formula determined by the underwriters. The notes are issued at monthly maturities. Every 30 days, a new interest rate is determined for the remaining life of the note. The noteholder has the option to redeem the note at any time before maturity. The issuer is obligated to purchase the note at par.

Municipal Warrants

Similar to corporate warrants, a municipal warrant will give the option to the holder to buy a stated number of bonds at a specified price within a specified period of time. These certificates are usually attached to the bond instrument at the time of the original issue. By exercising the warrants, the investor will purchase bonds at the same price and at the same interest rate as that of the original issue. The bonds with warrants usually yield lower coupon rates than a bond without the warrant.

Warrants may be detached from the bond certificate and sold separately. The warrant's market value is based on the prevailing interest rates for similar securities and the remaining life of the warrant. When interest rates drop, the value of the warrant increases.

The major advantage of bonds with warrants is the issuer's savings in interest cost. These bonds are generally sold at interest rates of 75 basis points lower than the prevailing market rates. But the issuer must be ready to borrow more funds when the warrants are exercised. This borrowing is made through the issuance of additional bonds to the warrant holder. The cost of issuing this second bond will be substantially lower than the public offering of the first bond. The issuer will save counsel's and underwriter's fees.

Super Sinker Municipal Bonds

Super sinkers are long-term bonds that can be retired well in advance of the maturity date by utilizing funds generated from prepayments and other sources of revenue. By issuing the super sinker, the issuer will offer a lower rate than a regularly structured bond.

Unlike the put bonds, super sinkers may have maturity dates well in advance of the actual date.

Super sinkers are generally used for housing and home mortgage issues. Their maturities range between 18 and 20 years with an estimated average life of three to six years.

Stepped Coupon Municipal Bonds

Stepped bonds issued by municipalities bear the same rate of interest; the rate of interest increases, however, in later years. This has its advantages and disadvantages. The principal disadvantage is to the investor who wishes to sell the bonds prior to maturity. He will receive a lower income because the interest is more heavily weighted in the more distant years. These bonds are inflation-oriented. It will cost the issuing municipality more to finance the high-interest payment in the later years. If the rate of inflation is reduced, it will cost more to the issuer to finance the "stepped coupon bond."

Stepped bonds also are known as Incremental Coupon bonds. They have less reinvestment risk to the investor than the regular coupon bonds.

Municipal Bond Funds

Municipal bond funds provide diversification. Instead of purchasing one municipal bond, an investor may choose to buy a share of a larger portfolio to reduce the risk by spreading the investment over a number of municipal bonds. In addition to reducing the risk, the investor will rely on the judgment of a professional bond manager. Municipal bond funds make it easier for a small investor to buy municipal bonds. The minimum investment in bond funds can be as low as $1,000.

Municipal bond funds are issued in two different types:

- Mutual Funds
- Unit Investment Trust

The mutual fund is an open-ended fund, featuring a managed portfolio of municipal bonds. The investor will purchase a share of the mutual fund. The return on the investment fluctuates with the performance of the fund. The mutual fund portfolio generally contains tax-exempt municipals. If it contains some taxable securities, the tax-exempt feature cannot be considered total.

The Unit Investment Trust is the more popular type of municipal bond fund. In the case of the unit trust, the customer invests $1,000 or $5,000 with the understanding that he will get the original investment back once all the bonds in the fund have matured, which can be in 3, 10, 25 or 30 years. In the meantime, the investors will get a fixed amount of interest monthly, quarterly, or semi-annually.

The customer may sell the unit trust in the secondary market. The price of the unit trust is based on the price of the underlying securities in the portfolio. Unit trusts carry a onetime sales charge that can range from 2 percent to 5 percent and annual fees of about 0.15 percent. The charges are factored into the yield quoted by the broker. By comparison, many municipal bond mutual funds do not have any sales charge but a larger annual fee than the unit trusts. The annual fee averages 0.8 percent.

Yields on this type of fund vary mainly because of the difference in the quality of the underlying securities. The higher the quality of the underlying security, the lower the yield.

CHAPTER FIVE

REVENUE BONDS

Revenue bonds are issued by public authorities that are created to perform a specific public function. These authorities are established by a special legislative act and have complete authority to perform duties imposed by authorizing legislation, including powers of eminent domain similar to those of other governmental divisions.

Revenue bonds are issued under a trust agreement, but the starting point is the authorizing statute that will sanction the construction of the revenue-supported project. The statutes regulate the powers to issue the bonds, and the attorneys draw up the trust agreement on the basis of these statutes.

After the trust agreement is prepared, the engineers prepare the report for the construction of the facility. This will include the construction cost, capital requirements, anticipated earnings and expenses of the project during the life of the bond and the management of the project.

After the bonds are issued, it is the investment banker's responsibility to sell them to the public. His concerns include: whether the bond indenture includes adequate protective covenants for the bondholders, whether the proceeds of the bonds are sufficient to complete the project, whether the authority has the ability to meet its debt service, and whether the security is priced in line with other comparable issues.

THE TRUST AGREEMENT

The trust agreement must have the necessary covenants that will form a part of the contract between the issuer and the bondholder. The trust agreement will include the name of the bond, the maturity date, the call features, the method in which the proceeds of the bond will be utilized, the method in which the revenues derived from the project will be applied, the rates, the fees, and charges of the facility, the method in which additional securities for the same project may be issued, the recourse of the covenants for insurance, fire, catastrophe, calamity rate, etc.

The issuer must assure the bondholder that the proceeds of the bond sale will be kept separate from all other funds and will be used solely for the project. Any excess funds must be deposited in the revenue fund to be used for debt service. The total cost of financing a revenue bond will be the flotation cost plus the cost of interest. The flotation cost is the underwriting and marketing cost of selling the issue. The marketing cost involves the counsel fees, fees to financial adviser, the accountants, the cost of printing notices and prospectuses, the cost of rating and signature. For general obligation bonds, in addition to these costs, the municipality will also incur the cost of election to receive the voter referendum. A recent study showed that the total marketing cost per $1,000 general obligation bonds is $8.61 and for a revenue bond, $15.51.

The trust agreement comes in two different types—open-end and closed-end. An open-end trust agreement allows for the issuance of additional parity bonds. The closed-end agreement allows for only a set number of bonds to be issued for the project.

THE REVENUE FUND

The trust agreement or the bond resolution must state that a revenue fund has been established. The revenue fund will be a reservoir of funds. All revenues from the project must be deposited in the fund and all disbursements must be made from the same fund. The order of priority of disbursing funds is based on the provisions of the trust agreement. There are two sets of priorities. One is a Net Revenue pledge and the other is a Gross Revenue pledge.

For a Net Revenue pledge, the order of priority for disbursing funds will be as follows:

1. The operating expenses and maintenance of the project.
2. The debt service. This refers to the amount of money needed to pay the interest and principal when due.
3. The debt service reserve fund. This is a special reserve fund to be used if in a given year the government is unable to meet its financial obligations.
4. The replacement fund. This is used to fund the replacement cost of certain items in the project, such as replacing the air-conditioning system.
5. The surplus fund. This is the excess fund after all payments have been met.

For a Gross Revenue pledge, the order of priority for disbursing funds will be the same, except Number 2 above will replace Number 1—the debt service requirement comes first and then the operating expenses and maintenance.

Revenue bonds are generally issued with a callable feature.

TYPES OF REVENUE BONDS

Public Power Revenue Bonds

Public power municipal bonds represent the largest portion of revenue bonds, and the public power authorities are the largest issuers of revenue bonds. The authorities are established to create public power facilities to provide electricity for the community. These facilities are at times in competition with private utility companies. The public power authorities will issue revenue bonds to finance their operations. These revenue bonds are secured by the revenue of the authority. New York State Power Authority and North Carolina Public Service Authority are examples of these entities.

There are basically four types of public power authorities: The first has its own facility to generate power, the second purchases power from a wholesaler and distributes it to the community, the third is the wholesale company itself, and the fourth is a combination of the second and third.

Housing Authority Revenue Bonds

To meet the housing needs of the people in the community, local governments issue housing authority bonds to finance the construction and the operation of dwellings and rental units. These bonds are secured by the rental income of the project.

The following types of housing authority bonds can be issued:

A. *Mortgage Purchase Bonds.* Here the government sells Mortgage Purchase bonds and uses the proceeds of the sale to purchase mortgages from savings and loan associations.

B. *Public Housing Authority Bonds (PHA).* These bonds are issued under the U.S. Housing Act of 1937 to finance the construction of apartment dwellings for low-income families or elderly people.

C. *Direct Loan Programs.* These bonds will help developers to build dwellings for low or moderate income people.

D. *Loan to Lenders Programs.* As with Mortgage Purchase bonds, these programs use the bond proceeds to make collateralized loans to lending institutions. The lending institutions will then make mortgage loans that are payable from loan repayments by the lending institution.

Moral Obligation Bonds

Unlike the general obligation bonds, the moral obligation bonds are not backed by the good faith or the credit of the political entity. They represent some sort of commitment by the local government to pay the principal and interest when due. They are issued to finance certain governmental projects.

Hospital Bonds

Hospital bonds are issued to finance the construction and the operation of hospitals. They are revenue bonds guaranteed by the revenue of the hospital.

Water and Sewer System Bonds

These revenue bonds are issued to finance the water and the sewer system for the residents and industries of a municipal region. The bonds are secured by the revenue of the project.

Industrial Revenue Bonds

Industrial revenue bonds are actually corporate bonds. They are, however, created as municipal securities. These bonds are issued to finance the construction and the operation of industrial and pollution control facilities. Corporations use this financing method to build convention centers, airport terminals, docks, pollution facilities, sewage disposal, and plants in economically depressed areas.

Special Assessment Bonds

The special assessment bonds are payable from tax assessment of the property benefited or erected by the utilization of the funds. Unlike the general obligation bonds, the good faith and the credit of the government are not pledged to secure this obligation.

Special Tax Bonds

These revenue bonds are secured by special taxes levied on certain items.

Taxable Municipal Bonds

Taxable municipal bonds are securities issued by municipalities in response to the Tax Reform Act of 1986. Under this Act, the interest on certain municipal bonds is taxable. State and local governments issue the taxable bonds to finance projects such as agricultural loans, aid to small businesses, or to issue certain industrial revenue bonds.

CHAPTER SIX

DISTRIBUTION OF MUNICIPAL BONDS TO THE PUBLIC

The municipal bond market has two components—the primary market and the secondary market. The primary market is the new issue market in which the underwriter accepts and purchases the security on a wholesale basis from the municipality and subsequently sells it to his customers. The secondary market is the trading market that starts immediately after the issuance of the security. The secondary market will last until the maturity date of the issue. During the first phase of the secondary market, the security will start trading on a "when issued" basis. This phase will last until the security becomes available to the public.

THE PRIMARY MARKET

When a municipality decides to issue a security, the distribution and selling of the security are done through an underwriting process. Instead of selling the security individually to investors, the municipality will sell it wholesale to a dealer. There are basically two types of underwriting—competitive bidding and negotiated arrangement. General obligation bonds are underwritten through a competitive bidding, and revenue bonds are generally offered through negotiated arrangements between the issuer and the underwriter. To issue the bond, the municipality must first receive a voting or statutory authority. After the authorization is obtained, the municipality will set the dollar face amount of the issue, the maturity date, and the time of issuance. The municipality will issue a document and invite dealers to submit their bids. The invitation to the dealers is generally done by advertising the security in a publication called the *Daily Bond Buyer*. If the municipality decides to sell the security through a negotiated arrangement, it will deal with one dealer or a syndicate of dealers to market the security.

Competitive Underwriting

If a dealer is interested in underwriting the issue, he will submit his bid to the municipality. He may decide to underwrite the issue alone, or, if the issue is too large, he may form a syndicate with other dealers. The dealers are usually commercial banks and investment bankers. As a syndicate, the underwriters will submit a bid to the issuer. This bid may be expressed in interest rate and/or the price of the bond. At a specified time, date, and place all bids are opened. The issuer will award the security to the syndicate with the lowest net interest cost to the municipality. The bonds will be delivered to the syndicate, and the municipality will receive the proceeds of the sale. The syndicate will then sell the security to the public at a predetermined price.

Commercial banks are the largest purchasers of general obligation municipal bonds. In making the decision to underwrite the bond, the bank will consider the risk involved, the yield, and the maturity of the issue. The latter is an important consideration for the overall liquidity requirements of the bank. Commercial banks are both purchasers and bidder–underwriters in the municipal bond market.

The municipality must prepare the following documents to initiate and complete the underwriting process:

- *The Official Statement*. Before issuing the security, the municipality must prepare the Official Statement. This is a document that summarizes the various features of the offering. It is similar to a prospectus of a corporate issue. There are no requirements, however, for the municipality to register the security with the SEC. The issuer will disclose the financial condition of the municipality in detail in the Official Statement.
- Before the issuance of the Official Statement, a *preliminary statement* may be published and distributed to the investment community. This is similar to a Red Herring prospectus of a corporate issue.

THE RATING OF MUNICIPAL BONDS

There are four financial service advisory agencies on the national level that determine the ratings of municipal bonds: Standard and Poor's Corporation, Moody's Investors Services, Fitch Investor Services, and White's Ratings.

The agencies determine the rating of a municipal bond based on the credit worthiness of the issuing municipality. Retail and institutional investors rely on these ratings to be able to chart their investment policies. The ratings influence the marketability and the interest rates of the bond. Insurance companies, commercial banks, and pension funds are not allowed to purchase bonds with a rating below investment grade.

S & P and Moody's analyze the municipality's credit worthiness, while White's ratings is concerned with the security's marketability. Fitch specializes in hospital bonds. In addition to these national agencies, there are many smaller local agencies that analyze municipal issues.

The rating agencies basically use the same criteria in

analyzing the financial condition of a municipality or a municipal facility. The criteria are based on the following:

1. Ability of the issuer to pay interest and principal when due
2. The characteristics of the obligation
3. Protection in the event of bankruptcy.

In providing this service, the agencies caution the investors that they assume no responsibility. The agencies do not make any recommendation to buy or sell the security or comment on the suitability of the security to an investor.

SYMBOLS OF RATINGS

	S&P	*Moody's*
Maximum grade	AAA	Aaa
Very good grade	AA	Aa
Good grade	A	A
Adequate capacity to pay interest and principal	BBB	Baa
Speculative	BB	Ba
Speculative	B	B
Speculative	CCC	Caa
Speculative	CC	Ca
Speculative	C	
Income bonds. Bonds pay no interest	D	C

AAA- to BBB-rated bonds are known as investment grade. Bonds rated AAA and AA are called high grades, and bonds rated A and BBB are considered low grades.

The rating agencies review the annual financial statements of most municipalities and update the rating based on current information available at the time. If the municipality fails to furnish financial information, the rating agency may suspend or withdraw the rating.

In evaluating the municipality's financial condition, the agencies will generally consider the following factors:

1. The municipality's debt and the debt ratio
2. The economic base of the municipality
3. The debt structure
4. The debt burden of the issuer
5. The ability of the municipality to reduce its debt
6. Per capita income
7. The employment mix of the municipality
8. The population growth
9. Building activity in the municipality
10. Retail sales in the community
11. Historical budget and audit reports
12. The municipality's resources and total revenues
13. The municipality's operating funds, general funds, and the debt service funds
14. The community's property taxes, assessed valuation, and tax delinquencies
15. The quality of management of the municipality

Because revenue bonds are secured by the revenue of a particular project, it is relatively simpler for the analyst to determine the rating of those bonds.

For revenue bonds, the analyst will consider the following:

1. The engineer's appraisal of the project
2. Legal protection to the bondholder
3. The interest coverage that is determined by:

$$\frac{\text{Net revenues}}{\text{Interest payments required}}$$

4. The debt service coverage that is determined by:

$$\frac{\text{Net revenues}}{\text{Debt service required}}$$

5. The operating ratio that is determined by:

$$\frac{\text{Operating expenses}}{\text{Operating revenues}}$$

6. The debt ratio that is determined by:

$$\frac{\text{Net debt}}{\text{Working capital plus plant}}$$

7. The net takedown that is determined by:

$$\frac{\text{Net revenues}}{\text{Gross revenues}}$$

The ratings have a direct impact on the bond's interest rates. The higher the rating the lower the interest rate will be, and vice versa. Ratings also affect the price of the bond in the marketplace.

In addition to AAA, AA, A, etc., the ratings may have different subclassifications, such as "strong double A-credit," "weak A-credit," and so on.

The analyst will issue warning signs when the following factors of a municipality exist:

- Increasing tax rate
- Delinquent taxes
- Reduced number of building permits
- Decreasing value of taxable property
- Budget deficit
- Expenditures in excess of inflation rate

- Expenditures in excess of approved budget
- Problems in the pension programs
- Problems with the cash management program
- The need to borrow to meet debt service requirements
- Population shift
- Poor quality of management

One difficulty in analyzing the financial condition of a municipality is the standards used to report financial data. There are differences among the various accounting methods used. The American Institute of Certified Public Accountants (AICPA) has suggested that municipalities adopt the accounting method and practices based on generally accepted accounting principles (GAAP).

Legal Opinion. The official statement is accompanied by an opinion of counsel as to the validity of the issue. The municipality will retain the services of a municipal bond attorney to render an opinion as to the authenticity of the security being issued. The attorney will examine the issue and will determine whether the municipality has statutory or constitutional authority to issue the bond. Even though municipal securities enjoy a high degree of safety, there have been times when municipalities have been in default to honor their debt obligation.* The history of municipal defaults goes back to the period immediately following the Civil War when, due to financial difficulties that plagued railroad companies, municipalities could not honor their obligations.

To rebuild the trust of the investing public, municipalities sought the opinion of outside counsel. Since that time, it has been a requirement to have a statement of legal opinion accompany the instrument of the bond in effecting a delivery.

---

*Defaults on tax-exempt municipal bonds have been relatively infrequent. Only 685 defaults have occurred since 1940, out of a total of 301,016 municipal bond issues.

The legal opinion may be issued twice. The first one will be a rough draft issued at the beginning of the underwriting process. The second one is the final version issued at the end of the underwriting process. In preparing the legal opinion, the bond counsel concerns himself only with the legality of the issue, its tax-exempt status, and its exemption from the registration requirement under the Securities Act of 1933. The legal opinion will not contain any information about interest rates and the market value of the security. The legal opinion may be *qualified* or *unqualified*. Qualified means there are certain legal reservations about the issue. Unqualified indicates that there are no legal constraints. Municipal bonds must be delivered with a copy of the legal opinion unless the trade is made *ex-legal*, in which case the buyer or the receiver of the bond will try to obtain the legal opinion himself. It will generally cost the buyer less to buy the bonds "*ex-legal.*"

Because of their minimum risk exposure, municipal bonds were not regulated by the federal government until the crisis of New York City in 1975 triggered Congress to amend the Securities Exchange Act of 1934. With this amendment, Congress made it mandatory for broker–dealers of municipal securities to register with the SEC. And in 1975, Congress created a board to oversee the municipal bond operation. The Municipal Securities Rule-making Board (MSRB) has a 15-member board of directors: five from the brokerage community, five from the banking community, and five from the public. As the rule-making authority, the MSRB is concerned with standards of professional practice, record keeping, qualification of broker–dealers, etc. The SEC's role in municipal bond operation is more administrative than regulatory. It protects the municipal bond investor from fraudulent activities.

Bond Indenture. During the creation of the security, the municipality must issue a statement citing the provisions of the bond indenture. The statement is in the form of a contract between the issuer and the lender of money who is the bondholder. The statement defines the terms of the security and the obligation of the trustee in representing the interests of the bondholders, and it contains remedies on default and other covenants. The statement must also include the description of the project, definition of the pledged revenue, application of the revenue, provisions for advance retirement of the bond, and the sinking fund.

The Rate Covenant. This statement includes the promise of the issuer that the rates of the facility (water, sewer, etc.) will be increased in line with rising costs to provide for the operational maintenance of the facility.

Financial Statement and the Annual Report. This financial statement of the issuer includes a "Cold Comfort Letter" prepared by an independent accounting firm. The "Cold Comfort Letter" reassures the bondholders that figures are correct, attesting to the financial performance of the issuer. Once a year the municipality must send a report of its financial condition to the holders of its debt obligations.

These are the necessary documents that are needed at the time of the creation of the security and before it is offered to the public for sale. Most of these requirements have been added after the crisis of New York City in 1975. Since 1975, municipalities have assumed greater responsibilities and have increased their legal exposure and liabilities. The crisis of 1975 has changed the roles of the participants in the municipal securities industry. The participants, the issuer, the accountants, the attorneys, the underwriters, etc., are now under the scrutiny of regulatory authorities and the bondholder.

To safeguard the interests of the bondholder, the issuer appoints a commercial bank to act as trustee. The trustee is responsible for assuring that the provisions of the bond instrument are met and the bondholder is protected.

To validate the issuance of the new bond, the issuer must also appoint a commercial bank to act as the authenticating agent. It is the responsibility of the authenticating agent to sign each certificate of bond. The authentication must be done before the securities are distributed to the public. In some cases, an officer of the municipality will sign the certificates authenticating their issuance.

Next, the issuer must appoint a paying agent and a registrar. The registrar will maintain the names and the addresses of the bondholders and the paying agent will prepare and mail the interest checks to the bondholders when due. As discussed above, bonds issued after July 1, 1983, must be in registered form, which means registered in the name of the bondholder. Prior to this date when the municipality was allowed to issue bonds in bearer-coupon form, the appointment of a registrar was not necessary. The requirement is to record the issue in a Bond Register that indicated the due dates, the denominations of the instruments, coupons, and interests. The Bond Register was usually kept at the municipality.

Once all these documents are assembled and the appointment of various agencies have been made, interested municipal bond dealers will submit their bids to the municipality if the underwriting is being made on a competitive basis. The account manager or the head of the syndicate group will submit the bid on behalf of the syndicate.

Competition is very keen, when bidding to underwrite an issue. The difference between one bid and another is between 5 to 10 basis points. One basis point is equal to 1/100th of 1 percent.

The bonds will be sold to the public at the Public Offering Price (POP) that had been previously determined by members of a syndicate. If the bonds were purchased from the issuer at $100, the syndicate member buys it from the syndicate at $110 and the Public Offering Price is $115. The difference between $100 and $115 is the *underwriting spread*; the difference between $110 and $115 is the *takedown*.

Before presenting the bid to the municipality, the account manager will hold a meeting with the members of the syndicate. The syndicate may be formed either through an Eastern account or a Western account. With the Eastern method, the underwriter is responsible for his proportionate share of the unsold portion. With a Western method, he assumes no responsibility once his allotment has been sold.

The final meeting is held to determine the *syndicate bid*. The underwriters will write a *scale*. This scale will determine the yield to the public with the profit to the syndicate factored in it. A *normal scale* is one that has longer maturities and higher yields. An *inverted scale* has shorter maturities and higher yields. During this meeting some syndicate members may drop out, if the syndicate letter had a "drop out" or a "market out" provision.

The presentation of the bid to the municipality is made in these ways:

- mail
- sealed bids sent by a special representative of the syndicate

The presentation of the bid will require a "Good Faith Deposit Check." The "Good Faith Deposit" ranges between 1 to 5 percent of the total par value of the bond. It is presented to the municipality for the purposes of covering the liquidating damages in the event the successful bidder does not pay for the bonds on the settlement date. These funds are returned within two business days after the settlement with the issuer.

Municipalities are extremely careful to observe the deadline. If the scheduled time for presenting bids is 10:00 a.m., any bids arriving at the designated place after 10:00 a.m. are ignored.

At the scheduled time, the municipal officer will open all the bids, and the bid with the lowest interest cost to the municipality will win. The bond certificates will be delivered to the account manager who, in turn, will deliver the appropriate amount of bonds to the members of the syndicate.

It is important for the underwriters to sell the bonds to their customers as soon as possible, particularly during a period of interest rate fluctuations. To help them sell the bonds, the underwriters may retain the services of dealers other than those who are members of the underwriting syndicate. These dealers will be members of the "selling group" and will receive a commission from the underwriters called the "Dealer's Concession." This commission generally ranges between 1/4 to 1 point ($2.50 to $10.00) per $1,000 bond. It is a percentage of the "takedown." They also are required to sell the bonds to the public at the public offering price. They are not allowed to charge commissions; their profit will be the amount of the concession.

Group Orders. A group order is an order for securities held in a syndicate for all members of the syndicate on a pro-rata method, which is based on the member's participation in the syndicate.

When submitting group orders to the syndicate, the municipal bond dealer must disclose the identity of the person for whom the order is being presented, the aggregate principal value of each maturity, and the maturity date of the securities. The manager of the syndicate, in turn, must disclose the identity of the account to other dealers within 10 days after the close of the order period. The syndicate must also establish priorities for different types of orders. The managing underwriter is allowed to change the order of priority if it is in the best interest of the syndicate. These priorities must be established before the syndicate submits its first offer to the issuer. The manager must notify the other members of the syndicate in writing if there are any changes in the priority order.

If the broker–dealer has any type of relationship with the issuing entity, that relationship must be disclosed in writing to the prospective customers who may be interested in purchasing the security. Otherwise, the broker–dealer is prohibited to execute the trade.

A copy of the final official statement must accompany the trade confirmation ticket that the broker will send to the purchasing customer. For negotiated sales, the broker–dealer must also send the customer confirmation about the underwriting spread, the initial offering price, and fees that the broker may have received in acting as agent. This information must also be submitted to other broker–dealers on request.

AFTER THE SALE OF THE SECURITY TO THE UNDERWRITERS

Immediately after the syndicate has purchased the issue from the municipality, the account manager will send a "Letter of Release" to each member of the syndicate. This letter will contain:

1. The purchase price of the bond from the issuer
2. A detailed statement of the underwriting terms, concessions, and the takedown
3. The final list of the syndicate members
4. Time and place to advertise the bond
5. The name of the printer who will print the circular
6. The amount of the "good faith deposit" required from each member
7. A notification to the members as to the delivery of the bond

The syndicate letter will indicate the following order of priorities to be used in the event the bonds are oversubscribed:

A. Presale orders.
B. Group orders.
C. Designated orders. Here the customer designates the municipal bond dealer to receive a sales commission.
D. Member orders. This is used by syndicate members for their customers.

E. Member-related orders. These are investment trusts or representatives of municipal bond dealers.

RESPONSIBILITY OF THE ACCOUNT MANAGER

The account manager is responsible for the following:

1. Advertising the issue
2. Preparing the offering circular
3. Maintaining records of sale
4. Keeping records for the unsold portion of the bonds
5. Confirming sales
6. Arranging delivery. Members of the syndicate will pick up their bonds from the account manager. The designated sales for other accounts are handled by the account manager. The manager will arrange with the municipality the time, place, and method of payment for the bonds.
7. Managing "closing day" procedures. On the closing day, the account manager's attorneys will examine all the documents and the full transcript of the proceedings, and exchange checks and bonds with the officials of the municipality.
8. Notifying for pickup. The manager will then notify other members of the syndicate that the bonds are ready for pickup. There are several service organizations and securities depositories that will help the syndicate members in the physical delivery and receipt of securities.
9. Accounting of the expenses. All expenses are shared by the syndicate members. These expenses include printing, counsel's fees, advertising, postage, insurance, telephone, clearance fees, and other miscellaneous items.

   The manager is required to send a statement on the profit and accounting to the syndicate members. This must be delivered within 60 days after the settlement or the delivery date of the security.
10. Filing income tax. The account manager will file the federal income tax on behalf of the syndicate.
11. Delivering the sales credit. The account manager

must deliver the sales credit to the syndicate members within 30 business days after the delivery date of the security.

An important factor in underwriting municipal bonds is the "placement ratio." The placement ratio is determined by the *Bond Buyer* through the use of the following formula:

$$\frac{\text{Dollar amount of new municipal bonds sold}}{\text{Dollar amount of new municipal bonds issued}}$$

The *Bond Buyer* will also publish the 30-day visible supply. These are new municipal bonds scheduled to be issued over the next 30 days.

SUMMARY OF THE UNDERWRITING PROCEDURE

1. First, a preliminary legal opinion must be prepared by bond counsel.

2. The municipality sends a cold comfort letter to the bondholders stating its financial condition.

3. The municipality advertises the issue in the *Daily Bond Buyer*.

4. The issuer prepares an official Notice of Sale describing procedures for bidding, the new issue, and the amount of good faith deposit required for bidding.

5. Interested underwriters form a syndicate or an account. The syndicate is formed by the managing underwriter.

6. The managing underwriter prepares the syndicate letter. The letter includes the participation of each underwriter or the bracket, the duration of the account (usually 30 days), indication that this is a joint account and not a partnership, the priority for allocating the oversubscribed bonds, and the type of account (Eastern or Western). The syndicate letter is sent to each member of the syndicate. The member must sign the letter if he accepts the provisions of the agreement.

7. The managing underwriter holds a meeting with the members of the syndicate to determine the bid, the public offering price, and the yield to the public. A preliminary meeting is held a day prior to the bid opening. During this meeting, the syndicate members determine the *scale*. The scale may be *normal* or *inverted*. Normal scale has longer maturities and higher yields. An inverted scale has shorter maturities and higher yields. During the meeting the members also decide the gross profit or the spread, and the coupon rate of the bond.

8. A final meeting is held shortly before the bid opening. At this meeting, the final bid scale and the profit margin is determined. The members will consider the municipal bond market in general, the *Daily Bond Buyer's* visible supply of forthcoming bonds for the next 30 days, the placement ratio of new municipal bonds offered and sold during the week, and the rating of the bond. The syndicate letter may have a "market-out" provision.

9. The bid is submitted to the issuer in a sealed envelope containing the good faith deposit check. The bid cannot be telegrammed to the issuer. The syndicate may use an agent to submit the bid.

10. The envelopes are opened. The issuer will determine the winning syndicate. A split-rate bid will have more than one rate of interest such as:

bonds maturing in 1991 – 8½%

bonds maturing in 1995 – 9% etc.

The syndicate with the lowest rate will win the award. If more than one bidder has the same rate, then the award goes to the bidder with the highest premium.

11. The issuer returns the good faith deposit checks to the unsuccessful bidders within two business days.

12. The winning syndicate buys the bond from the issuer on the settlement date.

13. The syndicate offers the bond to the public at the Public Offering Price (POP). The gross profit is the differ-

ence between the cost of purchase and the public offering price.

14. The syndicate member buys the issue from the managing underwriter. The difference between his cost of purchase from the syndicate and the Public Offering Price is called the "takedown." The takedown for all members will be the same.

15. The syndicate member may use another bank or broker to sell the bonds at the public offering price. These other brokers and banks are known as the selling group members. The syndicate member will give a percentage of his takedown to the selling group members. This is known as the "dealers' concession."

16. The bonds are delivered to the underwriters with a copy of the final legal opinion.

17. The underwriters sell the bonds to the investor and deliver the bonds with the legal opinion. The investor pays accrued interest calculated from the *dated* date until the settlement date of the trade.

18. If an Official Statement is published, the investor must receive a copy with the trade confirmation ticket. If a final official statement is not available, a summary of the statement or a preliminary official statement may be submitted to the investor. The official statement will disclose the underwriting spread, the initial offering price, and the fee to the brokers.

19. The selling broker must disclose to the customer any relationship he may have with the issuer (advisory, financial, contractual, or otherwise).

20. The syndicate account is settled. The managing underwriter sends a statement to each member within 60 days after the securities are delivered. The statement discloses the accounting and the syndicate profit. All sale credits must be delivered to the members within 30 business days after the securities are delivered.

21. The managing underwriter returns the good faith deposit check within two business days after the settlement with the issuer.

CHAPTER SEVEN

THE SECONDARY MARKET OF MUNICIPAL BONDS

The secondary municipal bond market is generally over-the-counter. Very few issues are listed on an exchange. The issues are advertised in the "Blue List." CRT terminals link the municipal bond dealers in the over-the-counter market. The dealers are brokerage houses and commercial banks registered with the Municipal Securities Rulemaking Board. Dealers specializing in certain issues will maintain inventory of bonds based on their size, financial standing, and marketing requirements. They will sell the bonds from their inventory. The profit will be the difference between the cost of their purchase and the price of sale.

The vast majority of small municipal bonds are purchased by a local bank. These bonds generally do not become part of the national bond market. The local bank will hold the bond until maturity and collect a tax-free income.

The buyers of municipal bonds may be categorized in the following manner:

1. Commercial banks
2. Broker–dealers
3. Individuals
4. Insurance companies

5. Corporations
6. Foreign investors

The bank's primary reason for buying municipal bonds is residual. When the bank's money manager has made loans and reached the loan demand level, he will purchase municipal bonds. Loans provide the primary revenue to the bank. Income generated from municipal bonds is secondary even though it is tax-exempt.

Insurance companies buy municipal bonds for investment purposes. They will keep enough funds to honor the insurance claims, and they will invest the rest in securities.

Individuals buy municipal bonds to take advantage of their tax-exempt status.

Trades in the secondary market are done in the regular way. They will settle on the fifth business day after trade. In certain cases instead of settling on the fifth business day after the trade, the settlement date may be agreed upon by both parties. The settlement includes accrued interest that's added to the cost of the transaction. If the bonds are in default at the time of the trade, the bonds will be sold "flat," which means they will be sold without any accrued interest. The unpaid past coupons must be attached to the bond at the time of delivery.

If the buyer and seller participate in a securities clearance with the depository organization, the delivery of the security will be effected through the depository medium. The depository company will debit the number of bonds from the seller's account and will credit the bond in the buyer's account.

UNITS OF DELIVERY

Coupon-bearer bonds: A bond is a good delivery if it comes in denominations of $1,000. Baby bonds of $100 and multiples of $100 are also considered good deliveries.

Registered bonds: Same as above but denominations

for delivery must not exceed $100,000 face value. If the trade is for $500,000 the delivery must be done in 5 × 100,000 and not 1 × 500,000.

If the bonds are interchangeable, that means registered bonds can be converted into coupon bonds and vice versa and contracts can be settled by the delivery of bonds in either form.

DELIVERY REQUIREMENTS FOR MUNICIPAL BONDS

For bearer bonds, the unit of delivery is $1,000 or $5,000. For registered bonds, the unit of delivery is $1,000 and multiples of $1,000 up to $100,000.

When the municipal bond is semi-mutilated, it still will be considered a good delivery if the certificate is validated by the bond trustees, the registrar, the transfer agent, the paying agent, or the issuing entity.

All coupons must be attached to the coupon bond for delivery.

For bonds in default, the deliverer must include all unpaid or partially paid coupons with the delivery.

If the settlement date of the trade is after the interest payment date, the delivery of the bond will not include the coupon.

If the delivery is being made 30 days prior to the interest payment, the deliverer must attach a due-bill or a bank check in lieu of the coupon.

A "called" bond is not a good delivery if the call notice was published on or prior to the delivery date, unless the trade is executed as "called" or the entire issue is being called.

A municipal bond without a copy of the legal opinion is not a good delivery, unless the trade is executed on the basis of "ex-legal."

For insured bonds, a document of insurance must accompany the certificates.

A due bill or a bank check must accompany the certificate if the transfer of the bond cannot be accomplished on or before the interest payment date. The same is true for securities traded "flat."

All expenses of shipment of the security is borne by the seller.

The delivery cannot be rejected for insignificant money differences.

All money differences must be solved by both parties within 10 business days after the settlement date. The accrued interest payment must be calculated with the contract price.

The receiving party may reclaim the item within one business day after the delivery for interest checks missing, mutilated certificates, and no legal opinion; within three business days following the receipt of the notice that the bank refuses to honor the interest check; within 18 months following the delivery for wrong issue, duplicate delivery, over-delivery, and rejection by the transfer agent.

The receiving party may reclaim the item at any time for counterfeit or stolen securities and for partially called bonds if the call notice was published on or before the delivery date, and the trade was not identified as "called."

All rejections and reclamations must accompany a notice explaining the rejection or the reclamation.

FACTORS INFLUENCING THE MARKET PRICE OF THE BOND IN THE SECONDARY MARKET

Many factors influence the market price of a bond:maturity, liquidity or the marketability, the nominal interest rate, the current interest rate, the quality of the issue, etc. The market price will fluctuate based on these factors. In general, when current interest rates go up, the market price of the bond will go down. The lower the nominal rate of a bond, the more widely the market price will fluctuate.

There are many professional and sophisticated analytical techniques used to forecast the future direction of interest rates. Many analysts attempt to predict the policies of the Federal Reserve System with regard to interest rates. Needless to say, forecasting interest rates are extremely difficult.

The market price of a bond also is affected by the quality of the issue. When the rating of a bond declines, the market price declines and the bond offers a higher yield.

The marketability of the issue influences the market price of the bond directly or indirectly. The more marketable a security is, the lower its market price will be; and therefore, it will offer a higher yield. In general, new issues yield more than a seasoned security. A seasoned issue is one that is being traded in the secondary market for a while. The U.S. government securities have unparalleled liquidity. Lots of $100,000 are *round lots* and lots under $100,000 face value are *odd lots*.

Charges may be levied on odd lot trades. This odd lot charge will lower the percentage return to the investor. The settlement dates for odd lots may also vary. An odd lot trade of a U.S. government security or a federal agency will settle on the fifth business day after the trade day, whereas a round lot transaction will settle on the business day following the trade day.

The sinking fund provisions of the bond may also affect the market price. The sinking fund is usually administered by the trustee bank. The issuer makes payments to the trustee periodically and the bank safeguards the interest of the bondholder. The market price of the bond with a sinking fund will be higher than one without this provision. The forces of supply and demand play a dominant role in the market price. If the issue is an attractive issue, the price will be higher than for a security with less investor interest. A *call* provision makes the bond less marketable. High premiums and deep discounts are less desirable than bonds trading near the par value. Bearer bonds are more marketable than registered bonds.

With the exception of revenue bonds, all municipal

bonds are quoted on a yield to maturity basis, whereas corporate bonds and U.S. government securities are quoted on a percentage-of-par basis. Corporate and U.S. government securities are quoted on a bid-asked basis in the following manner:

Bid	Asked
95½	96

This means the bid to purchase a $1,000 face value of a bond is $955.00 and the offer to is $960.00.

The price quotation system is different for a municipal bond. A 5 percent, 15-year-to-maturity bond may be quoted as:

Bid	Asked
5.40%	5.30%

To translate this quotation into dollar-terms, one has to consult the *Basis Book*. This book gives the dollar-price of the bid if the yield is known. The dollar-price of 5.40 percent bid for a 5 percent 15-year-to-maturity bond, as indicated in the *Basis Book* is $95.92. This means that the market price is $959.20 per $1,000 face value of the bond, and the offered yield of 5.30 percent is 96.92, $969.20 per $1,000 bond. The dealer's spread is $10 per $1,000 bond. The *Basis Book* also will indicate the accrued interest computed on a 360-day-a-year basis. The investor may be able to compute the dollar-price of a bond without the *Basis Book* by using the following formula:

$$\text{Dollar price} = \frac{\begin{pmatrix}\text{Face value}\\ \text{of bond}\end{pmatrix} + \begin{pmatrix}\text{Total interest}\\ \text{in one year}\end{pmatrix}}{1 + \text{Yield in decimals}}$$

In a secondary market, the bond dealer trades on a net non-commissioned basis. Brokers acting as agents generally charge a commission of $2.50 per $1,000 bond.

Coupon-bearer bonds are more easily marketable and, therefore, trade at a slightly higher price than registered bonds. Effective July 1, 1983, all new bonds maturing in one year or longer are issued in registered form in accordance with the requirements of the Tax Equity and Fiscal Responsibility Act of 1982.

Principal transactions in a customer account are made at an aggregate amount, including markups and markdowns. Agency transactions include commissions and service fees.

THE BASIS BOOK

The *Basis Book* is an important tool for fixed-income securities. Given the yield, one may find the dollar-price of the bond, or given the dollar-price, one may find the yield of the bond.

Using Table 7.1, let us determine the price or the yield of the securities:

TABLE 7.1. 2½%

Mat. Yield	*8½* Years	*9* Years	*9½* Years	*10* Years	*10½* Years	*11* Years	*11½* Years
1.90	104.69	104.94	105.19	105.44	105.69	105.93	106.17
2.00	103.89	104.10	104.31	104.51	104.71	104.92	105.11
2.10	103.10	103.26	103.43	103.59	103.75	103.91	104.07
2.20	102.31	102.44	102.56	102.68	102.80	102.92	103.03
2.25	101.92	102.03	102.13	102.23	102.33	102.42	102.52
2.30	101.54	101.62	101.70	101.78	101.86	101.93	102.01
2.40	100.76	100.81	100.84	100.88	100.92	100.96	101.00
2.50	100.00	100.00	100.00	100.00	100.00	100.00	100.00
2.60	99.24	99.20	99.16	99.12	99.09	99.05	99.01
2.70	98.49	98.41	98.33	98.26	98.18	98.11	98.03
2.75	98.12	98.02	97.92	97.83	97.73	97.64	97.55

EXAMPLE 1

What is the market price of a 2½ percent bond on a 2.25 percent basis maturing in 11 years?

To determine the market price, open the page in the *Basis Book* marked 2½ percent. This is the nominal rate of the bond. The question gives the basis or the yield at 2.25 percent. The first column of the page is the yield. Go down and find 2.25 percent. Find the market price in the 11-year column, opposite 2.25 yield. In this case, the price is $102.42.

Therefore, the market price of one bond with a face value of $1,000 is $1,024.20.

EXAMPLE 2

What is the market price of a 2½ percent bond on a 2.25 percent basis less 3/8 maturing in 11 years.

In this case, you are going to reduce the market price of $102.42 by 3/8. Three-eighths represents $.375 per $100. In this case the net price will be:

$$102.42 - .375 = 102.045$$

A $1,000 bond will cost:

$1,020.45

EXAMPLE 3

What is the market price of a 2½ percent bond on a 2.25 percent basis, maturing in 11 years and 3 months.

To solve this problem, one needs to do interpolation to determine the monthly value.

1. The price for 11 years and 6 months, 2½ percent on a 2.25 percent basis is $102.52.

2. The price for 11 years at 2½ percent on a 2.25 percent basis is $102.42.
3. Difference for 6 months is

$$\begin{array}{r} 102.52 \\ -102.42 \\ \hline .10 \end{array}$$

4. Difference for 3 months is .05 (1/2 of 6 months difference).
5. The price for a 2½ percent bond on a 2.25 percent basis maturing in 11 years and 3 months is $102.47.

$$\begin{array}{r} 102.42 \\ + \quad .05 \\ \hline 102.47 \end{array}$$

EXAMPLE 4

What is the market price of a 2½ percent bond on a 2.35 percent basis maturing in 11 years.

Since the first column of the *Basis Book* does not have 2.35 percent yield, one needs to do interpolation for an odd yield.

1. The price for a 2½ percent bond, 2.30 basis maturing in 11 years is $101.93.
2. The price for a 2½ percent bond on a 2.40 percent basis, maturing in 11 years is $100.96.
3. The difference for .10 basis is

$$\begin{array}{r} 101.93 \\ -100.96 \\ \hline .97 \end{array}$$

4. The difference for .05 basis is .485.
5. The price of a 2½ percent bond on a 2.35 percent basis, maturing in 11 years is 101.930 − .485 = $101.445.

EXAMPLE 5

What is the yield of a 2½ percent bond with a market price of $104.92, maturing in 11 years?

In this case, the market price is given and you need to determine the yield of the bond.

Under the 11 year column, find the closest possible price—in this case it is the actual price $104.92. Go to the left and find the yield—in this case, it is 2.00 percent.

EXAMPLE 6

What is the market price of a 2½ percent bond on a 2.15 percent basis, maturing in 11 years and 3 months?

To solve this problem, we must do interpolations of odd yield and monthly value combined.

1. The market price of

   11 year 6 months 2½ %, 2.10 basis is $104.07

2. The market price of

   11 year 6 months 2½ %, 2.20 basis is $103.03

3. The difference for .10 is 1.04
4. The difference for .05 is .52
5. The market price of

   11 year 6 months 2½ %, 2.15 basis is 103.55

   (104.07 − .52)

6. The market price of

   11 year 2½ %, 2.10 basis is 103.91

7. The market price of

   11 year 2½ %, 2.20 basis is 102.92

8. The difference for .10 is .99
9. The difference for .05 is .495
10. The market price of

    11 year 2½ %, 2.15 basis is 103.415 (103.91 − .495)

11. The difference between number 4 and number 9 is .135

    (103.55 − 103.415)

12. The difference for 3 months is .0675 (.135 ÷ 2)
13. The market price of 2½ percent bond on a 2.15 percent basis, maturing in 11 years and 3 months is 103.482 (103.415 + .0675)

BIDS AND OFFERS

In making his bids and offers in the secondary market, the municipal bond dealer is obligated to make only bona fide bids and offers. That means he must be prepared to buy or sell the security at the price quoted. He may, however, make a "nominal quote," which is made only for information purposes. The quotes must represent the fair or reasonable market value of the security. This will be based on the broker's inventory and the volatility of the security.

When the broker–dealer is participating in a joint account, he is not allowed to publish a quote if the security is being sold in multiple markets. Misrepresentation of quotations is prohibited. Reporting of the trade is not mandatory.

In executing an order, the broker must obtain the fair market value of the security. He may act as a broker–agent for his customer or as a broker acting on behalf of another broker.

If the broker is acting as a dealer in a transaction, the price must include any markups or markdowns and his expenses in the transaction. If he is acting as an agent, his commission or the service fees must be reasonable and fair.

INTEREST AND PRINCIPAL PAYMENTS ON BONDS

Bonds pay interest in either of two ways:

1. The bond may be issued and sold to the customer at a discount from the face value. These are generally non-interest bearing securities, such as zero bonds or U.S. Treasury bills. The customer purchases a $10,000 face value of the U.S. Treasury bills at $9,000 discount price but receives $10,000 at the time of redemption. The difference of $1,000 is treated as interest income.

2. The bond issuer will pay interest to the bondholder in accordance with a set schedule of payment. Most interest-bearing bonds pay interest every six months. Some, such as Eurobonds and Farmers Home Administration Notes, pay interest annually. Others, such as GNMA, pay interest monthly; and some Certificates of Deposit and tax-exempt notes pay interest at the time the principal is paid to the bondholder.

There are, therefore, two types of bonds—discounted and interest bearing. The method of interest payment has a lot to do with the yield of the security. A bond or a bill purchased at a price discounted from the face value will have a different yield calculation than a bond paying interest semi-annually or annually. If a discounted issue has a 6 percent interest rate, this means the customer has purchased the security at $100 - 6 = 94$. He has paid $94 for each $100 face value of the security. Therefore, one must calculate 6 percent, not on the basis of an investment of $100 but on investment of $94. This will mean 6.38 percent. For a GNMA security paying interest once a month, an 8 percent yield means, in fact, 8.13 percent actual yield.

METHOD OF PAYING THE PRINCIPAL

The issuer pays off the principal to the bondholder at maturity by using any one of the following methods:

1. If the bond or the note is a short-term instrument, the issuer will generally issue another security to refund the maturity issue. This is called "Roll-Over" or Refunding. The municipality may also do a prerefunding or advance refunding. In this case, the municipality will sell the new bond and hold the proceeds of the sale in an escrow account until the old bond is called or matured. The funds in the escrow account may be invested in government securities earning interest. The interest income will be used to pay the interest cost on the old bond.

2. Long-term bonds are retired by using cash reserves or the proceeds of a newly issued bond.

3. If the bond has a sinking fund provision, the issuer will retire a part or all of the issue by the maturity date.

4. The principal will be paid through a call. The issuer will redeem the bond prior to maturity. This may be done when interest rates in the economy have gone down. The issuer may call the bond by announcing the call in a financial publication 30 days prior to the call date. The bonds are usually called at a premium. The premium declines as the bond approaches maturity.

EXAMPLE

	Premium	*Price of Call*
1995	6%	$106
2000	5%	$105
2005	4%	$104

Bearer bonds are selected for call through a lottery procedure conducted by a trustee bank. The municipal bond may have a call protective feature. This means the bonds will not be called for a specified period of time.

5. The bondholder may tender the bond to the municipality at a tender price. The municipality has the right to accept or to reject the tender.

BOND INTERESTS AND CALCULATIONS

Interests on municipal bonds are computed on the basis of 360 calendar days a year, with each month having 30 calendar days. In the settlement of contracts the interest specified in the bond is added to the dollar price. The interest is computed up to but not including the day of the settlement on Regular Way trades and up to but not including the day of the transaction for cash trades.

All Regular Way transactions in bonds that are traded "flat" are done on the basis of "Ex-Interest" in the following manner:

1. The Ex-Interest date of the bond is the fourth business day before the record date in a Regular Way transaction. If there are no record dates established, the Ex-Interest date will be the fifth business day preceding the date on which an interest payment is to be made.

2. If the notice of payment of interest is not made sufficiently in advance of the record date, the Ex-Interest date will be on the first business day following the public notice of the record date, or the payment date, as the case may be.

The record date is a fixed date by the bond trustee for the purpose of determining the holders of the bonds entitled to receive interest payment.

Registered Bonds Traded with Interest

When the delivery of the registered bond traded "with interest" is made between the record date and interest payment date, a deduction equivalent to the full amount of the interest must be made on settlement.

Registered Bonds Traded "Flat"

When the delivery of the registered bond traded "flat" is made after the record date and if the trade is executed prior to the Ex-Interest date, a due bill check for the full amount of the interest must accompany the delivery.

In all transactions involving payment of interest, fractions of a cent are regarded as one cent. Fractions of a cent less than 5 mills are disregarded.

If the delivery is made too late to transfer the security on or before the record date, due bill checks for the interest on registered bonds must accompany the bond.

Examples of Accrued Interest Calculations

Issuers generally pay interest on bonds semi-annually on the first or the fifteenth of the two months in the following schedule:

January 1 and July 1	(J & J 1)
February 15 and August 15	(F & A 15)
March 1 and September 1	(M & S 1)
April 15 and October 15	(A & O 15)
May 1 and November 1	(M & N 1)
June 15 and December 15	(J & D 15)

For corporate and municipal bonds the accrued interest is calculated on the basis of 360 calendar days a year with each month having 30 calendar days. The seller of the bond must receive accrued interest from the buyer at the time of the settlement of the trade. The accrued interest is calculated on the basis of 30 calendar days each month starting from the last date the seller received his interest and continuing until the date of the settlement of the trade, but not including the day of settlement.

Customer A sells $1,000 Bee Corp. 6% due Jan 1, 2003:

Trade date:	September 13
Settlement date:	September 20
Price:	90½

This issuer will pay interest on January 1 and July 1 every year until the year 2003. The issuer last paid interest to customer A on July 1; therefore, the accrued interest calculation will be:

July has 30 days
August has 30 days
September has 19 days (up to but not including the date of settlement).

The seller must receive from the buyer accrued interest calculated on the basis of 79 days. $1,000 Bee Corp bond earns 6 percent interest every year, or $60. This is distributed to the holders in two installments—$30 on January 1 and $30 on July 1. ($60 a year on a 360 calendar-year basis means 17 cents a day.)

1. The seller sold the bond at 90½
2. The dollar amount of the trade excluding commissions is $905.00.
3. Accrued interest is 17 × 79 days = $13.43.
4. The seller must receive from the buyer $905.00 + 13.43 = $918.43.

When preparing the trade confirmation ticket, the broker must indicate the lowest of the yield. If it is a discount bond, the broker will use the yield to maturity. If the bond is a premium bond, the broker will use the yield to premium call, disclosing the first call date and the first call price. If it is a put or an option bond, the broker must determine the lowest yield. If the yield to par option is lower than the yield to put option, then the yield to put option must be indicated on the confirmation ticket.

BOND SWAPS

Through a procedure called Bond Swap, the investor sells a bond that has declined in value and uses the proceeds to buy other similar bonds. This is used to restructure a bond portfolio. The new bond may have a higher yield and a shorter maturity. For tax purposes, the Internal Revenue Service will consider this a Wash Sale and will disallow the loss to be used against other capital gains *if* two of the three factors are the same:

A. Maturity of the bond
B. Name of the issuer
C. Yield

If only one is similar, then the loss may be considered to be a tax-deductible item.

CLEARING OF MUNICIPAL SECURITIES

The securities clearing corporations have created a Bond Comparison System that enables the municipal industry to process municipal bond transactions. The advantages of trade comparison and clearance through a clearing facility are the cost-efficiencies and controls achieved through centralizing the processing of the trade—from a verbal commitment to a settled and paid contract. The system compares information submitted by both the buying and selling brokers or bankers, automatically matching the various details of the trade. The firms receive daily reports identifying matched trades and trades with discrepancies.

MUNICIPAL BONDS AS INVESTMENT VEHICLES

Municipal bonds are generally considered to be safe investments. There are certain risks, however, associated with them:

1. *Bankruptcy*. If the municipality goes bankrupt, it may not be able to pay the principal and interest to the bondholder.
2. *Delayed interest payments.*
3. *Loss of quality in credit ratings*—the reclassification of the bond by the rating company. The reclassification may lower the market price of the security.
4. *Lack of liquidity of the issue in the marketplace.*
5. *Possible risk*. There may be some risk associated with securities when the bonds are "called" or redeemed before the maturity date.

Return on Investment of Municipal Bonds

The interest earned on municipal bonds is tax-exempt, but any capital gains on the security are taxable under the federal tax laws.

The customer purchases a municipal bond with a face value of $1,000 that pays 6 percent a year interest:

A. Cost of purchase: $800.00
B. Interest earned: $60.00 a year (non-taxable)
C. The customer sells the bond at $1,000.
D. Profit on the transaction: $200.00 (taxable)

The return on investment of the bond is measured by various terms, such as Net Interest Cost (NIC), Yield to Maturity, Running Yield or the current yield, Yield to Call, etc.

1. Net Interest Cost. This is used for reducing bids from various underwriters to a standard of measurement.

2. Yield to Maturity. This is a measuring device for the percentage return of the investment if the bond is held to maturity. The yield to maturity is measured by:

- Amount of interest paid on the bond.
- The interest rate of the bond.

- The length of time to maturity of the bond: There are various Yield Tables used to get the Yield to Maturity of a bond. If Yield Tables are not available, the following formulas may be used:

Bonds Sold at Discount from the Face Value

$$\text{Yield to maturity} = \frac{\left(\begin{array}{c}\text{Total dollar}\\ \text{amount of}\\ \text{annual interest}\\ \text{per one bond}\end{array}\right) + \left(\begin{array}{c}\text{Total discount}\\ \text{divided by the}\\ \text{number of years}\\ \text{to maturity}\end{array}\right)}{(\text{Discount bond cost} + \text{par value}) \div 2}$$

EXAMPLE

The yield to maturity of \$1,000 bond – 7% maturing in 12 years purchased at \$95.

$$\frac{\$70 + (\$50 \div 12 \text{ years})}{(\$950 + \$1{,}000) \div 2} = .076\ (7.6\%)$$

Bonds Sold at Premium

$$\text{Yield to maturity} = \frac{\left(\begin{array}{c}\text{Total dollar}\\ \text{amount of}\\ \text{annual interest}\\ \text{per one bond}\end{array}\right) - \left(\begin{array}{c}\text{Total premium}\\ \text{divided by the}\\ \text{number of years}\\ \text{to maturity}\end{array}\right)}{(\text{Premium bond cost} + \text{par value}) \div 2}$$

EXAMPLE

The yield to maturity of \$1,000 bond 7% maturing in 12 years purchased at \$108.

$$\frac{\$70 - (\$80 \div 12 \text{ years})}{(\$1{,}080 + \$1{,}000) \div 2} = .06\ (6\%)$$

3. Current Yield or Running Yield. This is the interest rate divided by the price of the bond. It measures the current yield without any consideration as to maturity.

A $1,000 bond paying 7½% interest annually, purchased at $800 will have a current yield of $75/$800 = 0.093 (9.375%).

4. Yield to Call. This measures the yield of the bond up to the time the bond is called by the issuer. The issuer may call the bond if the current interest rates are lower than the nominal interest rate on the bond. The great majority of municipal bonds are non-callable, while some U.S. government and corporate bonds are callable.

There are several other terms used in conjunction with yields. One is Yield Differential or Yield Spread. Yield Differentials are the yield differences between varying types of bonds. It is used to compare the yields of different bonds or different groups of bonds. For instance, the Yield Spread between U.S. government securities and agency securities is 20 Basis Points (1 Basis Point is equal to 1/100th of 1%). 20 Basis Points means that if the yield on the U.S. government issues is 10.20 percent, the yield on the agency security will be 10.40 percent. This is a 20 Basis Point Yield Differential.

THE YIELD CURVE

The security analyst uses a chart to compare various yields. The chart is the Yield Curve, which indicates the relationship between yields and maturities of similar securities. The shape of the curve will determine the yield. One is Negatively Shaped Yield Curve, another is Positively Sloped Curve (Hump-Backed Yield Curve, Horizontal Curve, etc.). The curves are used to forecast future interest rate levels and help the investor to select the maturity of the bond. Figure 7.1 is an example of a Positively Sloped Curve.

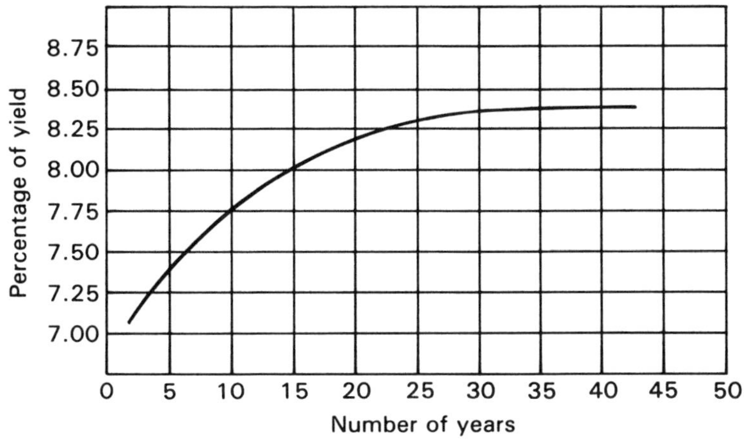

Fig. 7.1. A Positively Sloped Curve

HOW TO ANALYZE A MUNICIPAL BOND

To analyze a municipal bond, the investor will consider the following factors:

1. The legal opinion issued by the municipal bond counsel
2. The ability of the political entity to pay its obligations; its reputation and the track record of past performance
3. The population mix and the political stability
4. Retail sales per capita; the number of building permits issued during a given year
5. Taxes per capita, which is determined by dividing the amount of tax collected by the number of persons filing income tax
6. The quality of management of the municipality
7. The budget of the municipality

8. The debt service requirement of the municipality. This is the amount of the principal debt the municipality is required to pay every year. Is it increasing or declining?
9. What is the ratio of debt service vis-a-vis the annual revenue? As a general rule, it should not exceed 25 percent.
10. What is the floating debt of the municipality? The floating debt is the current liability of the municipality.
11. The ability of the municipality to collect revenues
12. The ratio of assets vs. liabilities
13. The market value and the assessed value of taxable real estate properties
14. The amount of bonded debt and self-supporting debt. The net bonded debt is equal to the total bonded debt self-supporting debt-sinking fund.
15. The amount of net direct debt, which is determined by:

$$\text{Net bonded debt} + \text{Floating debt.}$$

16. Does the municipality have any overlapping debt? This is a debt that the political entity owes to another political entity, usually within the same state.
17. The amount of the net overall debt, which is determined by:

$$\text{Net direct debt} + \text{Overlapping debt}$$

18. What is the debt per capita? This is determined by:

$$\frac{\text{Debt issued}}{\text{Number of residents}}$$

19. Employee fringe benefits and other unfunded liabilities
20. Does the municipality have any legal debt limits?
21. The tax delinquency rate. This is determined by:

$$\frac{\text{Amount of delinquent taxes}}{\text{Taxes due}}$$

The taxes due the municipality are measured by Ad Valorem tax. The Ad Valorem tax is determined by Mills.

$$1 \text{ mill} = \$.001 \text{ or } 1/10 \text{ of } 1 \text{ cent}$$

This is the tax per dollar of the assessed valuation of real estate properties.

$$\text{Tax due} = \text{Number of mills} \times \text{Assessed value}$$

BOND BUYER INDEXES

Indicators published by the *Bond Buyer* are based on price levels of various groups of municipal bonds. There are four different indexes:

11 Bond Index—Estimation of yield that would be offered on a 20-year GO bonds rated "Aa" or "AA."

20 Bond Index—Estimation of yield that would be offered on 20-year GO bonds rated "A."

25 Bond Index or Revdex—Estimation of yield that would be offered on a 30-year revenue bond of 25 issuers.

Bond Buyer Municipal Bond Index—This index represents an average of prices, which adjusts to an 8.0 yield basis of 40 recently issued municipal bonds.

The *Bond Buyer* utilizes a wire service called "Munifacts" to announce invitations to dealers for bids and awards.

MUNICIPAL BOND INSURANCE

The fiscal problems of New York City have created the need for municipalities and municipal bond underwriters to purchase insurance policies guaranteeing the payment of principal and interest to the bondholder. This provides an added safety to investors of municipal bonds. The bonds are generally insured by a consortium of insurance companies. There are stringent requirements that the municipality must comply with to qualify for the insurance. Once written, the policy becomes irrevocable. In the event of default, the insurance company guarantees to pay the principal and interest to the bondholder. Policies may be written for general obligation or revenue bonds.

There are two major carriers that provide insurance for municipal securities: the Municipal Bond Insurance Association (MBIA) and the American Municipal Bond Assurance Corporation (AMBAC). The municipality pays a one-time premium to buy the insurance policy. The coverage will be valid for the life of the security. Standard & Poor's Corporation assigns AAA to insured municipal securities, but Moody's Investors Services does not consider the insurance coverage to determine the rating.

STATE PROGRAMS

State governments may have programs that will guarantee or support the credit of local governments. This may be in the form of a general obligation pledge to pay the principal and interest or a grant to subsidize the debt service requirements of the local authorities. It will enhance the credit standing of a lower-rated local government if the state government is enjoying a higher-rated standing. Through this program, the local government will reduce the cost of financing the bond issue.

FEDERAL PROGRAMS

There are various federal programs that guarantee local municipal issues, particularly those in housing and urban developments, hospitals, rural projects, and defense-related facilities. These federal programs will lower the borrowing cost by local governments. The rating agencies will generally assign AAA to these issues.

CHAPTER EIGHT

MUNICIPAL NOTES

Municipal notes are short-term instruments issued by municipalities or local governments to finance a long-term capital acquisition or to meet the deficits in short-term operating cash flow.

Municipal notes are sold to the public in anticipation of receipt of taxes or revenues. These instruments are traded in the money market, whereas long-term municipal bonds are traded in the bond market. Notes are generally interest-bearing. They mature between one month and one year, with denominations from $5,000 to $5 million. As short-term instruments, they are not required to be issued in registered form. Most municipal notes are general obligations secured by the good faith and the credit of the municipality. They are rated by the rating service and the interest is tax-exempt from federal income tax.

TYPES OF MUNICIPAL NOTES

1. TANS—Tax Anticipation Notes. These are issued in anticipation of future tax receipts.
2. RANS—Revenue Anticipation Notes. These are issued in anticipation of future receipt of revenues.

3. BANS—Bonds Anticipation Notes. These are issued to finance a project which will eventually be funded by a long-term bond.

4. TRANS—Tax and Revenue Anticipation Notes.

Tax-Exempt Commercial Papers

Tax-exempt commercial papers (TECP) are short-term promissory notes. But unlike other anticipation notes, they are supported by a bank line of credit. And, unlike corporate commercial papers, the interest on municipal commercial paper is tax-exempt. The bank line of credit is different from the letter of credit issued by the bank. Through the line of credit, the bank agrees to lend funds to the municipality for a fixed time period. This will enable the municipality to meet future cash calls to redeem the commercial paper. A letter of credit is different. It represents the bank's commitment to make the payment of principal and interest as a guarantee for the debt obligation. The bank charges the issuer an annual fee to write the letter of credit. The fee is usually 1/2 percent of the amount of the authorized available funds. The bank may share its risk by syndicating the letter of credit to other banks. The rating agencies will step up the rating of issues backed by letters of credit. This means that if the bank writing the letter of credit is rated AA, then the commercial paper will also be AA.

Municipal commercial papers became popular in 1981 for their versatility and flexibility. Because of their varying maturities, they became attractive instruments for investors wishing to invest in short-term tax-exempt instruments. The largest purchasers are the money market mutual funds.

TECPs are usually sold at par and are redeemed at par plus interest at maturity. The municipality uses either general revenues or the proceeds of sale of a new commercial paper to redeem a maturing one. The principal and interest on the paper may be guaranteed by an irrevocable letter of credit issued by a bank, the state where the municipality is located, by an insurance company, or by a trust fund established to guarantee the paper.

Similar to other municipal securities, TECPs are rated by financial service organizations, such as Moody's, Standard & Poor's and Fitch. P-1 is the highest rating for Moody's, A-1 for Standard & Poor's, & F-1 for Fitch.

Tax-exempt commercial papers are issued through a disclosure statement known as Offering Memorandum, which is updated periodically as long as the municipality is in the TECP market.

Characteristics of Tax-Exempt Commercial Papers

- TECP carries a low-interest rate, usually half of the current prime rate. The interest rates are lower than other long/short-term municipal securities.
- Their maturities range from 1 to 270 days. This will enable the issuer to tailor its short-term borrowing needs, and also provide liquidity to the investor.
- The start-up and administrative costs for a TECP program are higher than for most other municipal securities. This is due to higher bond counsel fees, the bank line of credit, the underwriters fees, and overhead.
- Municipal commercial papers are issued with a minimum denomination of $100,000, but the average transaction is in $1 million or more.

Because of its short life, there is little secondary market available. The business is transacted between the hours of 9:00 a.m. & 12:30 p.m., with same-day settlement in federal funds.

MOODY'S SHORT-TERM MUNICIPAL RATINGS

Moody's Investors Services rates short-term municipal notes in the following manner:

MIG 1—Best quality notes

MIG 2—High quality notes

MIG 3—Favorable quality

MIG 4—Adequate quality. Notes carry some risks.

FDIC/FSLIC BONDS

FDIC/FSLIC Bonds are municipal bonds backed by the Federal Deposit Insurance Corporation (FDIC) or the Federal Savings and Loan Insurance Corp. (FSLIC). The bonds are issued by units of local governments that invest the proceeds in $100,000 Certificates of Deposit at banks or at S&Ls, which, in turn, lend the funds to the municipality for projects specified in the municipal bond issue.

The Procedure to Issue FDIC/FSLIC Bonds

1. Municipality sells bonds to the public.
2. Municipality invests the proceeds of the sale in $100,000 CDs issued by a bank or S & L.
3. The municipal bond owned by the public will be insured by the bank CD.
4. The bank CD is, in turn, insured by FDIC or FSLIC insurance.
5. The bank sells the CD to the municipality, takes the proceeds from the municipality, and lends the money back to the municipality for projects specified in the municipal bond issue.

This type of municipal bond matures in 10 or 15 years and since they are municipal bonds the interest is tax-exempt.

Standard and Poor's gives the issues a special rating—AAA-L. This is its highest rating but it's contingent on FDIC or FSLIC insurance.

Legislation has outlawed FDIC/FSLIC bonds issued after April 14, 1983. A secondary market for the existing issues, however, continues to exist.

MUNICIPAL TIGR'S OR MUNICIPAL MBEARS

Municipal TIGRs or Mbears are securities issued by investment banking firms as by-products of the Tax Reform Act of 1986.

Muni TIGRs are Municipal Tax-exempt Investment Growth Receipts and Mbears are Municipal Bond Exempt Accrual Receipts. They have two different names, but they are generally structured in the same way.

Muni TIGRs or Mbears are securities issued by investment banking firms representing ownership in a group of tax-exempt municipal general obligation or revenue bonds. The investment banking firm will purchase a group of tax-exempt municipal bonds and place the bonds at a commercial bank that will act as the custodian for the benefit of customers. The investment banking firm will then issue book-entry receipts evidencing ownership of future interest, principal, and the redemption premium on the municipal bonds. The municipal bonds, therefore, are stripped in the following manner:

1. *Coupon Municipal TIGR's.* Each Coupon Municipal TIGR evidences ownership of a direct interest in one of the semi-annual interest payments due on the municipal bonds in the portfolio. The investment banker will not make any payments on coupon Municipal TIGRs nor will the Coupon Municipal TIGRs be redeemable prior to their

maturities. At maturity, each holder will receive a single payment of the face amount of each Municipal TIGR.

2. *Principal Municipal TIGRs.* Principal Municipal TIGRs evidence ownership of the principal and redemption premium, if any, payable on the underlying municipal bonds in the portfolio. Here again, the investment banking firm will not make any payments on these TIGRs, nor will these TIGRs be redeemed prior to their maturities. At maturity, each TIGR holder will receive a single payment of the face amount of the Principal Municipal TIGR.

3. *Current Pay Municipal TIGRs.* Each Current Pay Municipal TIGR holder will receive a semi-annual interest payment and a final principal payment as do holders of regular municipal bonds. They are generally priced at par.

Tax Treatment

The discount accruing on the Municipal TIGRs purchased at a yield not exceeding the nominal interest rate of the municipal bonds in the portfolio is exempt from federal income taxation.

THE IMPACT OF THE TAX REFORM ACT OF 1986 ON MUNICIPAL BOND OPERATION

The Tax Reform Act of 1986 signed by President Reagan on October 22, 1986, has grouped municipal bonds, both general obligations and revenues, into three different categories with regard to their tax treatments:

First Category: These are tax-exempt municipal bonds issued by state and local governments and their agencies to meet an essential governmental purpose, such as highway construction, school financing, and so on. The interest on these bonds is tax-exempt.

Second Category: These are bonds issued by political entities for non-governmental purposes. Examples are housing authority or student loan bonds. These bonds will be identified as non-governmental municipal bonds if 10 percent or more of the proceeds of the sale are applied for non-governmental purposes. The interest on these bonds is taxable if issued after August 7, 1986.

Third Category: These are taxable municipal bonds such as certain Industrial Revenue Bonds, issued after August 7, 1986. The interest on Industrial Revenue bonds issued to finance the construction of docks, a mass commuting facility, waste disposal, airports (excluding hotels), a local electricity or gas facility, and facilities to furnish water is tax-exempt. The Tax Law, however, imposes volume limitations on state governments with regard to Industrial Revenue bonds. The face value of Industrial Revenue bonds for each state cannot exceed the greater of $50 per resident or $150 million per year.

CHAPTER NINE

MUNICIPAL SECURITIES RULEMAKING BOARD

Established by a Congressional Act in 1975, the Municipal Securities Rulemaking Board (MSRB) is charged with the responsibility of developing rules for the proper conduct of financial institutions engaged in trading, selling, and underwriting municipal securities. The Board is composed of members from the industry and the public. It is a self-regulatory entity similar to the NASD. But unlike the NASD, the MSRB does not have enforcement authority. Responsibility for enforcing the MSRB rules is assigned to the SEC, the NASD, the Comptroller of the Currency, the Federal Reserve System, and the FDIC.

MSRB's sole responsibility is to develop rules concerning:

1. Standards of professional qualification
2. Fair practice
3. Record-keeping
4. Compliance examinations
5. Municipal securities quotations
6. Sale of new municipal securities
7. Distribution of disclosure documents on new municipal securities

In addition, the MSRB has adopted a code of arbitration to resolve disputes among industry members and between broker–dealers and customers.

THE RULES OF MUNICIPAL SECURITIES RULEMAKING BOARD

The following rules of the MSRB are discussed in simplified terms. Rules with a prefix "A" pertain to the operation and administration of the Board. Definitional rules are identified by a prefix "D." General rules pertain to all other matters. They are identified by the prefix "G."

Rule A-13

Rule A-13 requires every municipal securities broker–dealer to pay to MSRB a fee equal to $.01 per $1,000 of the face amount of all municipal securities with a maturity date in excess of two years purchased from an issuer as part of an underwriting.

Rule A-14

This rule requires an MSRB member to pay an annual fee of $100.

Rule G-1

The day-to-day conduct of the department must be supervised by an officer assigned by the board of directors of the organization. The following municipal securities activities must be conducted in a special unit or division of the MSRB-member organization:

1. Underwriting, trading, and sales of municipal securities

2. Financial advisory and consultant services for issuers in connection with the issuers of municipal securities
3. Processing and clearing activities of municipal securities
4. Research and investment advice
5. Maintenance of records pertaining to municipal securities

Rule G-2

No municipal securities broker–dealer shall be qualified by the MSRB if he is expelled or suspended from membership in a stock exchange or the NASD.

Rule G-3

This rule establishes professional qualifications for municipal broker–dealers. The professional participants are in four categories: municipal securities principal, municipal securities sales principal, financial and operations principal, and municipal securities representative. These persons are required to pass an examination before performing their respective duties.

Every member-organization is required to have at least two municipal securities principals, except as follows:

A. A municipal securities broker–dealer who is a member of a stock exchange.
B. A municipal securities broker–dealer with less than 11 persons engaged in municipal securities activities.

Every municipal securities broker–dealer (other than a bank) shall have at least one financial and operations principal.

Any associated person of a member-organization who fails to pass a qualification examination is permitted to take the examination again after a period of 30 days has elapsed from the date of the previous examination. If the person fails the examination three or more times in succession, that person must wait six months to take another one.

Any person who first becomes associated with a municipal securities broker–dealer as a representative may not conduct any activity in municipal securities for a period of at least 90 days. This is known as the apprenticeship period. During this period, this person may not communicate with public investors regarding the sale of municipal securities.

Rule G-4

No municipal securities broker–dealer shall be qualified by the MSRB if he is expelled of suspended from membership in a stock exchange or the NASD.

Rule G-5

No municipal securities broker–dealer shall effect any transaction in any municipal security in contravention of any effective restrictions imposed by the Securities and Exchange Commission.

Rule G-6

Every member shall be required to carry a blanket fidelity covering officers and employees against losses in the following areas:

D. Fidelity
B. On promises
C. In transit
D. Misplacement
E. Forgery and alteration

F. Securities loss

G. Fraudulent trading

The broker–dealer must maintain coverage of not less than 120 percent of its required net capital up to $600,000. Minimum coverage for required net capital in excess of $600,000 shall be in accordance with the following table:

Net Capital Requirement Under SEC Rule 15C3-1	*Minimum Coverage*
$600,001– $1,000,000	$750,000
$1,000,001– $2,000,000	$1,000,000
$2,000,001– $3,000,000	$1,500,000
$3,000,001– $4,000,000	$2,000,000
$4,000,001– $6,000,000	$3,000,000
$6,000,001–$12,000,000	$4,000,000
$12,000,001–and above	$5,000,000

Every member shall review the adequacy of its insurance coverage at least once a year.

Each member shall report the cancellation, termination, or modification of its insurance policies to the stock exchange or the NASD.

Rule G-7

Every municipal securities broker–dealer shall obtain from its associated persons a questionnaire containing the following information:

1. The person's name, address, Social Security number, and the date of employment
2. Date of birth
3. Educational background
4. Business connections and employment history for the preceding 10 years
5. A record of any suspensions, expulsions, and convictions

Every municipal securities broker–dealer shall make an inquiry of all employers of the associated persons regarding the person's employment history.

The broker–dealer must maintain the employment questionnaire for at least three years after the person's employment has been terminated.

Rule G-8. Books and Records to be kept by Municipal Securities Broker–Dealers

Every municipal securities broker–dealer must maintain the following books and records:

1. Blotters and records of original entry
2. Account records
3. Securities records
4. Records regarding the securities in transfer, securities borrowed and loaned, securities to be validated, securities transactions not completed on the settlement date
5. Put options and repurchase agreements
6. Records for agency transactions
7. Records for transactions as principal
8. Records for syndicate transactions
9. Customer confirmation
10. Financial records
11. Customer account information
12. Customer complaints

All of the above must be clearly identified and maintained.

Municipal securities broker–dealers (other than banks) who are in compliance with SEC 17a-3 will be deemed to be in compliance with these requirements of the MSRB.

Rule G-9. Preservation of Records

A. *Records to be preserved for six years*
   1. Blotters and records of original entry
   2. Account records
   3. Securities records
   4. Records of syndicate transactions
   5. Customer complaints
   6. General ledgers pertaining to SEC Rule 17a-3

B. *Records to be preserved for three years*
   1. Records for securities in transfer, securities borrowed and loaned, securities to be validated, and securities transactions not completed on the settlement date
   2. Records of put options and repurchase agreements
   3. Records relating to agency transactions
   4. Records of transactions as principal
   5. Copies of customer confirmations
   6. Records of net capital computations
   7. Check books, bank statements and reconciliations, and wire transfers
   8. Bills receivable and payable
   9. Inter-office memorandum
   10. Power of attorney
   11. Records relating to employee fingerprinting

C. *Records to be preserved for life*
   1. Partnership agreement
   2. Articles of incorporation or charter
   3. Minute book and stock certificate book

D. All above records must be kept in an easily accessible place during the first two years.

E. Municipal securities broker–dealers (other than banks) who are required to comply with SEC Rule 17a-3 and 17a-4 will be deemed to be in compliance with this rule.

Rule G-10. Designation of Persons Responsible for Maintenance and Preservation of Books and Records

Every municipal securities broker–dealer shall designate one or more associated persons, who are either general securities principal or municipal securities dealers, to supervise the maintenance and preservation of books and records.

Rule G-11. Sales of New Municipal Securities

A. *Disclosure of Capacity.* Every municipal securities dealer who is a member of a syndicate that submits a purchase order to the syndicate shall disclose whether the securities are being purchased for his own dealer account, for the account of a related party, for a municipal investment trust sponsored by the dealer, or for an accumulation account established for the investment trust.

B. *Confirmation of Sale.* Sales of securities by a syndicate to a related account, municipal investment trust, or accumulation account for the investment trust shall be confirmed by the syndicate manager directly to such account.

C. *Disclosure of Group Orders.* Every municipal securities dealer that submits a group order to a syndicate shall disclose the identity of the person for whom the order is submitted.

D. *Priority Provisions.* Every syndicate shall establish priority provisions for the allocation of securities. The priority shall be in the best interest of the syndicate.

E. *Communication Relating to Priority Provisions and Order Period.* Prior to the submission of the syndicate bid, the managing underwriter shall furnish in writing to the other members of the syndicate the following information:

1. the priority provision
2. the procedure for changing the priority order
3. the procedure for allocation of securities
4. information on whether orders may be confirmed prior to the end of the order period

F. *Disclosure of Allocation of Securities.* Within 10 business days following the date of sale, the syndicate manager shall disclose to the other members of the syndicate the following information concerning the allocation of securities to orders submitted through the end of the order period, or if the syndicate does not have an order period, through the first business day following the date of sale.

1. The identity of each related account, municipal securities investment trust, or accumulation account, and the total par value and the maturity date of each security being allocated.
2. The identity of each person submitting a group order and the total par value and the maturity date of the security being allocated.
3. A summary, in the order of priority, of the allocation of securities to other orders that were entitled to a higher priority than a member's "Take down" order.

G. *Disclosure of Syndicate Expenses.* At or before the final settlement of a syndicate account, the managing underwriter shall furnish to the other members of the syndicate:

1. A statement of expenses incurred on behalf of the syndicate.
2. A summary statement indicating the total par values and prices of securities sold from the syndicate account.

Rule G-12. Uniform Practice.

This rule covers the establishment of uniform settlement dates for transactions in municipal securities, processing of trade comparisons, procedures for resolving trade discrepancies, requirements for good delivery, procedures for rejection and reclamation of municipal securities, close-out procedures, and the time periods within which good faith deposit checks must be returned, syndicate accounts settled, and credits from designated orders distributed.

This rule is designed to facilitate transactions in municipal securities.

A. *Scope and Notice*
   1. All transactions in municipal securities between member broker–dealers shall be subject to the provisions of this rule.
   2. A fail to deliver does not affect a cancellation of the transaction.

B. *Settlement dates*
   1. For "cash" trades—the trade date
   2. For "regular way" trades—the fifth business day following the trade date
   3. For "when, as, and if issued" trades—a date agreed upon by both parties

C. *Notice of Accelerated Delivery.* In the event the issuer gives notice of a pending delivery of securities within less than six business days before delivery, the syndicate manager shall give immediate notice to the members of the syndicate of the settlement date for transactions between the manager and the syndicate members.

D. *Dealer Confirmation*
   1. Dealers shall send trade confirmation to other parties within one business day following the trade date.

2. Cash trades must be confirmed on trade date.
3. For "when, as, and if issued" trades, initial confirmation shall be sent within two business days following the trade date. Confirmation indicating the final settlement date shall be sent by the seller at least five business days prior to the settlement date.
4. For transactions in new issues having a settlement date more than six business days, confirmation shall be sent within two business days following the trade date.
5. The following information shall be confirmed:
   a. Broker–dealer's name, address, and telephone number
   b. Contra party identification
   c. Purchase or sale
   d. Par value of securities
   e. Description of securities
   f. Cusip number
   g. Trade date
   h. Settlement date
   i. Yield at which the transaction was effected, and the resulting dollar price. If the securities are traded on the basis of dollar price or sold at par, only the dollar price needs to be shown. If the securities are priced to call or to par option, this must be stated with the call or option date and the price used in the calculation. If the transaction is effected on a yield basis, the dollar price shall be calculated to the lowest of price to call, price to par option, or price to maturity.
   j. Amount of concession
   k. Accrued interest
   l. Extended principal amount
   m. Total dollar amount of the transaction
   n. Instruments for receipt of delivery of securities and form of payment. For transactions in zero bonds the confirmation shall contain the rate of discount, and the resulting dollar price.

6. In addition, each confirmation shall contain:
   a. Dated date if it affects the price or interest calculation, and the first interest payment date if other than semi-annual
   b. Description of the security whether it is "registered," registered as to principal only, "bearer," or in book-entry form
   c. If the securities are called or preregistered, the date of maturity fixed by the call notice, and the amount of the call price
   d. Denomination of the security
   e. Special instructions or qualifications, such as "ex-legal," "flat," "in default," etc., and interest payment schedule if other than semi-annual

E. *Comparison and Verification of Confirmations.* Upon receipt of a confirmation, each party shall compare and verify information on the confirmation ticket. If there are any discrepancies, the party must promptly notify the contra broker. Confirmation must be returned to the contra broker within one business day after receipt.

F. *Delivery of Securities*
   1. Place and time of delivery. Delivery shall be made at the office of the purchaser, or its designated agent, between the hours established by the rule and practice.
   2. Securities delivered must have a cusip number if one is assigned.
   3. Delivery Ticket. A delivery ticket shall accompany the delivery of securities.
   4. Partial Delivery. The purchaser shall not be required to accept a partial delivery with respect to a single trade in a single security.
   5. Units of Delivery
      a. For bearer bonds—denomination of $1,000 and $5,000 par value.
      b. For registered bonds—denominations that are

multiples of $1,000 par value, up to $100,000 par value

6. Form of Securities
   a. Bearer and Registered Form
   b. Book-Entry Form
7. Mutilated Certificates. Delivery of a certificate that is damaged in such a way that any of the following is not recognized: name of issuer, par value, signature, coupon rate, maturity date, seal of the issuer, or the certificate number shall not constitute good delivery unless validated by the trustee, the transfer agent, or the issuer of the security.
8. Coupon Securities
   a. Coupon securities shall have all appropriate coupons attached to it.
   b. If the securities are traded "and interest" and the settlement date is on or after the interest payment date, such securities shall be delivered without the coupon payable on such interest payment date.
   c. If the securities are delivered on or after the thirteenth calendar day prior to an interest payment date, the seller may deliver to the purchaser a draft or a bank check payable not later than the interest payment date, or the delivery date, whichever is later, in an amount equal to the interest due in lieu of the coupon.
9. Mutilated or Cancelled Coupon. Delivery of a certificate with a damaged coupon shall not constitute good delivery unless the coupon is endorsed or guaranteed by the issuer or a commercial bank.
10. Delivery of certificate called for redemption. A certificate for which a call notice has been published on or prior to the delivery date shall not constitute good delivery unless the securities are identified as "called" at the time of trade.
11. Delivery without Legal Opinion. Delivery of certificates without legal opinion shall not constitute

good delivery unless identified as "ex-legal" at the time of trade.

12. Insured Securities. Delivery of insured securities shall have evidence of such insurance either on the face of the certificate or in a document attached to the certificate.
13. Endorsements for Banking or Insurance Requirements. A security bearing on endorsement indicating that it was deposited in accordance with certain banking and insurance requirements shall not constitute good delivery unless it bears a release signed by an authorized officer.
14. Delivery of Registered Securities
    a. Assignments. Delivery of a registered certificate must have an assignment on the reverse side of the certificate or a separate bond power.
    b. Bond Power. The bond power must be properly filled out with the name, the certificate number, and the par value of the bond.
    c. Power of Substitution. If the certificate has a power of attorney, a power of substitution shall be executed in blank.
    d. Guarantee. All assignments or endorsements must be fully guaranteed as acceptable by the transfer agent.
    e. Good Delivery. Certificates in legal form shall not constitute a good delivery unless cleared by the transfer agent.
    f. Payment of Interest. If a registered security traded "and interest" a delivery of such security made after the record date, a due bill check must accompany the delivery.
    g. Registered Securities in Default. If a registered security is in default a delivery of such security made after the record date, a due bill check must accompany the delivery.
15. Expenses of Shipment. Expenses of shipment of securities must be paid by the seller.

16. Money Differences. Following money differences may not be cause to reject the delivery:

Par Value of Bonds	*Money Difference*
$1,000- $24,999	$10
$25,000- $99,999	$25
$100,000-$249,999	$60
$250,000-$999,999	$250
$1 million and over	$500

G. Use of Automated Comparison, Clearance, and Settlement Systems. Transactions in municipal securities that are eligible for deposit at a securities depository organization may be settled through book-entry method of the depository.

H. Rejection and Reclamation
   1. Basis for Reclamation and Time Limit
      a. Reclamations must be made within one business day after receipt for the following items:
         i. The delivery does not have a coupon or interest check.
         ii. The delivery does not have a legal opinion.
         iii. The certificate or coupon is mutilated.
         iv. Bearer certificates are delivered instead of registered and vice versa.
      b. Reclamation must be made within three business days if the interest check is not honored.
      c. Reclamations must be made within 18 months following the date of delivery for the following items:
         i. Irregularity in delivery.
         ii. Transfer agent refuses to transfer the security.
      d. The following reclamations do not have time limitations:
         i. The delivered security is reported lost, stolen, or counterfeit.

ii. The delivered security is subject to call that was published on or prior to the trade date and the security was not identified as "called" at the time of trade.

2. Procedure for Rejection or Reclamation. The rejecting party shall provide a written notice indicating the reason of rejection.
3. Manner of Settlement of Reclamation. The party receiving the reclamation shall give the party making the reclamation either the correct securities or the money amount of the original transaction.
4. Effect of Rejection or Reclamation. Rejection or reclamation of securities shall not constitute a cancellation of the transaction.

I. Close-out

1. Close-out by Purchaser. With respect to a transaction that has not been completed by the seller, the purchaser may close-out the transaction in accordance with the following procedures:
   a. Notice of Close-out. The purchaser shall notify the seller not earlier than the settlement date of the trade his intention to close-out the transaction.
   b. Retransmittals and Transfer of Securities
      i. Retransmittals. Any party receiving a close-out notice may transmit the notice to another party from whom the securities are due.
      ii. Transfer of Securities. If the selling broker has submitted the securities in transfer, he may extend the close-out date by 10 business days.
   c. Contents of Notice
   d. Purchaser's Options. If the securities described in the notice of the close-out are not delivered by the date specified in the notice, the purchaser may close-out the transaction by taking one of the following actions:
      i. Purchase the security at the current market.

ii. Accept the delivery of the security from the seller.

iii. Require the seller to repurchase the security. The purchaser shall notify the seller stating the terms of the closeout after the execution of the trade.

e. Close-out not Completed

f. Completion of Transaction. If at any time prior to the execution of a close-out, the seller can complete the transaction within two business days, the seller shall give notice to the purchaser that the securities will be delivered within such a time period.

g. "Cash" Transaction. The purchaser may close-out transactions made for "cash" at the close of business on the day delivery is due.

2. Close-out by Seller. If a seller makes good delivery and the purchaser rejects delivery, the seller may close-out the transaction in accordance with the following procedure:

a. Notice of close-out to the purchaser

b. Contents of Notice

c. Execution of Close-out. If the purchaser rejects the item, the seller may sell out the transaction at the current market for the account and liability of the purchaser.

d. Acceptance of Delivery. The seller shall be entitled to recover from the purchaser all expenses incurred by the seller by reason of the purchaser's rejection of delivery.

J. Good Faith Deposit. Good faith deposits shall be returned by the syndicate manager within two business days following the date of settlement with the issuer. In the event the syndicate is not successful in purchasing the issue, the good faith deposit must be returned within two business days following the return of the deposit from the issuer.

Confirmations, Comparison, and Verification

Action Date	*Action by Purchaser*	*Action by Seller*
T + 1	Send confirmation	Send confirmation
Receipt date	Compare confirmation	Compare confirmation
Resolution of errors + 1	Send corrected confirmation	Send corrected confirmation
Settlement date	If no errors transaction settles	Transaction settles

Reclamations

Action Date	*Reason for Action*
Delivery date + 1	• Improper coupon or interest • Mutilated certificate or coupon • Legal opinion or documents missing
Receipt of notice + 3 Delivery date + 18 months	• Interest check not honored • Irregular delivery • Refused to transfer
No time limit	• Missing, stolen, counterfeit securities • Certificate called prior to trade date and not specified at the time of trade

Close-out by Purchaser

Action Date	*Action by Purchaser*	*Action by Seller*
Settlement date + 5	May give close-out notice	
Telephone notice + 1		Seller may transmit the close-out to a dealer failing to deliver the security.
Telephone notice + 10	Earliest delivery deadline (if no retransmittals)	
Telephone notice + 11–15	Earliest execution date (if no retransmittals)	
Settlement date + 90	Last day on which purchaser can initiate a close-out.	

K. Settlement of Syndicate. Final settlement of a syndicate shall be made within 60 days following the date of the delivery of security to the syndicate members.

L. Any credit designated by a customer due to a member of the syndicate shall be distributed to such member by the municipal broker–dealer handling such an order within 30 business days following the delivery of the securities to the customer.

Rule G-13. Quotations Relating to Municipal Securities

A. General Provisions

B. Bonafide Quotations. No municipal securities broker–dealer shall distribute or publish any quotations of municipal securities unless the quotation represents a bonafide bid or offer. A quotation is deemed to represent a bonafide bid or offer if the broker–dealer making the quotation is prepared to purchase or sell the security.

Rule G-14. Reports of Sales or Purchases

No broker–dealer shall distribute or publish any report of a purchase or sale of municipal securities unless the broker–dealer has reason to believe that the purchase or sale was actually effected.

Rule G-15. Confirmation, Clearance and Settlements of Transactions with Customers

A. Customer Confirmations

1. At or before the completion of the transaction, the broker–dealer shall send to the customer a written confirmation of the transaction containing the following information:

a. Name, address, telephone number of broker-dealer
b. Name of customer
c. Buy or sale
d. Par value of securities
e. Description of securities
f. Cusip number
g. Trade date and time of execution
h. Settlement date
i. Yield and dollar price as follows:
   i. For transactions effected on a yield basis, the yield at which the transaction was effected and the resulting dollar-price shall be shown. The dollar-price shall be calculated to the lowest of price to call, price to par option, or price to maturity.
   ii. For transactions effected on the basis of dollar-price, the dollar-price at which transaction was effected and the lowest of the resulting yield to call, yield to par option, or yield to maturity shall be shown.
   iii. For transactions at par, the dollar-price shall be shown.
j. Amount of accrued interest
k. Extended principal amount
l. Total dollar amount of transaction
m. Capacity in which the broker–dealer has effected the transaction
   i. As a principal for its own account
   ii. As an agent for the customer
   iii. As an agent for a person other than the customer
   iv. As an agent for both the customer and another person
n. Transactions regarding the receipt or delivery of securities.

2. In addition to this information, each confirmation shall contain the following data, if applicable:

a. Dated date
b. Form of certificate, bearer, fully registered, or book-entry
c. Description showing whether the securities are called or pre-refunded
d. If the securities are callable, designation to that effect
e. Denomination of certificates
f. Special instructions or qualifications—"ex-legal," "flat," "in default," etc.

3. Confirmation for transactions in zero bonds shall not be required to show the yield and dollar-price, nor the accrued interest. The confirmation should contain the rate of discount and resulting dollar-price.
4. Information requested pursuant to this rule shall be sent to the customer within five business days following the date of receipt of the request.

B. Settlement dates
1. For "cash" trade—the trade date
2. For "regular way" trade—T + 5
3. Deliveries to customer
   a. Securities Delivered
      i. All securities delivered shall be identical to information in the confirmation ticket.
   b. Delivery Ticket. A delivery ticket shall accompany the delivery.
      i. For bearer bonds—$1,000 or $5,000 par value
      ii. For registered bond—$1,000 up to $100,000 par value
4. Form of securities—bearer, registered as to principal or book-entry
5. a. Coupon securities shall have the correct sequence of all appropriate coupons.
   b. If the securities are traded "and interest" and the settlement date is on or after the interest payment date, such securities shall be delivered

without the coupon payable on such interest payment date.

   c. If the delivery of securities is made on or after the thirteenth calendar day prior to an interest payment date, the seller may deliver a due bill in an amount equal to the interest due.

6. Delivery of Certificates called for Redemption
   a. A certificate for which a notice of call has been published on or prior to the delivery date shall not constitute good delivery unless the securities are identified as "called" at the time of trade.
   b. A certificate for which a notice of call has been published on or prior to the trade date shall not constitute good delivery unless the securities are identified as "called" at the time of trade.
7. Delivery without legal opinion. Delivery of certificates without legal opinions shall not constitute good delivery unless identified as "ex-legal" at the time of trade.
8. Insured securities must have evidence of such insurance.
9. Endorsements for banking and insurance requirements. A certificate bearing such endorsements must have a release signed by an authorized officer.
10. Delivery of Registered Securities
    a. The certificate delivered to the customer shall be registered in the name of customer.
    b. Delivery to an agent of the customer may be registered in the name of the customer or in a "street name."
    c. Payment of interest. If a registered security is traded "and interest" and transfer cannot be completed over the record date, a due bill check must be attached to the certificate.
    d. Delivery/Receipt vs Payment
       i. RVP or DVP transactions shall be made in accordance with the following procedures:
          a. The broker–dealer must receive from the

customer prior to the execution of the order the name and address of the agent.

b. The customer must furnish the agent instructions with respect to the receipt or delivery of securities.

Rule G-16. Periodic Compliance Examinations

At least once every 24 months, each municipal securities broker–dealer shall be reviewed to determine whether the broker–dealer is in compliance with all the applicable rules of MSRB and the SEC.

Rule G-17. Conduct of Municipal Securities Business

In the conduct of his municipal securities business, each broker–dealer shall deal fairly with all persons and shall not engage in any deceptive, dishonest, or unfair practice.

Rule G-18. Execution of Transactions

Each broker–dealer, when executing a trade on behalf of a customer, shall make a reasonable effort to obtain a fair and reasonable price for the customer.

Rule G-19. Suitability of Recommendations and Transactions Discretionary Accounts

1. Account information
2. Knowledge of customer. The broker–dealer shall inquire about all essential facts of the customer's background.
3. The broker–dealer must have reasonable grounds to believe that the recommendation is suitable for the

customer based on the customer's financial background, tax statements, and investment objectives.

4. Discretionary Accounts. All discretionary accounts must have prior written authorization signed by the customer and accepted in writing by the broker-dealer.
5. Churning. No broker-dealer shall effect transactions in a discretionary account that are excessive in size or frequency.

Rule G-20. Gifts and Gratuities

1. Limitations on Value. No broker-dealer shall directly or indirectly give gratuity in excess of $100 per year to a person.
2. This rule shall not prohibit occasional gifts of meals or tickets to theatre or sporting events.
3. Compensations for Services. This rule shall not apply to contracts of employment to compensate for services rendered by another person, provided that there is an agreement between the broker-dealer and the person performing such services.

Rule G-21. Advertising

1. Professional Advertisements. No broker-dealer shall publish any advertisements concerning the facilities, services, or skills that is materially false or misleading.
2. Product Advertisements. No broker-dealer shall publish any advertisements about a product which is materially false or misleading.
3. New Issue Advertisements
   a. Accuracy at Time of Sale. A syndicate member who publishes any advertisement regarding the offering of a new issue may show the initial offer-

ing price or yields, even if the price or yield may have changed, provided that the advertisement contains the date of sale of the securities by the issuer to the syndicate. The date of sale is the date on which bids are required to be submitted to an issuer and in the case of a negotiated sale, the date on which the contract is executed.

b. Approval by Principal. Each advertisement must be approved in writing by the municipal securities principal prior to first use. Each broker-dealer shall make and keep current all records of such advertisements.

Rule G-22. Control Relationships

1. A control relationship with respect to a municipal security shall be deemed to exist if the broker-dealer controls or is controlled by the issuer of the security.
2. Discretionary Accounts. No broker-dealer shall effect a transaction for a discretionary account if such a broker-dealer has a control relationship with respect to such security, unless the transaction has been specifically authorized by the customer.
3. Disclosure. No broker-dealer shall effect a transaction for a customer if such a broker-dealer has a control relationship with respect to the security, unless the broker-dealer discloses to the customer the nature of the control relationship.

Rule G-23. Activities of Financial Advisers

1. Purpose
2. Financial Advisory Relationship. A financial advisory relationship shall be deemed to exist when a broker-dealer renders financial advisory or consultant services to an issuer.

3. Basis for Compensation. Each financial advisory relationship shall be evidenced by a written agreement, which must state the basis for compensation.
4. Underwriting Activities. No broker–dealer that has a financial advisory relationship shall acquire as principal, alone, or as a participant in syndicate any security from the issuer unless:
   a. The financial advisory relationship with respect to such issue has been terminated.
   b. The broker–dealer has disclosed in writing to the issuer at or before such termination that there may be a conflict of interest in changing from the capacity of financial adviser to purchaser of securities.
   c. Disclosure to Customers. If a broker–dealer acquires a new issue or participates in a syndicate, he shall disclose the existence of the financial advisory relationship to each customer who purchases such securities.

Rule G-24. Use of Ownership Information Obtained in Fiduciary or Agency Capacity

No broker–dealer having access to confidential information concerning a municipal security shall use such information for the purpose of soliciting purchases and sales of municipal securities.

Rule G-25. Improper Use of Assets

1. No broker–dealer shall make improper use of municipal securities or funds held on behalf of another person.
2. Guarantees. No broker–dealer shall guarantee a customer against loss.

3. Sharing Accounts. No broker–dealer shall share, directly or indirectly, in the profits or losses in a customer account.

Rule G-27. Supervision

1. Obligation to Supervise. Each broker–dealer shall supervise the activities of his associated persons in the conduct of his municipal securities business.
2. Designation of Supervisors. Each broker–dealer shall designate one or more municipal securities principals and financial and operations principals as responsible for supervising the activities of the organization.
3. Written Procedures. Each broker–dealer shall establish, maintain, and enforce written supervisory procedures to ensure compliance with the rules of MSRB and applicable provisions of the Securities Exchange Act of 1934. Such procedures shall include:
   a. The designation of at least one duly qualified municipal securities principal as responsible for supervising the activities of the organization.
   b. The prompt review and approval by the designated municipal securities principal of:
      i. The opening of each customer account
      ii. Each transaction in municipal securities
      iii. The handling of all written customer complaints
      iv. All correspondence pertaining to transactions in municipal securities.
   c. The prompt review and written approval of each transaction in a discretionary account.

   Municipal securities broker–dealers do not have to establish separate procedures for municipal securities if they have already established procedures in accordance with the Securities Exchange Act of 1934.

Rule G-28. Transactions with Employees and Partners of Other Municipal Securities Professionals

1. Account Instructions. No broker–dealer shall open an account for an employee of another broker–dealer or his immediate family, unless the broker–dealer first gives written notice to the employer of such persons. The broker–dealer must send duplicate copies of confirmation to the customer's employer.

Rule G-29. Availability of MSRB Rules

Each broker–dealer shall keep in each office a copy of MSRB rules, and shall make the rules available to the customers.

Rule G-30. Price and Commissions

1. Principal Transactions. No broker–dealer shall purchase municipal securities for its own account from a customer or sell for its own account to a customer except at an aggregate price that is fair and reasonable.
2. Agency Transactions. No broker–dealer shall purchase or sell municipal securities as agent for a customer for a commission in excess of a fair and reasonable amount.

Rule G-31. Reciprocal Dealings with Municipal Securities Investment Companies

No broker–dealer shall solicit transactions for an account of an investment company as compensation or in return for sales by such a broker–dealer of shares or units of such an investment company.

Rule G-32. Disclosure in Connection of New Issues

1. Disclosure Requirements. No broker–dealer shall sell, whether as principal or agent, any new issue to a customer unless, at or prior to sending the confirmation ticket, such a broker–dealer sends the following to the customer:
   a. A copy of the official statement if one is issued by the issuer.
   b. In connection with a negotiated sale of a new issue, the following information concerning the underwriting arrangements:
      i. The underwriting spread
      ii. The amount of any fee received by the broker–dealer as agent for the issuer.
      iii. The initial offering price

   If the official statement is not available in final form, a preliminary official statement may be sent to the customer. But when the final statement is published, that must be sent to the customer promptly.

Rule G-34. Cusip Numbers

Rule G-35. Arbitration

Every broker–dealer is subject to the following arbitration code:

Section 1. Matters Subject to Arbitration. The arbitration code shall apply to every claim, dispute, or controversy in connection with municipal securities activities.

Section 2. Persons Subject to the Provisions of the Arbitration Code

1. A municipal securities broker–dealer against another municipal securities broker–dealer

2. A non-broker–dealer against a municipal securities broker–dealer
3. A municipal securities broker–dealer against a non-broker–dealer

Section 3. Arbitration Committee

1. Appointment. The MSRB shall appoint an arbitration committee composed of seven members.
2. Duties. The arbitration committee shall establish and maintain a pool of arbitrators.

Section 4. Director of Arbitration

Section 5. Initiation of Proceedings. The procedure for arbitration is as follows:

1. The claimant shall file with the Director of Arbitration three executed copies of the Submission Agreement and three copies of the statement of claim of the controversy in dispute, together with the documents in support of the claim.
2. The respondent shall, within 20 business days of receipt, file with the Director of Arbitration one executed Submission Agreement and one copy of the answer, together with documents in support of his defense.

Section 6. Time Limitation upon Submission

1. No claim shall be eligible for admission to arbitrate where six years have elapsed from the occurrence of the act. This time limitation shall not apply when parties have submitted the dispute to a court of law.

Section 7. Denial of Arbitration. The Arbitration Committee may decline to permit the arbitration of any claim.

Section 8. Composition and Appointment of Panels

Section 9. Dismissal or Termination of Proceedings. The arbitrators may dismiss the proceedings and refer the parties to the remedies provided by law.

Section 10. Settlements

Section 11. Telling of Time Limitations for the Institution of Legal Proceedings.

Section 12. Designation of Number of Arbitrators

1. Claims up to $100,000: 3 to 5 arbitrators
2. Claims in excess of $100,000: 5 arbitrators

Section 13. Required Disclosure by Arbitrators. Each arbitrator shall be required to disclose any circumstances that might preclude him from rendering an objective and impartial determination upon any matter submitted for arbitration.

Section 14. Disqualification or Other Disability of Arbitrators

Section 15. Requirement for Hearing

Section 17. Representation by Counsel. Each party shall have the right to representation by counsel.

Section 23. Subpoena Process. The arbitrators or any counsel shall have power of subpoena process.

Section 31. Awards. Unless the law directs otherwise, all awards shall be deemed final and not subject to review and appeal.

MSRB RULES FOR RECORD-KEEPING

Broker–dealers must maintain proper record-keeping for all books and records.

Records for agency transactions must be kept for at least three years. These records must be kept separate from dealer transactions and must include all executed orders, date and time received, the price and date of execution, terms, conditions, and date of cancellations. All discretionary orders must be marked "discretionary."

Copies of customer confirmations must be kept for three years.

Customer account information must be kept for three years.

Customer account records and complaints must be kept for six years.

CHAPTER TEN

THE SECURITIES OF THE UNITED STATES GOVERNMENT

Since the beginning of the 12th century, governments have found it necessary to finance their administrations through the issuance of debt obligations. Kings discovered this method by borrowing from the public and promising to return the money at maturity. King William III of England made this a common practice in the 17th century with the full support of the Parliament. The guarantee of the Parliament made the people less hesitant to purchase the King's bonds. It was in the 17th century that an active bond market started to flourish at several trading centers in Europe. The most prominent was located in Antwerp.

PUBLIC DEBT OF THE UNITED STATES

In America bonds played a dominant role immediately after the Revolution for Independence. The government found it necessary and convenient to finance the wars and the economic expansion through the issuance of debt obligations. Public borrowing became part of American government's modus operandi.

The securities issued by the United States are guaranteed by the good faith of the federal government. The securities are the government's prime obligations. This governmental guarantee has two layers. Bonds, notes, bills, and certificates issued by the U.S. Treasury Department are supported by the full credit and faith of the federal government. The securities issued by federal agencies are backed by the issuing agency and depend upon the agency's ability to borrow money from the U.S. Treasury. Even though some agency securities have no federal guarantees or support, it seems improbable that in case of default the U.S. government would fail to safeguard the bondholder's interests.

The U.S. Treasury securities have a high degree of acceptance by the public investors. This—coupled with the federal government's unlimited power of taxation—makes these securities practically riskless. They have tremendous liquidity and a wide range of maturities—from a few days up to 30 years.

The Treasury Department sells U.S. government securities to finance the deficit condition in the federal budget. Deficit condition in the budget varies during the course of the year. The government spends money throughout the year, but the Treasury's revenue—in the form of tax collection or otherwise—has irregular schedules. Tax collections peak in the April through June calendar quarter, but expenditures are generally steady through the year. In issuing securities, the Treasury Department borrows money from the public to finance these various gaps between revenue and expenditure. It also must raise funds to finance the federal agencies whose expenditures and revenues are not included in the federal budget.

The U.S. government received its authority to issue Treasury securities by the enactment of the Second Liberty Bond Act of 1917. The Act limits to $400 billion the outstanding total face amount of securities issued by the United States. This $400 billion ceiling also includes securities sold on a discount basis, such as Treasury bills. Through the years, Congress has raised the $400 billion debt limit several times. The total outstanding debt of the United States government today is in excess of $3 trillion.

The Treasury Department has complete authority to issue its securities in any form or type. The Tax Equity and Fiscal Responsibility Act of 1982 forbids the issuance of securities in bearer form if the life to maturity is in excess of one year. Some of the securities are sold on a competitive basis and some through a negotiated arrangement. There is no limit as to the interest rates offered by the Treasury Department. There is, however, a long-standing limit of 4¼ percent rate of interest on long-term U.S. Treasury bonds, but Congress has provided exemption from this limit several times.

There are basically two types of Treasury securities—marketable and nonmarketable. Marketable securities are Treasury bills, notes, and bonds with varying dates of maturity. Bills are issued on a discount basis and carry no interest; the others are issued with the promise to pay interest at specified intervals, plus the principal amount at maturity. Nonmarketable securities are savings bonds, trust funds, Retirement Plan Bonds, Depositary Bonds, special issues sold directly by the Treasury Department to various agencies, securities issued for foreign monetary authorities and local governments, REA series issued in connection with financing the Rural Electrification Administration, etc.

Today, most of the marketable securities are issued in a book-entry form. There are no certificates issued. They are held in a computerized accounting method at the Federal Reserve Bank on behalf of financial institutions. The Federal Reserve will transfer title of ownership through a "book-entry" method. It will debit the seller's account and credit the buyer's account by entering the number of bills or bonds transacted between the two parties, and then credit the appropriate funds in the seller's account.

The bulk of the U.S. public debt is in marketable securities. The Treasury securities may be called by the Treasury Department if they are callable instruments. The Department must give four months advance notice before calling the security.

There is a reciprocity in taxation between municipal securities and U.S. Treasury securities. The interest on municipal bonds is exempt from federal taxation and interest on Treasury securities is exempt from state and local taxation. The interest on Treasury securities, however, is subject to federal income tax.

THE MARKET OF U.S. GOVERNMENT SECURITIES

Although some bonds are listed on the New York Stock Exchange, most of the trading of U.S. government securities is made in the over-the-counter market. Dealer banks and non-bank dealers maintain inventory of U.S. government securities and deal primarily with institutional accounts and customers interested in trading U.S. government issues. In addition to primary government dealers, there are government bond brokers acting as agents between the customer and the primary dealer. Brokers do not maintain a position in government securities. They match the bids and offers placed by the primary dealers. There are approximately 40 primary government dealers. Their trade organization is known as the Association of Primary Dealers in Government Securities. The dealers report their security positions daily to the Federal Reserve Bank of New York, and the Fed conducts its Open Market Operations through these recognized and approved primary government bond dealers.

The over-the-counter trading hours are from 9 a.m. to 4 p.m., Eastern time. Trading is done through a telecommunication system in which quotes and positions are displayed on computer terminals.

Government securities are quoted on the basis of 1/32nds of 1 point. 1 point means $10. The Bid price means somebody wishes to purchase the security at that price, and the offer or the Asked price means somebody wishes to sell the security at that price.

Bid	Offer
98.8	99.18

Since the quotes are made in terms of 32nds of 1 point, the above quotation will read:

Bid	Offer
\$980 + 8/32nd of 1 point (\$10)	990 + 18/32nd

Government securities are also quoted in terms of 64ths of 1 point. This is identified by a + sign next to the quoted price. Thus,

Bid	Offer
98.8+	99.16+

means \$980 + 17/64ths of 1 point (\$10) and \$990 + 33/64ths of 1 point (\$10). Whenever the quotation denotes a + sign, double the fraction after the decimal point, add 1, put that figure over 64, and calculate as to \$10. Therefore, 98.8+ becomes:

$$8 \times 2 = 16$$

$$16 + 1 = 17$$

17/64ths of \$10 to be added to \$980 for the quotation of a \$1,000 face value of a government security.

The U.S. Treasury bills are quoted in terms of a discount rate.

Government dealers buy and sell government issues with no commissions added to the price. Their profit margin is the spread between the bid and the offer. The quotations are for round-lot transactions. A round-lot is a trade of \$100,000 face value of an issue and multiples of \$100,000. Amounts under \$100,000 face value are odd-lots and the dealers generally charge an odd-lot differential and/or a service fee.

For example, in terms of 32nds, the spread will be:

Bid	Offer
99.26	99.30
(990 + 26/32nd)	(990 + 30/32nd)

This is a spread of 4/32nds. Translated in dollars and cents, this means that the dealer will make $1,250 per $1 million on a two-year U.S. Treasury note. The longer the maturity of the issue, the greater the spread will be between the BID and the OFFER.

In terms of percentage, the quotation is done on a basis point. 1 basis point is equal to 1/100th of 1 percent.

Bid	Offer
14.42%	14.38%

This quotation for a 91-day U.S. Treasury bill has only a four Basis Point spread. The dealer will earn $100 per $1 million face value of a 91-day Treasury bill. Transactions in U.S. Treasury securities normally settle on the business day following the trade day. If the trade is done in "Cash," the settlement will be on the day of the trade. The odd-lot trades are settled on the fifth business day after the trade day. The trades are settled always in federal funds and not in the clearing house method.

In addition to the regular trading of U.S. government securities, the commodity exchanges also provide the trading of future contracts in U.S. government bills, notes, and bonds. These are financial future contracts by which an agreement is made to purchase or sell specified securities on a date in the future at a specific price. The delivery and payment specifications are made by the commodity exchanges.

The Federal Reserve Bank provides telegraphic transfers of book-entry Treasuries for unmatured marketable securities through a nationwide communications network. No transfers are done on the day of maturity or on the interest record date. The transfer fee is usually $3 per recipient per one issue for interdistrict transfers.

The Federal Reserve will lend securities from its portfolio to primary dealers if the dealer wishes to accomplish a delivery of a security. The usual charge for these securities loans is 1½ percent. The procedure is for the dealer to return the security to the Fed within five business days.

Even though U.S. Treasury securities are secured by the good faith and credit of the U.S. government, they are subject to the same variation in market values during a period of fluctuating interest rates. The volatile swings of interest rates in recent years have produced extreme variations in market values of these securities.

The following will be a detailed discussion of the securities of the United States.

U.S. TREASURY BILLS

The Treasury Department sells U.S. Treasury bills through a public auction every Monday of the week. If that Monday is a holiday, the bills are sold either on Friday preceding Monday or on Tuesday following Monday. These weekly bills are issued in two denominations: One will mature in three months and the other will mature in six months. They are offered to the public on a given Monday but are dated on Thursday following the Monday's auction. The payment for the purchase of the bill is due, therefore, on Thursday following the auction date. Thursday will also be the maturity dates of the old bills sold three months and six months earlier. The holders of the old bills will redeem their bills on that Thursday when the payments for the new bills are due from the owners of the new bills. The amounts of the new bills sold on Monday may be greater than, less than, or equal to the amounts of the old bills maturing on Thursday. The arithmetic is based on the Treasury's cash requirements. This procedure for refunding the old bills by raising new funds through the issuance of new bills is called "Roll-over."

If on that Thursday the total amount due the holders of the old bills is $11 billion, the Treasury, for instance, will auction new bills for $12 billion. It will use $11 billion out of $12 billion to redeem the old bills, and the rest of the money, $1 billion, is referred to as "Fresh Money."

The schedule for the weekly three-month and six-month bills is as follows:

1. The U.S. Treasury will announce late Tuesday afternoon, preceding the Monday's auction, that it will auction the weekly bills.
2. On the following Monday, the two maturity bills will be auctioned to the public.
3. The bills will be dated Thursday following the Monday auction. The payment is due on Thursday.
4. The maturity dates of the new bills will be on a Thursday, three months and six months later.
5. Between Monday and Thursday, the new bills will be traded on a When-Issued basis. This is the period of the primary market.
6. After the settlement date on Thursday, the new bills will be traded in the secondary market until the date of maturity. The forces of supply and demand and the prevailing interest rates will dictate the price of the bills in the secondary market.

Every four weeks, the Treasury Department will auction U.S. Treasury bills maturing in 52 weeks. The auction day for these bills is usually on a Wednesday, with payments due the following Tuesday. On that Tuesday, the 52-week bills sold 52 weeks earlier will mature and the Treasury will employ the same roll-over procedure used for three-month and six-month bills.

The schedule for this monthly auction is as follows:

1. The U.S. Treasury Department will announce the

monthly offering on Thursday preceding the Wednesday's auction.

2. The Treasury will sell the bills in a public auction on Wednesday.

3. The 52-week bills will be dated on Tuesday following Wednesday's auction. The trade will settle on this Tuesday and the payment is due from the purchasers on that day.

4. The maturity date of the new bills will be Tuesday, 52 weeks later.

5. Between Wednesday and Tuesday, the new bills will be traded on a When-Issued basis. This is still the primary market.

6. After the settlement date on Tuesday, the 52-week bills will be traded in the secondary market until the day of maturity.

Therefore, the Treasury Department issues weekly bills with maturities of three months and six months 52 times a year, and monthly bills with maturities of 52 weeks 12 times a year. The daily, weekly, and the monthly schedules of the Treasury Department with regard to Treasury bills are generally routine. The Department, however, may deviate from these schedules and procedures, and it has occasionally done so.

The U.S. Treasury bills are non-interest bearing. They are issued on a discount basis, which means the purchase price will be less than the face value or the redemption price. They come with minimum denomination of $10,000 face value. The investor, for instance, will pay $9,000 to purchase it. He will receive $10,000 at maturity. The difference in money will be a payment of interest. But the bills, themselves, pay no interest. If a bill is due, for example, on Thursday, November 1 and the customer fails to redeem the bill on that day but redeems it at some future date, he will only receive what he would have received on the redemption day. He will not receive interest for the period between the due date and the day the bills were redeemed.

According to tax laws, the Treasury bills are excluded from consideration as capital assets; therefore, the difference between the cost of purchase and the redemption value is treated as ordinary income, and not as capital gains. As discussed above, this income is subject to federal income but exempt from state income tax.

The Primary Market of Treasury Bills

The U.S. Treasury bills are issued in terms of dollar discounts expressed as a percentage of par value, or the face value, computed on a 360-day-a-year basis. They are issued through a competitive bidding by the Federal Reserve Bank of New York in behalf of the Treasury Department. The procedure for the public auction is the following:

1. The Treasury issues a notice with respect to the new offering.
2. The Treasury will invite tenders under competitive and non-competitive bidding. For this auction bidding, the Fed will only recognize approved government dealers.
3. If it is a competitive tender, the dealer must express the price for the bill on the basis of 100 with no more than three decimals. Example: 99.665.
4. If the tender is non-competitive, the Fed will accept the tender without a stated amount (usually up to $500,000) at the average price of the accepted competitive bids.
5. The dealers will accept the bills from the Fed and sell them to the public.

The Computation of the Discount Price

The discount price of a Treasury bill is computed on the basis of the actual days to maturity on 360 days per year by using the following formula:

$$D = F \times \frac{r}{100} \times \frac{t}{360}$$

$$F - D = P$$

where

D = the discount amount

F = the face or the par value of the bill

r = the rate of interest

t = the number of days to maturity.

EXAMPLE

A Treasury bill is quoted as follows:

Bid	Offer
13.55%	13.05%

The Bid percentage is higher than the Asked percentage because these are expressed in terms of discount price from the face value. Larger discount means lower dollar-price, as we shall illustrate by using the above formula for a $10,000 bill maturing in 90 days.

What is the dollar amount when the Bid is 13.55%?

$$D = \$10{,}000 \times 0.1355 \text{ (the rate in decimals)} \times \frac{90}{360}$$

The answer is $338.75. This is the amount of the discount. The purchase price will be, therefore:

$$10{,}000 - 338.75 = \$9{,}661.25$$

You will use the same formula for the Asked percentage of 13.05.

$$D = 10{,}000 \times 0.1305 \times \frac{90}{360}$$

The answer is 326.25. This is the amount of the discount. The price for the $10,000 90-bill will be:

$$10{,}000 - 326.25 = \$9{,}673.75 \ .$$

The Bid and the Asked, in dollar terms means: somebody is bidding to purchase a $10,000 90-bill at $9,661.25, and somebody is offering to sell at $9,673.75.

The full discount per $10,000 par value is $338.75 on the Bid side and $326.25 on the Asked side. The investment return on an annualized yield basis of these two discount prices is higher than the discount basis calculated on a 365-day basis.

EXAMPLE

Let us say the investor purchases the $10,000, 90-day bill at the Asked percentage of 13.05 percent. Using the above calculation, he will earn $326.25 in 90 days. On an annualized basis, this discount of 326.25 would be:

$$\$326.25 \times \frac{365}{90} = \$1{,}323.125$$

This amount is earned by investing $9,673.75, which was the dollar-price for the $10,000, 90-day bill. To determine the yield one would use the following formula:

$$Y = \frac{D}{P} \times \frac{365}{t} \times 100$$

where

Y = the yield on an annualized 365 days-year basis

D = the discount amount

P = the dollar-price, which is $F - D$

F = the par value of the bill

t = the number of days to maturity.

Therefore, using the above example the yield would be:

$$Y = \frac{326.25}{9{,}673.75} \times \frac{365}{90} \times 100$$

$$Y = 13.677\% \ .$$

Compare this with the Asked percentage of 13.05 percent.

The investor may use a conversion table, which will convert the discount percentage into annual equivalent yields.

The Secondary Market of Treasury Bills

The customer does not have to wait until the date of maturity to redeem his bills. He may sell them at any time before the maturity date in the secondary market. The secondary market is over-the-counter. The trading of government securities usually opens at 10:00 a.m. and closes at 3:30 p.m., Eastern time. The trading in the over-the-counter market is done by telephone, telex, or through computer terminals. The government dealers are the market makers and the brokers who act as agents for their customers.

If the customer sells his bills prior to maturity, he may apply the following formula to determine the annualized equivalent rate of return:

$$Y = \frac{S - P}{P} \times \frac{365}{D} \times 100$$

where

S = dollar-price when sold

P = dollar-price when purchased

Y = annualized equivalent rate of return

D = the number of days that the customer held the bill.

EXAMPLE

The customer purchases a $10,000, 90-day bill for $9,673.75 and sells it in the secondary market for $9,793.75 after holding it for 45 days. The equivalent rate of return on an annualized basis is:

$$Y = \frac{9{,}793.75 - 9{,}673.75}{9{,}673.75} \times \frac{365}{45} \times 100$$

$$Y = 10.06\%$$

CASH MANAGEMENT BILLS

Cash Management bills are issued by the Treasury Department to finance the interim cash needs of the government. They are issued at irregular intervals with maturities ranging from a few days to about six months. They are generally issued when government spending is the heaviest, and they mature shortly after major tax receipt dates, such as March, April, June, September, and December. At times they are issued with maturities to coincide with those of outstanding bills. They are issued in large blocks with a minimum denomination of $1 million.

U.S. TREASURY NOTES

The U.S. Treasury notes are securities issued by the Treasury Department, with maturities ranging from one year to 10 years. The notes are generally issued on a regular basis. Notes, bonds, and Treasury Certificates are offered to the public for cash subscription or in exchange for maturing securities. Offerings are announced a few weeks before the issue date. They are sold at a set price that's established by the Treasury Department, or at a competitive bid in an auction market similar to the public auction for Treasury bills. (The bidding for these securities is done in terms of yield rather than dollar-price.) Commercial banks may submit subscriptions to the Treasury to purchase Treasury notes. Other purchasers are primary dealers, savings and loan associations, government entities, companies, and so on. The Treasury Department will make an allotment of notes on a percentage basis.

The following are different types of Treasury notes:

1. *Two-year Treasury Notes.* These are auctioned a week or so before the end of each month. They are dated and mature as of the end of the month. The amount to be sold may be greater or less than the amount of the old notes maturing on that day.

2. *Three-Year Treasury Notes.* These are issued on an irregular basis. In recent years they are issued at the end of each quarter—February, May, August, November. They are usually announced on the last Wednesday of the preceding month, but dated on or near the 15th of the issuance month.

3. *Four-Year Treasury Notes.* These notes are sold in the last month of each quarter and mature at month's end.

4. *Five-Year Treasury Notes.* These are issued in the final month of each quarter.

5. *Seven-to-Ten-Year Treasury Notes.* These notes are issued by the Treasury Department to accommodate maturity and refunding requirements of other issues. They are dated and mature on the 15th of the month.

U.S. Treasury notes are issued in minimum denominations of $1,000. There are no certificates issued. Ownership is identified through a book-entry system of the Federal Reserve Bank.

Interest income on U.S. Treasury notes is taxable under federal tax law, but tax-exempt from state and local taxes. They are traded in the secondary market usually over-the-counter.

The Treasury notes are traded on the basis of fractions of one point, either in 32nds or 64ths. The following is an example of the quotation of a Treasury note in the secondary market:

Rate	Mat	Date	Bid	Asked	Yield to Mat
10⅛	1996	Sept.	98.18	98.22	15.16

If there are no + signs next to the quotation, the notes are traded on the basis of 1/32nd of 1 point. 98.18 will mean:

$980 + 18/32nd of $10

The investor will add 18/32nd of $10 to $980, and that will be the price to sell or purchase $1,000 face value of a U.S. Treasury note. If there is a + sign next to the quotation (98.18 +), that means the notes are traded on the basis of 1/64th of $10.

98.18 + will mean:

$980 + 37/64th of $10

U.S. TREASURY BONDS

Treasury bonds are long-term federal government obligations, with maturities ranging from 10 to 30 years. They are offered to the public either through an auction process or through the use of subscriptions. The bids for bonds are required to be on a yield rather than on a dollar basis.

Treasury bonds are issued in a minimum denomination of $1,000 with a fixed interest payable semi-annually. Some of the issues may be callable by the Treasury Department before the maturity date. The callable issues will be identified as 8½ percent May 15, 1994–99. This means the maturity date is 1999, but the bonds may be called in 1994.

There are no certificates issued. Ownership is identified through a book-entry method of the Federal Reserve Bank.

Treasury bonds are traded in the over-the-counter market. The market quotation system is similar to U.S. Treasury notes. Interest income is subject to federal income tax, but exempt from state or local taxes.

U.S. TREASURY FLOWER BONDS

The Treasury Flower bonds are purchased at a substantial discount from the face value. They mature into full face value at the death of the bondholder. They are redeemable at par with accrued interest. The beneficiary of the estate will use the security to pay federal estate taxes. The U.S. Treasury Flower bonds are no longer issued but they may be purchased in the secondary market until 1997, when the last Flower bond, issued in 1974, will expire.

NON-MARKETABLE SECURITIES OF THE UNITED STATES

1. *United States Savings Bonds.* The U.S. Treasury Department has promoted the sales of savings bonds to raise funds for the U.S. government. Series EE and HH bonds are the only issues now offered by the Treasury. The Series EE and HH savings bonds are non-callable and non-transferable. Series EE bonds are sold at 50 percent of the face value in denominations from $50 to $10,000 and subject to an annual purchase limit of $15,000 (issue price) per investor. These bonds may not be used as collateral for a loan.

Series HH bonds are sold at face value in denominations of \$500 to \$10,000, and are subject to annual purchase limit of \$20,000 per investor.

2. *Retirement Plan Bonds.* The Retirement Plan bonds are issued by the U.S. Treasury Department in denominations of \$50, \$100, \$500, and \$1,000. Purchases in any one calendar year are limited to \$10,000 per investor. They are purchased in connection with bond purchase programs and pension and profit-sharing plans. Retirement Plan bonds are subject to federal income tax.

3. *Individual Retirement Bonds.* The Individual Retirement bonds are designed for investment by persons who are not covered by a retirement plan. They are sold in denominations of \$50, \$75, \$100, and \$500. The bonds mature when the bondholder reaches the age of 70½ years.

4. *Government Account Series.* The U.S. Treasury Department sells these securities directly to government agencies and trust funds.

5. *Depositary Bonds.* The Depositary bonds are sold to designated depositaries and financial agents of the U.S. Treasury Department for the purpose of providing an offset to the cost of providing service to the U.S. government.

6. *State and Local Government Series.* The state and local government series securities are issued by the U.S. Treasury Department and sold to state and local governments that wish to reinvest the proceeds of advance refundings of their tax-exempt debt.

7. *Foreign Series.* The Foreign Series securities are special non-marketable securities issued by the U.S. Treasury Department and sold to foreign governments and monetary authorities. They are issued in two different types:

a. Dollar-denominated foreign series

b. Foreign currency denominated series. This is denominated in the currency of the country purchasing the security. The securities may be in the form of bills, CDs, notes, or bonds.

TAX TREATMENT FOR U.S. GOVERNMENT SECURITIES

Generally, the interest on U.S. government securities is subject to federal income tax and exempt from state and local tax.

Any increment in value of savings bonds represented by the difference between the purchase price and the redemption value, whether at or before maturity, is considered as interest. The U.S. Treasury bills are also treated in the same way.

Purchase price: $8,700

Redemption value: $10,000 .

Interest earned is $1,300 and subject to federal income tax. No capital gain (or loss) is afforded to the Treasury bills.

CHAPTER ELEVEN

FEDERAL AGENCY OBLIGATIONS

Federal agency obligations are instruments of the U.S. government created by various congressional acts to meet the demands of the nation's economic growth. Ever since the enactment of the Federal Farm Loan Act of 1916, the number of federal agency securities has grown substantially creating a sizable secondary market. As with the Treasury obligations, these securities are issued by congressional Acts and usually with the approval of the Secretary of the Treasury. They are exempt from SEC registration requirements.

Federal agency securities are not the direct obligations of the U.S. Treasury Department, but they carry specific federal sponsorship or guarantees. These guarantees come in various forms. Some of these securities are supported by the full faith and credit of the United States, some are guaranteed by the Treasury Department and others are backed by the agency's ability to borrow funds from the U.S. Treasury. Regardless of the form of these guarantees, or even the lack of them, the federal government plays a dominant role in marketing, distribution, and the administration of these securities. They are considered to be legal investment instruments for federally chartered banks and institutions and may be accepted as collateral for advances of the Federal Reserve Banks. In several cases, the interest earned on the securities are exempt from state and local taxation and some are exempt from federal income tax. Some securities are issued and payable through the Federal Reserve Banks. Most agency obligations are eligible for purchase by the Federal Reserve in its Open Market operations in the secondary market.

FEDERAL FINANCING BANK

The Federal Financing Bank (FFB) was created in 1973 to consolidate and reduce the cost of financing a variety of federal agencies. Its main purpose is to reduce the government's cost of borrowing. Most federal agencies finance their activities through FFB. The FFB is authorized to purchase the obligations of the federal agency with instructions from the Secretary of the Treasury, who is the chairman of a five-man board of directors. The FFB is managed and staffed by the employees of the Treasury Department. The FFB is not authorized to finance the operation of the Farm Credit System, the Federal Home Loan Banks, the Federal Home Loan Mortgage Corporation, and the Federal National Mortgage Association. It is authorized to finance the General Services Administration, the Small Business Administration, TVA, the United States Postal Service, and other smaller agencies.

The FFB will finance its operation by issuing securities and selling them either to the public or to the Secretary of the Treasury. These securities, like the U.S. Treasury obligations, are general obligations of the United States.

THE "BIG FIVE"

The following federal agencies are called the "Big Five":

- The Federal Home Loan Bank
- The Federal National Mortgage Association
- The Banks for Cooperatives

- The Federal Land Bank
- The Federal Intermediate Credit Corporation

Bonds and debentures of these agencies are offered periodically through the dealers and banks. The creditworthiness of these securities is comparable to the direct obligations of the U.S. Treasury. The issuance of these securities is generally done through an underwriting group. The group receives an allotment from the agency at a discount and sells the security to the public at par. The spread is the underwriters' profit.

The underwriting process is divided into several periods:

1. *The announcement date* — The agency announces the type of financing.
2. *The pricing date* — The agency announces the coupon rate of the issue.
3. *The offering date* — The agency officially offers the package to the public.
4. *The dated date* — The bonds are issued, the payment is received, and the owners begin accruing interests.

There are usually two weeks between the offering date and the dated date. The trading usually starts on the day following the offering date.

FARM CREDIT SYSTEM

The Farm Credit System provides credit to American farmers, ranchers, and producers to run their operations and raise agricultural products. These services are accomplished through the following agencies:

- The Federal Land Banks
- The Banks for Cooperatives

- The Federal Intermediate Credit Banks
- The Production Credit Associations

There are 37 Farm Credit banks throughout the country located in 12 Farm Credit districts: 12 Federal Land Banks, 12 Federal Intermediate Credit Banks, 12 Banks for Cooperatives, and one Central Bank for Cooperatives in Denver, Colorado.

Through its fiscal agent in New York, the Farm Credit System sells the securities to the public. The entity is run by the Farm Credit Administration, as an independent agency of the United States government. The interests of the securities are subject to federal taxation, but are exempt from state or local taxes.

The following is a description of the agencies in the Farm Credit System:

1. *Banks for Cooperatives.* The Banks for Cooperatives were organized in 1933 under the Farm Credit Act. They provide loans to cooperative associations that are owned by farmers and are engaged in marketing agricultural products and farm supplies. The banks issue bonds to finance their operations. The bonds are normally issued on the first of each month with a six-month maturity date. Securities with maturity of up to 10 years are sometimes offered.

2. *Federal Land Banks.* Federal Land Banks were organized in 1917 under the Federal Farm Loan Act. They provide loans to farmers and ranchers for a variety of agricultural purposes. Each borrower is required to purchase stock in the Federal Land Banks Association in an amount equal to 5 percent of the loan. He will then pledge the stock with the association as collateral for the loan. The stock is retired when the loan is repaid. The Federal Land Banks will issue bonds on a quarterly basis with maturities that range from a few months to up to 20 years.

3. *Federal Intermediate Credit Banks.* Federal Intermediate Credit Banks were authorized by the Agricultural Credit Act of 1923. They provide short and intermediate

loans to banks, agricultural credit corporations, livestock loan companies, and other financing institutions. They issue bonds to finance their operations. The bonds are issued on the first of each month with a maturity date of nine months. Longer maturities of up to 10 years are also issued.

4. *Farm Credit Consolidated Systemwide-Discount Notes.* These discount notes are the secured obligations of the 37 Farm Credit Banks. These notes are issued in denominations of $50,000, $100,000, $500,000, $1,000,000, and $75,000,000, with maturities of 5 to 270 days.

The Farm Credit System will issue the discount notes for purposes of interim financing between bond sales.

5. *Federal Farm Credit Banks Consolidated Systemwide Bonds.* These bonds are the secured obligations of the 37 Farm Credit Banks. They are issued every month with 6 months and 9 months maturity dates. Longer term bonds are also issued.

The Farm Credit Banks are authorized to issue bonds and notes in an amount not exceeding 20 times the capital and surplus of the banks.

The Consolidated Bonds are considered eligible investments for state and national banks, for credit unions, and for federal savings and loan associations. They are accepted as collateral for advances of the Federal Reserve Banks and are eligible securities for Federal Open Market Operations.

The interest on these bonds is subject to federal taxation but is exempt from state, municipal, and local taxation. Gain from the sale of the bonds is subject to federal and state taxation.

FEDERAL HOME LOAN BANKS

Federal Home Loan Banks were created by the Federal Home Loan Act of 1932. There are 12 Federal Home Loan Bank districts under the supervision of the Federal Home Loan Bank Board in Washington, D.C. The Board provides a permanent system of reserve bonds for its members, which are mostly savings and loan associations that are engaged in home financing in their respective communities. The stock of the Federal Home Loan Bank is owned by member-institutions.

The principal function of the Federal Home Loan Bank is to provide advances to the member organizations to meet withdrawal demands and provide home mortgages to the public. These advances are generally secured by home mortgages or by U.S. government obligations. Unsecured advances of one year or less may be extended if the member institution's credit liabilities do not exceed 5 percent of its assets.

The Federal Home Loan Banks obtain their funds from three sources: sale of capital stock to member organizations, deposits from member organizations, and sales of securities to the public.

Although the notes and bonds of the Federal Home Loan Bank are not guaranteed by the United States, they are the obligations of the Bank that operates under the federal charter. The banks are required to maintain secured advances, guaranteed mortgages, U.S. government securities, or cash in an amount at least equal to the consolidated bonds and discount notes outstanding.

The bonds are issued in book-entry form with a minimum denomination of $10,000 and increments of $5,000 thereafter. They mature generally from one to 10 years. The interest on the bonds is subject to federal taxation but exempt from state and local taxes. The bonds are considered as lawful investments for all fiduciary, trusts and public funds, for savings banks, savings and loan associations, insurance companies, and national banks. Gain from the sale of these securities is subject to federal and state taxation.

FEDERAL HOME LOAN MORTGAGE CORP.

The Federal Home Loan Mortgage Corp. was created on July 24, 1970, by Title III of the Emergency Home

Finance Act of 1970. It was created to help maintain the availability of mortgage credit for residential housing through the secondary market in conventional mortgages. The corporation, known as Freddie Mac, purchases conventional residential mortgages and sells them by means of mortgage-related investment instruments. These instruments come in two types: Guaranteed Mortgage Certificates (GMC) and Mortgage Participation Certificates (PC).

1. *Guaranteed Mortgage Certificates* (GMC). Guaranteed Mortgage Certificates represent undivided interests in conventional residential mortgages previously underwritten by the Mortgage Corporation. GMCs guarantee the return of the principal once a year in guaranteed minimum amounts without regard to the status of the underlying mortgages. It pays interest semi-annually. The final payment date is 30 years from the date of issuance, but the bondholder may redeem the bond at face value 15, 20, or 25 years after issuance.

The certificates are issued in denominations of $100,000, $500,000, and $1 million. The Federal Reserve Bank of New York is the transfer agent and the registrar for these securities.

2. *Mortgage Participation Certificates* (PC). Mortgage Participation Certificates distribute a pro-rata share of the principal payment collected on the mortgage in the underlying pool to the security holders every month. It guarantees the payment of interest and principal regardless of the status of the underlying loan. The security matures in 30 years but the weighted life is assumed to be around 12 years.

Mortgage Participation Certificates are sold by FHL Mortgage Corp. directly to the public or through selected securities dealers. They are issued in denominations of $100,000, $200,000, $500,000, $1 million, and $5 million.

The interest on securities of the Federal Home Loan Mortgage Corporation is subject to federal and state income taxation.

FEDERAL NATIONAL MORTGAGE ASSOCIATION (FNMA)

The FNMA is a government-chartered corporation but owned by public stockholders. It is authorized to render assistance to the secondary market of federally insured mortgages. These securities are popularly known as Fannie Mae's.

Mortgages insured by Federal Housing Administration or the Veterans Administration are purchased by FNMA. The FNMA borrows funds to buy mortgages. It does not insure mortgage loans. It merely manages the portfolio of mortgages.

The short-term notes of FNMA are issued in denominations of $5,000, $10,000, $25,000, $100,000, $500,000, and $1 million.

The obligations issued by FNMA are accepted as security investment for fiduciary, trusts, and public funds. FNMAs are subject to federal and local income taxes.

The Federal National Mortgage Association was created under the National Housing Act of 1938. It was partitioned into two entities—one is the present FNMA engaged in providing mortgage funds in the secondary market, and the other emerged as the Government National Mortgage Association (GNMA) that became a governmental corporation in the Department of Housing and Urban Development (HUD). GNMA is engaged in providing mortgage funds in the primary market.

The issues of FNMA are lawful investments for fiduciary, trusts, and public funds. The debentures are issued in denominations of $10,000, $25,000, $50,000, $100,000, and $500,000.

FNMA also issues short-term discount notes, similar to commercial papers, that mature from 30 to 270 days. They are issued in denominations of $5,000, $10,000, $25,000, $100,000, $500,000, and $1 million. These notes may be purchased by national banks as part of their investment portfolio.

GOVERNMENT NATIONAL MORTGAGE ASSOCIATION

The Government National Mortgage Association, popularly known as Ginnie Mae, is a wholly owned corporate entity of the United States government within the Department of Housing and Urban Development (HUD). It was created in 1968 by the partition of the old FNMA. As a separate entity, GNMA took over the assets, liabilities, and the operation of the special assistance, management, and the liquidating functions of the FNMA.

The GNMA makes commitments to purchase mortgages from private lenders at favorable prices in order to help promote the growth in housing in the United States. It also raises funds by issuing securities backed by pools of mortgages under the authority of the Department of Housing and Urban Development. Under this authority, GNMA guarantees the timely payment of the principal and interest on trust certificates.

GNMA issues its securities in the following manner:

1. The mortgage banker lends funds to the people in the community to purchase real estate property.
2. The banker will then assemble a pool of eligible mortgages.
3. All the mortgages in the pool must be insured by one of the following federal agencies:

    - Federal Housing Administration
    - Farmers Home Authority
    - Veterans Administration

4. The mortgages in the pool must be for single family residential properties.
5. The mortgages in the pool must aggregate to at least $1 million.
6. All mortgages in the same pool must have the same maturity date.
7. All mortgages in the same pool must have the

same stated rate of interest (usually the FHA/VA interest rate then in effect).

8. After assembling all these mortgages, the mortgage banker will submit an application to the Government National Mortgage Association.

9. The GNMA will authorize the issuance of GNMA securities with a coupon rate of 50 basis points below the rate of the underlying mortgages in the pool. If the mortgage rate is 13 percent, the GNMA security will have an interest rate of 12½ percent.

10. GNMA securities will be sold to the public. The GNMA security holder, therefore, will have a proportionate interest in the pool of mortgages. The securities issued by the GNMA bear the good faith and credit of the United States government. They are issued in denominations of $25,000, $100,000, $500,000, and $1 million. They are considered legal investments for federally chartered credit unions.

Under a "pass-through" program, the principal and interest payments collected on mortgages in specified pools are "passed-through" to the holders of GNMA securities, after the service fees are deducted. The pass-through certificates have maturities equal to those of the underlying mortgages, ranging between 12 and 40 years. Due to prepayment of mortgages, the actual maturities are considerably less.

The following are some of the functions of the Government National Mortgage Association:

1. *Special Assistance Functions.* Through this program GNMA provides special assistance for financing certain types of home mortgages. The program is operated under a "Tandem Plan," which means GNMA purchases mortgages from private lenders at a price more favorable than available in the market. And in order to reduce the cash outlay for these purchases, GNMA works "in tandem" with investors by selling the mortgages to them at prevailing market prices and, as a subsidy, absorbing the difference between the GNMA price and the market price.

2. *Mortgage-Backed Securities Program.* The GNMA may raise funds for the mortgage market by guaranteeing securities backed by pools of mortgages as described above. There are two types of guaranteed mortgage-backed securities:

a. One is mortgage-backed bonds issued by FNMA and the Federal Home Loan Mortgage Corporation. Mortgage-backed bonds are issued with maturities ranging from one to 25 years.
b. The other is the pass-through securities issued by government-approved mortgages, as described above.

3. *Management and Liquidating Functions.* Under this program, GNMA has issued Participation Certificates (PCs) for various governmental agencies:

- PCs for Government Mortgage Liquidation Trust
- PCs for Federal Assets Liquidation Trust
- PCs for Federal Assets Financing Trust

These certificates represent beneficial interest in future payments of the principal and interest on a pool of mortgages from the inventory set aside for that purpose. They carry maturities, ranging from one to 20 years and issued in denominations of $5,000, $10,000, $25,000, $100,000, $500,000, and $1 million.

While GNMA securities are issued in minimum denominations of $25,000, some brokerage houses sell GNMA investment trusts with units of $1,000 each. The major assumption in purchasing GNMA securities or investment trusts is that the mortgages in a particular pool will be paid off in the early years.

Statistics compiled by the Federal Housing Administration have shown that the average life for all FHA mortgages is 11.2 years. Therefore, GNMA securities prices are pegged to an assumed average life of 12 years. Prices of securities rise and fall with mortgage interest rates. Purchasing a Ginnie Mae security at a discount gives the investor a built-in increase in the eventual yield if the mortgages in the pool are prepaid.

The anticipated yield on a Ginne Mae security is only a guesswork based on the historical "pay-down rate" for each individual pool. If the mortgages in the pool are paid off faster than projected, the yield will be more. If the pay-off takes longer, the yield will be less. This is called "FHA Speed" or "FHA Experience."

An astute investor may locate pools of mortgages that are likely to pay off rapidly. This can be in a geographic area of the country with high turnover in housing based on economic trends, the housing cycle, interest rates, and the availability of mortgage funds.

The interest on GNMA securities is subject to federal, estate, gift, excise, state, and local taxes.

Definition of Terms

GNMA Factor Book This book of factors is issued each month by GNMA and expresses in decimal terms the outstanding remaining percentage of the principal amount of each pool.

Graduated Payment Mortgage This is a mortgage that provides for the deferred payment of a portion of the interest due monthly on the mortgage loan during its early years.

Guaranteed Coupon This refers to a term in the contract for the purchase or sale of mortgage-backed securities that states that the securities to be delivered pursuant to the contract will bear an agreed-upon Interest Rate.

Par Amount The Par Amount is the face value or the original principal amount of a mortgage-backed security.

Par/Price Cap This refers to a provision in a contract for the purchase or sale of Mortgage-Backed securities that limits the payment for Mortgage-Backed securities to the Par Amount or the contract price, whichever is higher.

Principal and Interest Payment Date This term, when used with respect to a GNMA security, refers to the 15th day of the month following the month of issue, and the 15th day of every month thereafter over the life of the GNMA security. The term, Principal and Interest Payment Date, when used with respect to a FHLMC security, refers to a date on or before the 15th day of the second month following the month in which a purchaser becomes a registered holder, or a date on or before the 15th day of each month thereafter.

Record Date The record date is the last business day of the month. The Record Date determines the name of the person entitled to receive payment of principal and interest on a Mortgage-Backed security.

Yield This is the annual percentage return that is earned.

Yield Maintenance Yield maintenance refers to a provision in a contract for the purchase or sale of Mortgage-Backed securities permitting the seller to deliver securities bearing an interest rate that will produce a corresponding yield given the price agreed to by the parties to the transaction.

STUDENT LOAN MARKETING ASSOCIATION

The Student Loan Marketing Association, created in 1972 under the Higher Education Act of 1965, is a private, for-profit corporation established to provide liquidity for insured student loans under the Guaranteed Student Loan Program. The Corporation provides a secondary market for loans made by commercial banks, savings and loan associations, colleges, and universities. The corporation is popularly known as "Sallie Mae."

Sallie Mae issues common stock and sells the stock to financial and educational institutions. This stock is considered to be an eligible investment for national banks, federal savings and loan associations, and other financial institutions. The Sallie Mae stock is exempted from SEC registration requirements. It finances its programs through the Federal Financing Bank.

UNITED STATES POSTAL SERVICE

The United States Postal Service is an independent entity in the executive branch of the United States government. As such, it has the power to issue debt obligations to finance capital expenditures and run the operation of the Postal Authority. Postal Service bonds are lawful investments for fiduciary, trusts, and public funds. They are exempt from all state and local taxes except estate, inheritance, and gift taxes. The Postal Service generally finances its programs through the Federal Financing Bank.

FEDERAL HOUSING ADMINISTRATION

The Federal Housing Administration was established under the National Housing Act of 1934 to encourage the flow of private capital into residential financing and to provide a system of mortgage insurance as an aid to builders and buyers of homes.

The FHA finances its operation through the issuance of bonds. The FHA bonds are issued in denominations of $50, $100, $500, $1,000, $5,000, and $10,000. They are fully guaranteed by the United States and as such are considered lawful investments for fiduciary, trusts, public funds, and national banks.

NEW COMMUNITIES DEBENTURES

The New Communities Debentures are issued under the Housing and Urban Development Act of 1970. Through this Act, the federal government provides assistance to new communities. The debentures are issued in registered form in denominations of $5,000. These securities are legal investments for surplus and reserve funds of the Federal Home Loan Banks. Income of the bonds is subject to federal and state income taxes.

PUBLIC HOUSING NOTES AND BONDS

The Department of Housing and Urban Development provides financial assistance to local public housing agencies. The local public housing agencies issue short-term project notes and long-term bonds. The short-term notes are known as Project Notes. Both the Project Notes and Bonds are backed by the full faith of the United States with the payment of principal and interest guaranteed by the United States government. The interest on bonds is tax exempt.

EXPORT-IMPORT BANK OF THE UNITED STATES

The Eximbank aids in financing exports by extending loans and providing export credit insurance. The Eximbank acts as an independent corporate agency of the United States government. It finances its obligations through the Federal Financing Bank.

FARMERS HOME ADMINISTRATION

The Farmers Home Administration (FMHA) is an agency in the Department of Agriculture. Its primary purpose is to extend loans to farms and community facilities in rural areas. The agency finances its programs through the Federal Financing Bank.

GENERAL SERVICES ADMINISTRATION

The General Services Administration manages the governmental properties, including construction and operation of buildings, distribution of supplies, etc. Its financing is done through the Federal Financing Bank.

MARITIME ADMINISTRATION

The Merchant Marine bonds and notes are obligations guaranteed by the full faith and credit of the United States.

SMALL BUSINESS ADMINISTRATION

The Small Business Administration (SBA) is an instrumentality that provides financial and management assistance to small business concerns. The SBA makes loans to Small Business Investment Companies (SBIC) that, in turn, lend money to small businesses. The SBA finances its obligations through the Federal Financing Bank.

TENNESSEE VALLEY AUTHORITY

The Tennessee Valley Authority is a wholly-owned corporate agency of the United States government established in 1933. Its objective is to strengthen the regional development of Tennessee Valley and adjacent areas. TVA's power system supplies power to Tennessee, Northern Alabama, Northeastern Mississippi, Southeastern Kentucky and portions of Georgia, North Carolina, and Virginia.

Bonds sold to the public are issued in denominations of $1,000 and $5,000. Income on bonds and notes is subject to federal income taxes, but exempt from state and local taxes.

WASHINGTON METROPOLITAN AREA TRANSIT AUTHORITY

The Washington Metropolitan Area Transit Authority (WMATA) was created in 1967 to develop, finance, and operate a mass transit system serving the greater Washington Metropolitan area.

The bonds of WMATA are issued in denominations of $5,000, $10,000, $25,000, $100,000, and $500,000. The bonds may be subject to redemption prior to maturity. Interest income is subject to federal and state income tax.

ASIAN DEVELOPMENT BANK

The Asian Development Bank was established in 1966 with a membership of 43 countries. Its purpose is to foster economic growth in Asia by lending funds and promoting investments to member countries in the region.

The Bank issues bonds and notes, and sells them to the public. The bonds and notes are issued in registered form in denominations of $1,000. Interest paid to nonresident aliens and foreign corporations is not subject to federal income tax.

INTER-AMERICAN DEVELOPMENT BANK

The Inter-American Development Bank is owned by 26 regional and 15 non-regional countries. Its objective is to foster economic and social development of its regional developing member countries.

It issues bonds to finance its operation. Interest paid to non-resident aliens and foreign corporations is not subject to federal income tax.

INTERNATIONAL BANK FOR RECONSTRUCTION AND DEVELOPMENT (WORLD BANK)

The International Bank for Reconstruction and Development was established at the Brettan Woods Conference in July of 1944. Its purpose is to promote the economic development of member countries by providing loans for specific projects and technical assistance. Loans made by the Bank must be used for productive purposes. The Bank issues bonds and notes to finance its operation. The securities are issued in denominations of $1,000, $10,000, and $100,000. The interest paid on the bonds is fully taxable. They are considered legal investments for commercial banks, savings banks, insurance companies, trust funds, etc.

CLEARING FACILITY FOR MORTGAGE-BACKED GOVERNMENT SECURITIES

An organization called Mortgage-Backed Securities Clearing Corporation (MBSCC) facilitates the processing and settlement of trades. The Clearing Corporation nets all the trades for its participating organizations in the same way that a securities clearance is done for equity instruments. Instead of handling each trade separately, the Clearing Corporation offsets the purchases against the sales and the participant will only be required to deliver and receive the net balances with corresponding netting of the funds in the transaction.

CHAPTER TWELVE

THE MONEY MARKET INSTRUMENTS

The most important aspect of the money market is its ability to provide liquidity for investors, financial institutions, corporations, and governments. The securities in the money market are short-term instruments to meet the liquidity needs of investors, institutions, and corporations.

The money market is a conglomeration of many different markets. There are many participants and products. The players are the U.S. Treasury Department, foreign and domestic banks, corporations, federal agencies, insurance companies, brokerage houses, pension and endowment funds, states and municipalities, etc. The market is vast and specialized. Each participant is specialized only in a certain field.

Billions of dollars worth of instruments are traded daily at different financial centers around the world. Vast sums of money are shifted constantly between one market player and another. An important aspect of the market is the professionalism of the players. Their professional integrity has helped maintain the market's viability and vitality.

The money market is innovative and versatile. New products and instruments are constantly introduced and it has become increasingly complex to understand all the intricacies of the products in the marketplace.

Banks use the money market to manage their cash and utilize the technique of asset-liability management.

In the wholesale market of money instruments, the traders apply techniques of arbitrage to make a profit or to manage cash. Arbitrage is used in the securities business in the following methods:

1. The trader purchases a security at an exchange and sells it at a different exchange. The difference in money will be the trader's profit or loss.
2. The trader purchases a convertible bond and sells the common shares to which the bond may be converted.
3. The trader purchases a convertible preferred stock and sells the common stock to which the preferred stock may be converted.
4. The trader purchases rights and sells the stock.
5. The trader purchases the security of a company to be acquired and sells the comparable shares of the acquiring company.

If the trader purchases and sells the securities simultaneously, it is called a *bona fide arbitrage*. If he purchases first, waits and sells it later, it is called a *risk arbitrage*.

The instruments of money market are:

- Short-term government securities
- Short-term federal agency securities
- Short-term state and local notes
- Repurchase and Reverse repurchase agreements
- Federal funds
- Letters of Credit
- Bankers Acceptances
- Commercial Papers

- Certificates of Deposit
- Eurodollars
- Money Market Funds
- Eurocurrency
- Credit union shares

The trading is done in the over-the-counter market. Modern techniques of communication are used to buy and sell money market instruments. Money market dealers purchase for their own accounts, and the money market brokers act as agents between the dealer and the customer. The dealers are the market makers. They stand ready to bid and offer and ready to purchase and sell for their own account. The margin of profit is very thin. A 1 Basis Point spread between the bid and the offer means a profit of 27.78 cents per $1 million per one day. 1 Basis Point profit for $1 million for a 90-day instrument is $25.00.

The same arithmetic is applied for financing a Repurchase Agreement. If the security used in the Repurchase Agreement yields 15.50 percent and the cost of the financing of the Repurchase Agreement is 15.10 percent, the dealer will make a profit of 40 Basis points. This means $11.11 per day per $1 million.

The day-to-day trading profits are watched very carefully, whether buying long or selling short. The real profit comes from the dealer's ability to position blocks of securities. To stay profitable a dealer seeks:

- maximum return
- maximum liquidity
- and minimum risk

Massive sums of money are sometimes used to establish money market positions. Some dealers are conservative and some have speculative objectives. It is not unusual for a dealer in the money market to establish a securities position of 500 times the bank's capital, which makes the dealer operation an extremely important area in the organization. In establishing positions, a dealer must be aware of the following parameters:

1. types of instruments
2. the percentage of portfolio that can be invested
3. the credit risk of the security
4. the maturity of the security for liquidity purposes

He must be knowledgeable enough to forecast future interest rates, and maintain a confidence level.

In trading money market instruments, two terms must always be considered—*intermediation* and *disintermediation*.

When a bank is acting as an intermediary to raise money, it is known as *intermediation*. When investors remove funds from banks and invest them in money market instruments to enjoy a higher rate of interest, it is known as *disintermediation*.

The following is a detailed study of the instruments of the money market.

FEDERAL FUNDS

Federal funds are reserve bank balances held on deposit with the Federal Reserve Bank. They represent the legal reserve that a member bank is required to maintain at the Federal Reserve Bank in a specified ratio to its deposits. To operate its cash utilization program, a member bank will sell excess federal funds or purchase funds to meet its reserve requirements.

Billions of dollars of federal funds are traded by member banks across the country every day. The buying and selling are done at rates of interest established by the parties in the transaction on a negotiated basis. Federal funds are money market instruments and the trades are done in the money market.

The Federal Reserve Bank debits the balance in the federal funds account when checks drawn on the bank are collected, and credits the balance when the bank receives payment for checks drawn on other banks.

In Fig. 12.1, the Federal Reserve Bank will credit $100 for the federal funds account of the First National Bank and will debit the same amount from the federal funds account of the Chase Bank.

The federal funds balances, therefore, are predicted on the action of the bank depositors and the lending and the investment operations of the bank. The most important task for the bank's money manager is to make sure that after all these activities are taken into account, the bank has sufficient federal funds in its account at the Federal Reserve to meet its legal requirements. The task of maintaining the reserve requirements and utilizing the excess federal funds is difficult. The money manager must calculate the money

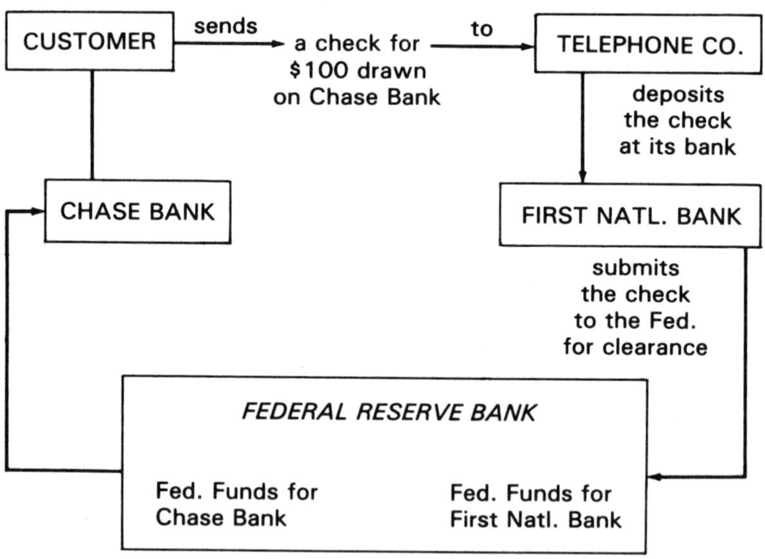

Fig. 12.1. Federal Funds Flowchart

positions daily and maintain enough liquidity to satisfy unexpected withdrawals.

The rate of interest for federal funds transactions is based on the forces of supply and demand. If there is too large a supply of federal funds and banks wish to sell the excess balances, the rates will decline. Conversely, if the banks have deficit condition and they must buy federal funds to satisfy their reserve requirements, the rates will go up.

The selling and buying of federal funds are processed through the Fed's book-entry system. The seller of the federal fund will make a one-day commitment of surplus funds at a set rate of interest to the buyer of the federal fund. The seller will record the transaction as *federal funds sold*, offset by a reduction in the reserve account of the federal funds balances at the Fed. Conversely, the buyer will record the transaction as *federal funds purchased*, offset by an increase in the federal funds balance at the Fed.

Many banks use the federal funds market for reserve adjustments to meet the requirements of the Federal Reserve regulations. Other banks use the market as a source of additional revenue. They do arbitrage in federal funds by purchasing small amounts of funds from smaller banks at lower interest rates and selling them as a large block to a city bank at a higher interest rate.

Most of the federal fund trading is done on an overnight basis. There is, however, a futures market that has developed in recent years, where the trader will sell the federal funds on a given day for delivery in the future. He sells the federal funds, for instance, on Friday, for delivery on Tuesday. This may be done in connection with an arbitrage in Eurodollars. He will sell the Eurodollars one day and deliver the corresponding federal funds two or three days later.

Even though the federal funds market is strictly a U.S. market linked with the Federal Reserve operations, foreign banks also may participate in buying and selling federal funds. A foreign bank, for example, will sell Eurodollars on a Friday to a U.S. bank, and will cover this by delivering the corresponding amount of federal funds on Monday. Since the foreign bank is not a member of the Federal Reserve, it uses a clearing bank to process the federal fund transactions in its behalf.

The federal funds may also be traded on a term basis. A bank's money manager, for instance, will sell an amount of federal funds for a term of 30 days, 60 days, or 90 days. If he expects to have surplus funds for an extended period of time, he will sell the funds at a specified rate of interest. These are called *Term Federal Funds*. The bank purchasing the term funds wishes to maintain a long-term money position in its banks. Purchasing a term federal fund may be more advantageous than issuing Certificates of Deposit (CDs). CDs are considered to be deposits, and, as such, the issuing bank must maintain a ratio for its reserve requirement and pay an FDIC insurance premium. Purchasing federal funds, however, is considered to be a borrowing of funds; therefore, there are no reserve requirements and no FDIC fees.

Term federal funds may not offer attractive arrangements for smaller banks because of the danger of losing liquidity for a period of time. They may be attractive, however, for foreign banks in these ways:

1. A foreign bank will issue CDs and sell them to the public. Since they are foreign institutions, there are no reserve requirements and no FDIC fee for the CDs.
2. The foreign bank will use the proceeds of the sale of the CDs to sell term federal funds through its clearing bank.

Other participants of federal fund trading are the savings and loan associations and corporations. The savings and loan associations will sell federal funds either through the Federal Home Loan Bank or directly to a commercial bank. Corporations are not allowed to trade in federal funds as direct participants; they do so, however, by utilizing their operating banks as intermediaries.

The Mechanics of Trading Federal Funds

Federal funds are unsecured overnight loans. One bank lends funds to another. After the two parties agree as to the terms of the contract, the transaction will be effected by an immediate debit and credit in the respective bank's federal funds account at the Federal Reserve. This is done at the Transit Department of the Federal Reserve on instructions from the buying and selling banker. If the two parties are located at different Federal Reserve districts, the funds are transferred through the Fed's wire transfer facility.

On the following business day, the transaction is reversed if this is an overnight trade. The bank that purchased the federal funds returns them to the selling bank through the same facility.

CERTIFICATE OF DEPOSIT

A Certificate of Deposit, or CD, is a money market instrument issued by a bank. A bank will issue a certificate of deposit to finance its short-term obligations or its money supply. A CD is a negotiable receipt for funds deposited at a bank for a specified period of time earning a specified rate of interest. The owner of the CD will redeem the certificate at the time of maturity and receive the principal and interest. He may also sell the CD in the secondary market.

Certificate of Deposit became popular starting with the decade of the 1960s. The creation of this instrument is due largely to the rising interest rates in 1961 and the competitive posture of the banks to service their corporate customers by offering them high yielding money market rates. It was at this time that corporate treasurers sought liquidity for their cash balances by investing in U.S. Treasury bills, finance papers, repurchase agreements, and so on.

Through the issuance of CDs, banks were able to effectively compete for short-term funds.

A Certificate of Deposit is generally issued in a book-entry form. The usual denomination is $100,000. Denominations of less than $100,000 and more than $10 million are not uncommon. The term life of a CD is from seven days to five or seven years. The majority of CDs are issued with maturities of less than one year. There is no limit on the maturity that banks are permitted to offer.

The interest rate on a CD is based on competitive money market rates and the financial standing of the issuing bank. If the CD is issued by a "prime name" bank, it will offer a lower rate of interest. The rate of interest on a CD is not dictated by the Federal Reserve, which imposes certain ceiling requirements for the funds in a bank account.

The secondary market is dominated by "Prime CDs"—CDs issued by prime banks. CD dealers generally trade prime CDs in denominations of $1 million or more. Rates in the secondary market fluctuate in response to money market conditions. Trades are settled either on a cash basis or regular way. A cash transaction settles on the day of the trade; the regular-way transaction settles on the business day following the trade date. Payment is usually made in federal funds. The trading in the secondary market is done on a bid and asked basis. A dealer will bid more aggressively for CDs if he thinks rates will fall. A normal round-lot trading unit is $1 million.

As in federal funds, bankers may use the CDs to adjust their reserve requirements. Unlike federal funds, however, a CD is considered to be a deposit of funds. A bank sells a CD, receives the funds, and places it on deposit. As such, the bank is obligated to pay FDIC premium for these funds and remove a percentage of the deposit to comply with the Fed's reserve requirement. The federal funds are not subject to these requirements. If a bank elects to adjust its money position by purchasing a term federal fund, it is not required to pay the FDIC fee, and the term federal fund is not reduced to comply with the reserve requirements. The bank's money manager, therefore, has several choices at his disposal to adjust his money position:

1. Borrow from the Fed's Discount window
2. Buy federal funds—there are no FDIC fees and no reserve requirements.
3. Liquidate short-term assets
4. Repurchase agreements
5. Issue a CD. The bank must pay the FDIC fee and remove a percentage from the CD funds for reserve requirements.

CDs are also used by banks to tap the domestic market for funds.

Agencies or branches of foreign banks also use Certificates of Deposit. A foreign bank CD may offer a higher rate of interest because the foreign bank is not required to pay FDIC fee nor deduct a percentage for reserve requirement.

Banks are not allowed to purchase their own Certificates of Deposit. There are also certain restrictions of lending funds against a CD held as collateral. A bank may sell a CD to another bank without any restrictions.

Types of Certificates of Deposit

1. *Fixed Rate CD.* The rate of interest of these CDs is fixed at the time of issuance. The holder will receive the funds at maturity, plus the interest income. On CDs with maturities up to one year, the interest is paid at maturity.

2. *Variable-Rate CD.* The interest rate on the Variable-Rate CDs is adjusted every 30 or 90 days. Variable-Rate CDs are usually issued with maturities of one year or less.

3. *Term CDs.* These CDs are issued with maturities in excess of one year. They generally pay interest every six months.

4. *Roly-Poly CDs.* These are a series of six-month CDs issued to cover a period of two years or more. The purchaser makes a contractual agreement to buy the Roly-Poly CDs upon maturity of each six-month certificate until the contract expires. The buyer may sell the contract in the secondary market before it expires. There are two types of Roly-Poly CDs:

A. Fixed Rate Roly-Poly CD. This CD carries an interest rate that is fixed for the life of the contract.
B. Floating-Rate Roly-Poly CD. Here the interest rate is changed every six months.

5. *Eurodollar CDs.* The Eurodollar CDs are certificates issued on Eurodollars, which are U.S. dollars located abroad. The Eurodollar CDs are issued by foreign banks or by foreign branches of American banks. The Eurodollar CDs may offer a higher rate than its domestic counterpart because there are no reserve requirements against these funds, even though they may be issued by the foreign branch of an American bank. There is an active secondary market centered in London. The transaction is settled in Clearing House funds on the second business day following the trade day. The First National Bank of Chicago has established a Clearing Center in London to facilitate the processing of Eurodollar CDs.

6. *Eurodollar CD Futures.* The Eurodollar CD futures are futures contracts to buy or sell the Eurodollar Certificates of Deposit.

7. *Floating Rate Eurodollar CDs* (FRCD). These are term CDs with maturities in excess of one year. The interest rate on these instruments are adjusted every three or six months. The *Libor rate* is used to determine the interest rate. Libor is the official rate for Eurodollar and stands for London Interbank Offered Rate.

8. *Asian Dollar CDs.* These are Certificates of Deposit issued by Singapore branches of U.S. and Japanese banks. The rates are based on SIBOR (Singapore Interbank Offered Rate). They are issued in denominations, ranging from

$100,000 to $1 million. The center of activity for these instruments is in Singapore. The transactions are settled in Clearing House Funds generally on the second business day following the trade day.

9. *Zero-Coupon CDs.* Some investment firms offer zero-coupon CDs. Here the investor will buy the CD at a discount from the face value, but will collect the face value at maturity. The Zero-Coupon CDs are generally used for tax-deferred retirement accounts.

Calculation of Sales Proceeds and Accrued Interest for Certificates of Deposit

1. *Certificates of deposit maturing in one year or less.* For these certificates, the interest is calculated on the basis of 360 days a year.

EXAMPLE 1

The customer owns a 90-day CD with a face value of $1 million paying 9 percent interest. How much money would he receive at the time of redemption? The bank will apply the following formula:

$$\begin{pmatrix}\text{Proceeds}\\ \text{at time of}\\ \text{redemption}\end{pmatrix} = \text{Principal} + \begin{pmatrix}\text{Interest}\\ \text{income}\end{pmatrix} \times \frac{\begin{matrix}\text{Number}\\ \text{of days to}\\ \text{maturity}\end{matrix}}{360}$$

$$1{,}000{,}000 + \left(90{,}000 \times \frac{90}{360}\right) = \$1{,}022{,}500$$

EXAMPLE 2

The customer owns a 90-day CD with a face value of $1 million bearing an interest rate of 9 percent. The customer wishes to sell the CD in the secondary market 20 days short of maturity.

What will be the amount of accrued interest he would receive from the buyer of the CD?

The accrued interest will be calculated on the basis of the number of days he held the CD.

$$90 \text{ days} - 20 \text{ days} = 70 \text{ days}$$

The accrued interest for 70 days is the following:

$$\$90{,}000 \times \frac{70}{360} = \$17{,}499.99$$

EXAMPLE 3

The customer sells a 90-day CD with a face value of $1 million bearing an interest rate of 9 percent on a 8.5 percent basis.

The customer sells the CD in the secondary market 20 days short of maturity.

What will be the proceeds of the sale? The bank will apply the following formula:

$$\left(\begin{matrix}\text{Sale}\\\text{proceeds}\end{matrix}\right) = \frac{\text{Principal} + \left(\begin{matrix}\text{Interest}\\\text{income in}\\\text{dollars}\end{matrix}\right) \times \dfrac{\begin{matrix}\text{Number}\\\text{of days to}\\\text{maturity}\end{matrix}}{360}}{1 + \left(\begin{matrix}\text{Interest}\\\text{\% sold}\end{matrix}\right) \times \dfrac{\left(\begin{matrix}\text{Number}\\\text{of days to}\\\text{maturity}\end{matrix}\right) - \left(\begin{matrix}\text{Number of}\\\text{days before}\\\text{maturity}\end{matrix}\right)}{360}}$$

$$\frac{1{,}000{,}000 + \left(90{,}000 \times \dfrac{90}{360}\right)}{1 + \left(8.5\% \times \dfrac{20}{360}\right)} = \$1{,}017{,}694.20$$

2. *Fixed-rate CDs maturing from one to five years.* For CDs maturing from one to five years, the calculation for proceeds of sale and redemption is somewhat difficult. The following example illustrates the method of computing the interest of the CD. The calculations are for a CD maturing in three years with annual interest payments at the anniversary of the issue. For CDs that pay interest semi-annually, the calculations will be the same as shown below but half-years are taken instead of whole years.

EXAMPLE 1

The customer owns a CD with a face value of $1,000,000 bearing an interest rate of 9 percent and maturing in three years. What is the amount of interest for each year?

The interest is calculated on the basis of the actual number of days in the year, 365 days, and 366 for leap year, by using the following formula:

$$\frac{\text{Principal} \times \begin{pmatrix}\text{\% interest} \\ \text{on CD}\end{pmatrix} + \begin{pmatrix}\text{Number of} \\ \text{days in year}\end{pmatrix}}{360} = \$91{,}250$$

The interest income for each of the three years will be $91,250. If one of those three years was a leap year, the interest for that year would be:

$$\frac{\$1{,}000{,}000 \times 9\% \times 366}{360} = \$91{,}500$$

COMMERCIAL PAPER

Commercial papers (CP) are money market instruments issued by corporations. They are short-term promissory notes issued to finance the interim needs of the corporation. Commercial papers may be secured or unsecured. The pioneer of this type of financing was GMAC, the financial subsidiary arm of the General Motors Corporation. GMAC started to issue commercial papers in 1920, and today it is one of the largest issuers of these instruments.

Corporations will sell commercial papers either directly to the public or through commercial paper dealers. The dealers will purchase the paper directly from the corporation on a wholesale basis and sell it to the public. The difference in price will be the dealer's spread. The dealers also provide a secondary market for these instruments. Corporate treasurers of industrial, commercial, or finance companies use commercial papers as an alternate source of financing. Today, there is an active primary and secondary market for these instruments. The corporate treasurers consider this method of financing more advantageous and economical over a bank loan. The interest cost to the corporation on commercial papers is generally lower than the bank's prime lending rate on bank loans. As interest rates fall, corporate borrowing through the commercial paper market becomes relatively cheaper and corporate treasurers shift from bank loans to commercial papers.

Commercial papers are exempt from the registration requirements under the Securities Act of 1933. To maintain this exemption status, the life of a commercial paper may not exceed 270 days. Short-term commercial papers may be used as collateral to borrow money from a bank.

There are approximately 900 corporations that issue commercial papers on a regular basis. They use the funds to finance current operations or to provide a working capital. Most of the CPs are rated by Standard & Poor's or Moody's Investors Services. The paper is generally supported by unused bank credit line. They are mostly sold at a discount from the face value. The difference between the discount price and the redemption value will be the investor's profit. At the time of maturity, the corporation will roll its commercial paper, which means it sells new paper and obtains funds to pay off the maturing paper.

A round-lot transaction is $100,000. Some CPs are

issued in denominations of $25,000 or $50,000. They are mostly issued in bearer form; some come registered in the name of the customer. The corporation usually appoints a commercial bank to act as the paying agent. At maturity, the paying agent bank will redeem the paper. Transactions in the secondary market settle in federal funds on the day of the trade.

The dealers maintain the market of the CPs in their inventory. They stand ready to buy back the paper when the investor wishes to sell it before maturity.

The gain or income on commercial papers is subject to federal and local income tax.

Bank Financing and Commercial Papers

Commercial papers with fixed interest rates have created some financing problems in recent years because of the fluctuating interest rates in the marketplace. It is difficult for a corporate treasurer to accept a market rate risk when issuing a commercial paper. Long-term financing at the current interest rate may be risky when interest rates decline. Treasurers, therefore, tend to stay flexible in their corporate financing strategies. They have increased their dependence on short-term credit—whether through the issuance of commercial paper or bank loan—that might carry a fixed rate for a short period of time but can be rolled over regularly to adjust to new interest rates. Because of the difficulty in forecasting future interest rates, corporations may have a hard time making decisions on capital expenditures, pricing, expansion, and long-term capital investment.

The trend, therefore, is toward short-term and floating rate borrowing. Banks may be able to satisfy this corporate need by lending money to corporations on a "matched funding" basis. This means the bank may be able to link a specific corporate loan to a source of funds with similar characteristics. This is an innovative system of banking. The "matched funding" system will be able to break a large pool of money into smaller pools with rates and maturities matched to a particular corporate borrowing need. Through this method, pools of fixed-rate deposits will be matched to a fixed rate loan. The banks will require fixed rate deposits from institutions and will match these to a corporate loan.

One of the most creative techniques used to correct mismatches of funds is the trading of the financial futures contract. The bank will hedge fixed rate loans in the financial futures market. Since the price of a financial futures contract changes with interest rates, a gain on a futures transaction may be used to offset a loss in interest income, or vice versa. Banks may also use financial futures to convert floating rate corporate loans. The result of this transaction is known as a "Synthetic Fixed Rate Loan."

LETTERS OF CREDIT

The use of letters of credit by commercial banks for shipment of goods and issuance of bonds and money market instruments is widespread. In issuing a letter of credit, a bank makes a commitment to pay. Letters of credit are used for municipal bonds, housing agency securities, industrial revenue bonds, commercial papers, banker's acceptances, and other securities. In a securities offering, a bank guarantees payment of interest and principal to the investor. The issuing entity pays a fee to the bank for the issuance of the letter of credit. The letter of credit brings an improved credit rating for the security by the rating organization. The bank charges an annual fee ranging from 0.25 percent to 3 percent of the amount guaranteed, depending on the degree of risk involved. If a bank has outstanding letters of credit in the amount of $15 billion at 1 percent annual rate, the bank will earn $150 million a year. Unless the bank is called to make good on the agreement, the letters of credit will not immobilize the bank's capital nor will it affect its reserve requirements. Only banks are allowed to issue letters of credit, not securities firms.

BANKERS' ACCEPTANCES

As money market instruments, bankers' acceptances represent a class of credit instruments known as bills of exchange. Bills of exchange are orders to pay a specific amount of money at a specified time drawn on a financial institution. When the drawee acknowledges his obligation to honor the order, he writes the word "accepted" with an authorized signature on the order. At this point, the bill of exchange becomes a bankers' acceptance. This "acceptance" represents the liability of the bank to pay the specific amount at a specified time.

Bankers' acceptances are used to finance domestic and international trade.

The use of a bankers' acceptance may be illustrated by the following example:

1. A U.S. merchant buys merchandise in Hong Kong.
2. The U.S. merchant may decide to finance the purchase and shipment of the merchandise through a bankers' acceptance. This means he will request his U.S. bank to issue a letter of credit in favor of the Hong Kong merchant.
3. The letter of credit issued by the U.S. bank will state the particulars of the shipment and the value of the merchandise. This becomes a draft on the U.S. bank.
4. The U.S. merchant will agree to pay his bank a specified amount at the maturity of the draft. This occurs when the shipment is received and the conditions are verified. In accepting the letter of credit, the Hong Kong merchant remains liable until the shipment is received in the United States.
5. The Hong Kong merchant, in order to finance his own operation, will discount this U.S. bank draft at his local bank. For instance, if the draft is for $100,000 at maturity, he will receive $95,000 from the Hong Kong bank and will start utilizing this cash.

6. After acquiring the draft and the shipping instructions from the Hong Kong merchant, the Hong Kong bank will forward the draft to the U.S. bank. The shipping documents are released to the U.S. merchant against a trust receipt, thus allowing the merchant to sell the merchandise.

7. On receipt of the draft, the U.S. bank will stamp "accepted" across the face of the draft and include an authorized signature. At this point, the draft becomes a *bankers' acceptance* (BA) and it becomes an obligation of the "accepting" bank. Usually the Hong Kong bank will discount the "acceptance" with the U.S. bank.

8. The U.S. bank may elect to hold the acceptance as an asset or sell it to a dealer or to an investor. When the bank sells a bankers' acceptance, that means the new holder of the BA is financing the shipment of the merchandise. The "accepting" bank earns both commissions charged for issuing the letter of credit and the interest that it will charge the customer purchasing the instrument.

Some banks prefer to hold bankers' acceptances issued by other banks. This is called *three-name paper*. The three names are the drawer and the two banks. A bank may sell its bankers' acceptances to another bank and purchase the other banks' acceptances for its portfolio. This practice is known as "swaps."

Maturities of bankers' acceptances range from 30 days up to 270 days.

From the banking standpoint, bankers' acceptances have an important advantage over direct loans. Financing the customer's credit demands through a bankers' acceptance does not involve a charge on the bank's cash reserves.

The gain or income on bankers' acceptances is subject to federal and local income tax. The Federal Reserve uses bankers' acceptances in its repurchase agreements with BA dealers. These bankers' acceptances used by the Fed are known as Prime BAs.

Bankers' acceptances are bought and sold on a discount basis, just like the Treasury bills.

EURODOLLARS

Eurodollars are deposits denominated in U.S. dollars placed with banks outside the United States. An American corporation or a merchant purchases merchandise from a foreign corporation and will pay a check denominated in U.S. dollars. The foreign corporation will place these funds in a foreign bank or a foreign branch of a U.S. bank. These funds are referred to as Eurodollars. The Eurodollars are placed in the bank in the form of a time deposit. The foreign bank may lend these dollars to another bank in Europe or in America.

As money market instruments, Eurodollars are traded regularly around the world. The trading may involve substantial pyramiding of Eurodollar deposits. This pyramiding effect may be illustrated by the following example:

1. A European bank A holds a deposit in a U.S. bank B.
2. The European bank A makes a Eurodollar deposit with European bank C.
3. European bank C may, in turn, deposit the proceeds with European bank D, and so on.
4. Each redeposit creates a new Eurodollar deposit liability on the banks of the foreign banks involved. The original deposit in the U.S. bank B may be several times larger than what the actual amount is.

Eurodollars became popular in the early 1960s, and London became the center for Eurodollar trading activity. Other centers around the world are Hong Kong, Singapore, Bahrein in the Middle East, Paris, Switzerland, New York, San Francisco, Nassau and Cayman Islands in the Bahamas, and Tokyo.

The Federal Reserve Board has established rules to have some of these Eurodollars flow back to the United States. Effective December 3, 1981, the New York City banks were allowed to establish special accounts for Eurodollars. The Fed considers New York City to be a free banking zone allowing banks to compete in the huge Eurodollar market and bringing the dollars back to the United States. Other states have also established free banking zones for this purpose. There are also "offshore" international banking facilities in the Bahamas and elsewhere. These facilities allow customers to deposit Eurodollars.

Ironically, the concept of the Eurodollar trading was created in the late 1950s by the Soviet Union. For political reasons, the Soviet Union feared placing its U.S. dollars in banks in the United States. The Russians convinced the European banks to accept the dollar balances, and the European banks began to lend the balance to other banks and borrowers. The Soviet Union, through its banking facilities around the world, conducts a sophisticated arbitrage trading in Eurodollars today.

Eurodollars have a fixed term. They have a wide range of maturities—from overnight to five years. Most of them are issued in maturities of six months or less. As Clearing House funds, they mature into federal funds overnight. The rate on Eurodollar is based on London Interbank Offered Rate (LIBOR) published every business day in London.

A U.S. bank depositing Eurodollars in a foreign branch will avoid certain restrictions on the uses of funds and rates. As money market instruments, Eurodollars play a very important role in the international trade, balance of payments, and money management. The result has been the development of an international interest rate with no national money market restrictions. Commercial banks use these Eurodollars to adjust their liquidity positions.

Transactions in Eurodollars are recorded through a book-entry system. Eurodollars never leave the United States. Since they are Clearing House funds, they clear into federal funds through the Fed's settlement system. The only time that the Eurodollars leave the United States is when paper currencies are taken out of the country and deposited abroad. This may be illustrated by the following example (see Fig. 12.2):

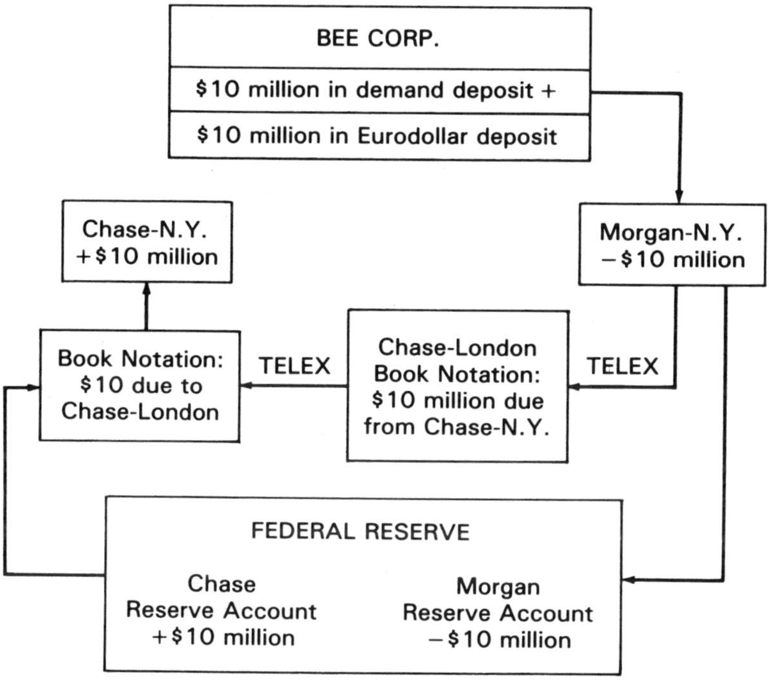

Fig. 12.2. Eurodollar Flowchart

1. Bee Corp. advises Morgan Guaranty in New York to remove $10 million from the account and deposit it at Chase Manhattan's London branch.
2. Morgan will make this deposit by sending a telex to Chase–London.
3. Upon receipt of the telex message, Chase–London will make a book-entry stating that $10 million is due from Chase Manhattan in New York.
4. Simultaneously, Chase in New York will make a book-entry stating that $10 million is due to Chase–London.
5. After telexing the funds to Chase–London, Morgan in New York will advise the Federal Reserve Bank in New York to debit its reserve account $10 million and credit Chase–New York's reserve account $10 million.

6. The funds never leave the United States. It is merely a shifting of funds from one bank account to another bank account in the Federal Reserve Bank. The funds abroad in the form of Eurodollars are only entries in the bookkeeping system of the respective banks.

Even if the Eurodollars are being used by a non-American organization, the situation will still be the same. Assuming Chase–London lends the Eurodollars to a foreign corporation, the foreign corporation will use the funds to purchase natural gas from Algeria. Algeria will receive the payment in Eurodollars and deposit it at Citibank–London. Citibank–London will make a book notation marking the amount due from Citibank–New York. The Fed in New York will debit and credit the reserve accounts of the respective banks.

Eurodollar Loan Syndication

For large projects, a European bank may decide to syndicate a Eurodollar loan. Loan syndication of this type is used to limit the liability of a bank. The procedure for syndication is the following:

1. The borrowing entity accepts the terms of the loan.
2. The lead bank guarantees the borrower.
3. The lead bank will arrange the loan syndicate with other banks.
4. The borrowing entity will receive the loan. The procedure usually takes a week.

Eurocurrency

The Eurocurrency is the general term referring to a deposit denominated in the currency of another country. Eurodollars are an important ingredient of the Eurocurrency market. Foreign currencies, such as Swiss francs, British pounds, French francs, German marks, Italian lira,

Japanese yen, and Canadian dollars, are part of the Eurocurrency market. Traders conduct arbitrage and Eurocurrency swaps, converting one type of currency into another to make a profit or to meet their liquidity requirements.

REPURCHASE AND REVERSE REPURCHASE AGREEMENTS

As a money market instrument, a repurchase agreement consists of two transactions:

- Selling the security with the agreement to repurchase it at the same price at some future date; the seller will agree to pay a stipulated interest charge to the buyer
- Purchasing the security with the agreement to return it and receive the money back plus the stipulated interest charge

The repurchase agreements are used by banks, financial institutions, and dealers to realize a profit or to finance their obligations. The securities used in the agreements are generally U.S. Treasury and Agency securities and some money market instruments.

The RPs or Repos, as they are popularly known, have a wide range of maturities—from overnight to several months. The latter is known as Term RP.

The rate of interest on Repos is based on the prevailing money market rates. In selling the security, the dealer will pay the interest to the buyer of the security for the duration of the term. The interest is calculated on a 360-day basis and the transactions are settled in federal funds. The usual denomination is $1 million.

A reverse repurchase agreement is the reverse of the RP. The dealer buys the security with the agreement to sell it back at the same price at some future date.

Sometimes, both in Repo and Reverse Repo, the two

parties agree to return the security at a different price than the original price in the transaction. The difference between the two prices will be the investor's interest earning.

RP transactions done by banks to finance the purchase of U.S. government and Agency securities are exempt from the Fed's reserve requirements. But RPs done to finance CDs, BAs, and loans are subject to the reserve requirements.

State and local governments also use RP financing. State of California, for instance, sells $1 billion long-term bonds through an underwriting process. The State receives $1 billion and will immediately invest it in an RP transaction until the money is needed.

The Federal Reserve also uses the repurchase agreements to maintain the equilibrium in the money positions. Through its Open Market Operations, it sells U.S. Treasury securities to primary dealers with the agreement to buy them back. These Repos are made at the initiative of the Fed and represent an important complement to purchases and sales of securities by the Fed. The Fed uses the Repo to increase the money supply for a few days if the Federal Open Market Committee believes that the money increase is needed only for a short period of time.

Procedures for Repos and Reverse Repos

Repurchase Agreement

1. Dealer A lends government securities to Bank B.
2. Dealer A will receive federal funds from Bank B against the security.
3. Dealer A will utilize the federal funds—sell the federal funds or finance his trading operation.
4. Dealer A agrees to buy back the security from Bank A at the end of a specified period at the price specified at the time of the agreement.

5. Dealer A, upon receipt of the security and in addition to the transaction money, must also pay an interest to Bank B.
6. If there is a record date involved, the accrued interest must also be calculated as part of the transaction.

Reverse Repurchase Agreement

1. Dealer A borrows government securities from Bank B.
2. Dealer A agrees to return the same security back to Bank B at the end of a specified period at a price specified at the time of the transaction.
3. Bank B must pay interest to Dealer A.
4. If there are record dates involved, accrued interest must be taken into consideration as part of the transaction.

Dealer A may use this reverse REPO for his arbitrage activity. After borrowing the security from Bank B, Dealer A sells the security to another dealer and then utilize the proceeds of the sale to generate a profit. Dealer A may even sell the security short after borrowing it from Bank B. He will utilize the accrued interest in his arbitrage strategy. Dealer A will sell the security short at a high price just before an interest record date and buy back to cover his short immediately after the record date when the market price hopefully has declined. He will be in trouble, however, if the securities go up unexpectedly after the record date. This will force him to cover the short at a higher price.

Retail Repurchase Agreements

Banks and savings and loan associations offer retail repurchase agreements to their customers. It basically works this way:

1. The customer, when buying a retail REPO from the bank, is effectively making a short-term loan to the bank.
2. The bank agrees to repay the loan to the customer within one to 89 days, depending on the term of the agreement. The interest that the bank will pay the customer will be based on prevailing money market rates. These rates may be fixed or variable for the term of the agreement.
3. The bank is required to set aside enough government securities to cover the value of its outstanding retail REPOs. If the bank goes bankrupt, the securities will be sold and the proceeds will be used to repay the REPO holders.

The laws of certain states vary as to the bank's procedure of setting aside a group of government securities for the protection of the REPO holders. According to laws of some states, if the bank goes bankrupt, these securities might have to be used to pay off the general creditors. The only full protection the REPO customer may receive if the bank places the government securities with an independent trustee or custodian.

MONEY MARKET MUTUAL FUNDS

The money market mutual funds are financial entities specialized in investing the customer's funds in various money market instruments. An investor with only $500 may invest in a money market mutual fund and earn an interest rate prevailing in the money market. Most funds offer check writing services. The customer may withdraw funds at any time or write a check on the balance.

The growth of the money market mutual funds was explosive and phenomenal in the 1970s. Until December 14, 1982, these funds were the exclusive domain of brokerage houses and other non-bank financial institutions. In 1982,

Congress enacted a law allowing the banking institutions to offer money market funds to their retail customers. The money market funds offered by banks are insured by the FDIC; and in the case of savings and loan associations, they are insured by the FSLIC.

SWAPPING

Swapping is a procedure through which one security is sold and with the proceeds of the sale another security is purchased. In the case of bonds or interest bearing instruments, swapping is done to take advantage of the yield spread between one security and another. Swapping has become a very useful tool for portfolio managers.

There are several different techniques in swapping:

1. Yield Pickup Swap
2. Substitution or a Replacement Swap
3. Intermarket Swap
4. Yield Anticipation Swap

Let us study each one.

YIELD PICKUP SWAP

By applying the Yield Pickup Swap, the portfolio manager will replace lower yield security with a security offering a higher yield. Both securities will have the same quality and maturity date.

SUBSTITUTION OR REPLACEMENT SWAP

In a Substitution Swap, the portfolio manager replaces one type of security with another yielding a higher interest.

INTERMARKET SWAP

In an Intermarket Swap, the portfolio manager replaces a high quality bond with one of lower quality to take advantage of the yield spread. For example, replace a bond rated AAA with one rated A. The A-rated bond will have a higher yield.

YIELD ANTICIPATION SWAP

In a Yield Anticipation Swap, the portfolio manager replaces a security with another one in anticipation of a yield change in the future. For example, if he expects interest rates to decline, he would replace short-term maturity bonds with bonds having longer maturities.

CHAPTER THIRTEEN

MORTGAGE-BACKED SECURITIES

One of the most phenomenal movements in the securities business in recent years has been the dynamic growth of mortgage-backed securities. Fluctuations in interest rates in the capital market as well as the housing market since the late 1970s forced financial institutions to seek new avenues to maintain liquidity and reduce the risk associated with mortgages on real estate. One of the avenues open to financial institutions was the restructuring of the outstanding real estate mortgages into a pool and issuing securities supported by the pool. The securities issued on the mortgage pools came to be known as mortgage-backed securities.

This chapter will discuss the creation and types of different mortgage-backed securities and their operating procedures. But first let us discuss different types of mortgages available in the market today.

WHAT IS A MORTGAGE

A mortgage is a pledge of a collateral to secure a loan to buy a property. A person wishing to purchase a house or a commercial property will go to a financial institution and apply for a loan. The institution will assess the property and the financial background of the prospective borrower, and will make a determination on whether to grant a loan. If the loan goes through, the property will be pledged and the property owner will be required to make a monthly payment to pay off the principal and interest on the loan until the date of maturity.

The life of a mortgage can be between 12 and 40 years. A conventional type mortgage is one that has a fixed rate of interest, with a life of 30 years. This type of mortgage is known as Fixed Rate Mortgage (FRM). The property owner is referred to as the *mortgagor* and the lending institution as the *mortgagee*. For FRM mortgages the monthly payment is *level*. That means the monthly payments are always the same. The monthly payment that the mortgagor is required to make has two components—one toward the payment of principal and the other toward the payment of interest. For a traditional mortgage, the monthly checks for the early years constitute mostly the interest on the loan. The principal portion in the payment increases over time until maturity. At maturity the monthly payment is almost entirely the principal.

The principal portion of each monthly check is used to repay the loan. And if this is a 30-year mortgage, the loan is *amortized* for 30 years. The principal payment of each monthly check is referred to as the *Amortization Payment*, and the amount of the outstanding balance of the principal at a given time is called the *mortgage balance*.

Let us assume the property owner's monthly payment is $450.00. In the early years, the interest payment will be higher than the principal. For example, $400 will be the interest and $50 will be used to repay the principal. The amortization payment is $50. The following month, the $450.00 check will be composed of $390.00 in interest and $60 to repay the principal. The total amount of the monthly payment remains the same. The components in the check vary from month to month.

In any month the interest portion of the check is computed by multiplying the interest rate (computed on a monthly basis) with the mortgage balance at the beginning of the month. The borrower's equity in the property is the difference between the current market value of the property minus the mortgage balance.

Equity = Current market value − Mortgage balance

The property owner is free to pay more than the required monthly amount. This additional amount will reduce his mortgage balance. This is called a *prepayment*. The prepayments are always applied to the mortgage balance.

HOW TO QUALIFY FOR A MORTGAGE

In making a determination to make a mortgage loan to a prospective property owner, the lending institution applies certain parameters as to the financial background of the applicant, his creditworthiness, and the value of the property. The rule of thumb is that the monthly mortgage payment should not exceed 25 percent of the borrower's monthly income, less other obligations he may be required to make.

The lender requires the borrower to make a downpayment on the property. This is usually an amount equal to between 5 percent and 25 percent of the value of the property.

One of the most important criteria for the lender is to determine the Loan to Value Ratio (LTV). The LTV is the ratio of the mortgage balance to the current market value of the property. It is determined by:

$$\text{LTV } \% = \frac{\text{Mortgage balance}}{\text{Current market value}} \times 100$$

The lower the LTV percentage, the greater the safety to the lender will be. The LTV decreases as the mortgage balance is reduced or the property value is increased.

MORTGAGE INSURANCE

Most banks require the property owner to carry insurance to cover the amount of the mortgage balance. In the event of death, the insurance company will pay off the outstanding mortgage balance and the beneficiary of the homeowner will have a fully paid-up house.

The mortgage insurance is like a life insurance policy. Life insurance policies are issued in one of two kinds: term life policy and whole life policy. If a person purchases a term life policy, he will make an annual premium payment until the maturity date of the policy. When he dies the beneficiary will receive the face amount of the insurance. The term life policy has no cash value, and the person receives no interest on the amount of the annual premium. The whole life policy earns interest and the policy builds up cash value as the person makes the annual premium payments. The whole life premiums are higher than the premiums on the term life. But because of its cash value, the person may borrow money from the insurance company at a favorable interest rate. At the expiration date of the policy, the person, if still alive, will receive the full cash value of the policy. If he dies at any time before the expiration date, the beneficiary will receive the full face value of the policy.

Mortgage insurance is like a term-life policy—but it is a *decreasing term insurance*. The insurance premium that the homeowner is required to make will remain the same but the face value of the insurance will be reduced gradually as the homeowner pays off the principal every month. The face value of the policy is the amount that the homeowner owes to the bank at a given point. Mortgage insurance, therefore, is a decreasing-term insurance. It covers only the remaining mortgage balance at a given point. It has no cash value and pays no interest to the homeowner.

The mortgage policy may be written in one of two ways. In the first one, the beneficiary will be the beneficiary of the homeowner; in the other, the beneficiary will be the lending institution itself. In the latter case, the lending institution gets the money directly from the insurance company in the event the homeowner dies. The lender will use the money to retire the mortgage. In the first case, the homeowner's beneficiary will receive the money directly and it will be up to the beneficiary to pay off the mortgage. This policy may be a more attractive one particularly when mortgage interest rates are on the rise and the homeowner's beneficiary decides not to pay off the existing mortgage. The beneficiary will receive the insurance payment, invest it elsewhere, and continue to make the monthly mortgage payments to the bank. In both cases, the amount of the insurance premium that the homeowner is required to make is generally the same.

In addition to a mortgage life insurance, the lending institution may require the homeowner to carry a regular homeowner's policy against fire, damages, and liabilities.

Certain lenders also require the homeowner to carry bankruptcy coverage in case the homeowner declares bankruptcy under Chapter 13, which allows the homeowner to renegotiate the terms of the loan with the lender.

There are also government insurance guarantees to cover the outstanding mortgages, such as FHA and VA.

THE MORTGAGE CREDIT SUPPLY

Where does the mortgage money come from? Until 1970, the primary source of mortgage credit was the local financial institution—thrift organization such as a savings and loan association or the savings bank. The thrift institution accepted deposits from the local resident and lent to another resident for mortgage when the second resident wanted to purchase a property.

Since the turn of the century, Americans have always relied on mortgage credit for the purchase of property. The system allowed them to pledge the property for the loan and pledge their future income to repay the loan and the interest. Borrowing money to purchase a real estate property has become one of the most dominant facets of American life. As a result, today, 2 out of 3 Americans own their homes. To help the customer repay the interest on the loan, the federal government has allowed the homeowner to deduct the cost of interest from his taxable income.

Until 1970, the mortgage activity was a local affair. If the local bank did not have enough deposits, it stopped making mortgage loans to local residents. But if it had excess deposits, it used the additional funds to buy mortgage loans from outside its area. Even though the demand for a mortgage was predictable, the supply for a mortgage was not. The increased people mobility in the 1970s created severe imbalances in the supply and demand for mortgage credit around the country. This problem was partially alleviated when mortgage bankers came into existence. The mortgage banker acted as agent or an intermediary. He originated the mortgage loan but sold the loan to investors or lenders in other localities where mortgage capital exceeded mortgage demand.

There developed a very active secondary market for mortgages in which banks and thrift institutions purchased and sold existing mortgages to alleviate the cyclical shortages of funds in the mortgage markets. The intervention of the mortgage banker was not enough, however, to solve the problem of imbalances in the mortgage credit.

In the early 1980s, it became necessary for institutions to assemble a pool of outstanding mortgages, transfer the pool to a trust to create a security based on the value of the pool, and then sell the securities to investors. These securities came to be known as mortgage-backed securities with investment characteristics that appealed to pension fund managers, insurance companies, money managers, and individual investors.

Federal National Mortgage Association and Federal Home Loan Mortgage Corporation played dominant roles in this secondary market. Fannie Mae purchased and sold FHA- and VA-backed mortgages in the secondary market, and Freddie Mac bought and sold mortgages without any FHA and VA guarantees.

In addition, the high interest rates in the U.S. economy in the early 1980s gave rise to different types of mortgages. Traditionally banks lent on the basis of a fixed mortgage rate for the duration of the mortgage loan. The fixed-rate mortgages, however, caused a serious financial and liquidity problem for the lending institution in an atmosphere of rising interest rates. Banks started to package other types of mortgages that collectively came to be known as Alternative Mortgage Instruments (AMI).

With the introduction of AMIs, other financial institutions became interested in making mortgage loans. Today commercial banks, insurance companies, and pension funds participate in the mortgage market in an unprecedented manner. The market has ceased to become the exclusive domain of thrift institutions.

ALTERNATIVE MORTGAGE INSTRUMENTS (AMI)

AMIs offer nontraditional mortgage programs to consumers and prospective property owners. AMI's do not have level monthly payments. They are created primarily to reduce the risk to the lender as well as the borrower.

Most of the following types of mortgages or AMIs are fairly new:

1. *Graduated Payment Mortgage (GPM).* The Graduated Payment Mortgage does not have a level payment. The monthly payments are not the same. The monthly payments that the property owner is required to make start at a low level and rise later on. The actual number of years that the payments rise and the percentage of the annual increase depend on the type of GPM. There are basically five types of GPMs. GPM I, GPM II, GPM III, GPM IV, and GPM V.

GPMs appeal to those homeowners who could not afford the large monthly payments of a traditional type mortgage loan. By borrowing a GPM, the homeowner can make lower payments in the beginning; but as his personal income rises, he will be able to afford the increased monthly payment of the GPM.

2. *Pledged Account Mortgage.* The Pledged Account Mortgage is created by taking the property owner's down payment and depositing it at the bank. The savings account is pledged for the mortgage loan, but it also serves as an interest-earning account for the homeowner. The homeowner may withdraw funds from the account to make his monthly mortgage payments.

3. *Rollover Mortgage (ROM).* ROMs are mortgages that are popular in Canada. Its entry into the U.S. is fairly recent. At times they are referred to as RRMs (Renegotiated Rate Mortgages). ROMs are 30-year mortgages with interest rates being negotiated every 3 or 5 years.

4. *Reverse Annuity Mortgage (RAM).* In a RAM type of mortgage, the *bank* makes a monthly payment to the homeowner, just the reverse of a regular mortgage arrangement. If the homeowner has a cash flow problem but has a large equity in the property, the RAM provides a method of converting the equity into a monthly income stream. The bank sends a monthly check to the homeowner based on the current equity of the house and charges an interest. In effect, the bank is making continuous series of monthly loans for a period of time, which may extend up to 10 years. The bank takes the house as collateral, and the homeowner uses the money to cover his expenses. This type of mortgage is attractive for elderly people who need a monthly subsidy to support themselves.

5. *Shared Appreciation Mortgage (SAM).* Through a Shared Appreciation Mortgage, the bank agrees to provide a mortgage at a greatly reduced rate of interest. In return, the property owner agrees to share the appreciated increase in the property value with the bank when the loan matures or the property is sold. Let us assume that the prevailing mortgage rate in the market is 9 percent. The bank lends the loan at 6 percent, which is a reduction of one-third of

the going rate. In return, the homeowner gives the bank one-third of the appreciated increase of the property value when the loan matures or the property is sold, whichever comes first. With this type of mortgage, the homeowner will be able to afford to buy the house and the bank will make a potential profit at the end. This is similar to an *equity Kicker*.

6. *Adjustable-Rate Mortgage (ARM)*. In an Adjustable Rate Mortgage, the interest rate is adjusted at regular intervals, which can be every six months, three years, or five years. Currently, most of the single-family dwellings are financed through ARMs. For ARMs the initial interest rate is usually lower than the prevailing mortgage rate in the market.

FIXED-RATE MORTGAGE-BACKED SECURITIES

The pool of mortgages used to create a mortgage-backed security usually contains Fixed Rate Mortgages, mainly because the other type of mortgages discussed above lack standardization and uniformity. The level payments of the FRM make the calculation of the payment of principal and interest to the security holder relatively easy.

The mortgage-backed securities are created based on the value of the mortgages in the pool. The pool may contain up to 300 mortgages, issued by a single institution or by many institutions. The size of each loan ranges between \$100,000 to \$150,000. Loans in excess of \$500,000 are usually not used for mortgage pools.

Mortgage-backed securities are issued on pools containing only quality mortgages.

High quality mortgages have the following characteristics:

1. The property is a single-family, owner-occupied detached dwelling.
2. The property is located in the United States.

3. The mortgage loan has an original maturity of no more than 30 years.
4. The property is located in a good geographic location.
5. The loan to value ratio (LTV) is not more than 80 percent.
6. Mortgages are insured.
7. The mortgages are seasoned. A seasoned mortgage is one with a life of more than five years (defaults in mortgages usually occur during the first five years).
8. The pool contains mortgages diversified in different parts of the country.

Poor quality mortgages are:

1. Mortgages on vacation homes
2. Mortgages on attached properties or condominiums
3. Mortgages on manufactured houses
4. Mortgages on multi-family units
5. Mortgages on nonowner-occupied housing units
6. Mortgages on mobile homes
7. Mortgages with maturities of less than 30 years

TYPES OF MORTGAGE-BACKED SECURITIES

Pass-Through Securities

Pass-through securities represent the largest class of mortgage-backed certificates. They are issued on pools of mortgages that are mostly fixed rate, 30-year conventional mortgages. (Although occasionally one may find a pool containing some GPMs and 15-year mortgages.)

To create a pass-through security, a financial institution will assemble a pool of mortgages and sell the pool to investors in the form of pass-through securities. The financial institution acting as the sponsor, the originator, or the creator will transfer the mortgages to a trust against the receipt of certificates and then sell the certificates to investors. Pass-through securities represent a sale of assets by the issuing bank. The bank will sell the mortgage loan and records the loan off its books. The difference between the mortgage loan and the proceeds of the sale of the pass-through is considered as a profit or loss to the bank. Any cash flow from the mortgage loan is passed-through to the security holder with the bank acting as an intermediary between the homeowner and the security holder. To continue to service the mortgage loan, the bank charges a servicing fee to the security holder, which is usually 50 basis points annualized. This means if the mortgage rate is 9 percent the security holder will get 8½ percent interest on his security. The ½ percent will be applied to cover the bank's servicing fee.

The security holder holds a pro-rata interest in the mortgage pool. The pass-through security is not an obligation of the issuing bank. The homeowner continues to be obligated to pay the monthly principal and interest to the bank, which then passes the payment to the security holder after deducting the servicing fee, the pool administration fee, insurance, and guarantee fees. These fees are fixed over the life of the pool in such a way that the security holder is assured to receive a fixed pass-through rate every month.

The trust holds the pool but the owners of the mortgages are the security holders.

To induce the investor to purchase a pass-through security, the originating bank will seek an agency to guarantee that the security holder will receive the monthly payment of principal and interest regardless of whether the homeowner makes the payments or not. The originator will file the necessary documents with the guarantor-agency and issue the pass-through securities backed by the guarantor.

There are three federal agencies that guarantee payments for pass-through security holders, GNMA, FNMA, and FHLMC.

There are four different types of pass-through securities: Ginny Mae Pass-Throughs, Freddie Mac Participation Certificates, Fannie Mae Mortgage-backed Securities, and private pass-through securities. Let us study each one:

1. Ginny Mae Pass-Through Securities

The mortgage pools of Ginny Mae Pass-Through Securities contain FHA- or VA-secured mortgage loans. These pass-through securities are backed by the full faith and credit of the U.S. government. GNMA is a wholly owned U.S. government corporation within the Department of Housing and Urban Development (HUD). Ginny Mae guarantees the payment of principal and interest to the security holder, regardless of whether the mortgage payment is received by the bank.

There are six different types of GNMA Pass-Throughs:

A. *GNMA I.* The GNMA I's represent approximately 80 percent of all the pass-through securities in the market. The mortgages in the pool of GNMA I are single issuer (issued by the same bank) with the same rate of interest and the same maturity date. The minimum size of the pool is $1 million.

B. *GNMA II.* The GNMA II's are issued on multiple issuer pools (mortgages in the pool are issued by different banks). This allows small mortgage lenders to pool together smaller mortgage loans to make up the $1 million unit requirement of GNMA. Mortgages in GNMA II may have different interest rates. The minimum pool size is $7 million.

C. *GNMA Midget.* The GNMA Midget is a 15-year security with an assumed life of seven years for purposes of quoting yields. The minimum pool size is $1 million.

D. *GNMA–GPM.* The GNMA–GPM is a pass-through security based on graduated payment. The minimum pool size is $1 million.

E. *GNMA–Mobile Home Pass-Through.* The GNMA Mobile Home Pass-Throughs are based on mortgages for mobile homes. Due to the fact that the lending bank requires closer supervision to monitor and maintain this type of mortgage, the servicing fee charged the security holder is usually higher than for other types of pass-through securities. The minimum pool size is $½ million.

F. *GNMA–FHA Projects.* The GNMA–FHA Projects are pass-through securities based on 40-year, multi-family mortgage loans. The pricing of the security is based on an assumed life of 18 years. The minimum pool size is $½ million.

2. FHLMC–Participation Certificates

After GNMA, Freddie Mac is the second largest issuer of pass-through securities. Its pass-through is called Participation Certificates. The PCs are based on conventional single-family residential mortgages, but, unlike GNMA, these mortgages are not secured by FHA or VA. They yield a higher rate than Ginny Mae Pass-Throughs. The payment of principal and interest to the PC holder is not guaranteed by the U.S. government. They are guaranteed only by FHLMC. The minimum pool size is $100 million. (For Guarantors Programs, the minimum pool size is $5 million.)

3. FNMA–Mortgage-Backed Security

The FNMA–Mortgage-Backed Security is a recent entry into the pass-through market. It is similar to Freddie Mac PCs. The payment of principal and interest to the mortgage-backed security (MBS) holder is guaranteed only by Fannie Mae. The minimum pool size is $1 million.

4. Private Pass-Through Securities

Private pass-throughs are issued by commercial banks or savings and loan associations with no guarantee as to the payment of principal and interest. The issuing bank will generally charge 50 basis points to the security holder for collecting payments from the property owner and monitoring the status of the mortgage loan. As in other types of pass-throughs, this is again a sale of assets to the security holder who will have a pro-rata ownership in the pool of mortgages.

METHOD OF PAYMENT

The cash flow of the pass-through security is related to the cash flow generated from the pool of the underlying mortgages, but the two payments are not the same. The payment to the security holder is less than the payment received from the property owner because of the servicing fee that the bank charges the security holder. The monthly cash flow from the pool is level, but the payment to the pass-through holder is not. This is due to the calculation of the servicing fee. The servicing fee is a percentage of the outstanding principal. The dollar amount of the fee is reduced as the principal declines each month.

In addition, there is an initial delay of payment to the security holder. This delay is a result of the payment schedule of the homeowner who is not required to send the first check on his mortgage loan until the beginning of the second month, after the origination date of the mortgage. Consequently, the holder of the security does not receive his first payment until sometime into the second month. The GNMA security holder will receive his first payment on the 15th of the second month from the origination date of the mortgage.

For trading purposes, the schedule for initial payment is: 45 day delay for Ginnie Mae Pass-Throughs, 54 day delay for Fannie Mae MBS, and 75 day delay for Freddie Mac PCs.

The industry standard for quoting pass-through securities is 12 years. According to an analysis conducted by FHA, mortgages are paid on average in the 12th year after origination. This is called the FHA Experience. Since the average life to prepayment is 12 years, the mortgage cash flows are also evaluated on a 12-year basis. Prepayments occur when the property owner sells the property or refinances the mortgage due to prevailing low interest rates in the market.

Calculation of Monthly Payments for Pass-Through Securities

The sum of principal and interest that the security holder expects to receive every month is not the same. The components of the principal and interest in the check vary. Generally, the amount of interest will decrease and the principal will increase as the mortgage loan ages toward maturity. This is because interest is paid on the remaining balance of the loan that is continuously decreasing as the property owner is making his monthly payments.

The *monthly interest payment* on a pass-through is calculated by:

$$\begin{pmatrix}\text{Remaining balance}\\ \text{of the principal}\end{pmatrix} \times \begin{pmatrix}\text{Monthly interest}\\ \text{rate in decimal}\end{pmatrix}$$

The return on investment on a pass-through varies from pool to pool, depending on the type of security, the age, prepayment expectations, and so on.

How to Calculate the Remaining Balance of the Mortgage Loan

The following formula is used to calculate the remaining balance in the mortgage loan:

$$D = \left[1 - \left[\frac{(1 + 1)^t - 1}{(1 + I)^m - 1}\right]\right] \times M$$

where

D = remaining dollar balance of the mortgage at a given point

I = monthly mortgage interest rate (in decimal)

t = number of months the mortgage has been paid

m = number of months of the mortgage at original maturity

M = original loan amount

Let us assume a $50,000, 30-year mortgage that has aged five years has a mortgage interest rate of 10 percent. What is the remaining dollar balance of the mortgage loan?

10% on a monthly basis is .0083333. 5 years is 60 months, 30 years is 360 months.

$$\left\{1 - \left[\frac{(1 + .0083333)^{60} - 1}{(1 + .0083333)^{360} - 1}\right]\right\} \times 50{,}000 = \$48{,}287.15$$

How to Calculate Monthly Interest Payment

The following formula is used to calculate the monthly interest payment:

$$IP = D \times I$$

where

IP = interest payment

D = remaining dollar balance of the mortgage at a given point

I = monthly interest mortgage rate in decimal

In the above example, the monthly interest payment on the security will be:

$$48{,}287.15 \times .0083333 = \$402.39$$

If the security has a servicing fee, the formula will be:

$$IP = D \times (I - S)$$

where S is the servicing fee in decimal. If the servicing fee is .50 percent a year, this will be .00041667 a month.

Therefore,

$$IP = D \times (.0083333 - .00041667)$$

$$= 48{,}287.15 \times (.0083333 - .00041667) = \$382.2$$

How to Calculate the Monthly Principal Payment

The following formula is used to calculate the monthly principal payment:

$$P = D - D_{+1}$$

In the example above, D represents the dollar amount on the 60th month. D_{+1} will be the dollar amount of the remaining mortgage on the 61st month. Calculate the D_{+1} by using the same formula:

$$D_{+1} = \left\{1 - \left[\frac{(1 + .0083333)^{61} - 1}{(1 + .0083333)^{360} - 1}\right]\right\} \times 50{,}000$$

$$= 48{,}250.76$$

The monthly principal payment will be, therefore,

$$D - D_{+1}$$

$$48{,}287.15 - 48{,}250.76 = 36.39$$

The total monthly payment to the security holder will be the sum of both the principal and interest.

$$IP + P = \text{Monthly payment}$$

MORTGAGE-BACKED BONDS

In the late 1970s, banks and savings and loan associations created certain debt obligations based on a pool of mortgages similar to corporate bonds. These securities came to be known as Mortgage-Backed Bonds (MBBs). Unlike the pass-through securities, the MBBs are the direct obligation of the issuing bank with a set date of maturity paying interest every six months and with the principal paid at maturity. The bonds are supported and secured by the mortgages in the pool. The aggregate face-value of the bonds is less than the value of the underlying pool of mortgages. By issuing the bonds, the bank is able to raise funds at a low cost without the necessity of selling the underlying mortgages, as in the case of a pass-through security.

The sale of a pass-through security is a sale of assets. The property owner has the obligation to make the monthly payments to the bank that acts as agent to distribute the payment to the security holder. In issuing a pass-through security, the bank assumes no obligation to make the payment. The guarantor–agency, such as GNMA or Freddie Mac, will guarantee that the security holder receives his monthly checks of principal and interest on a timely basis.

When issuing a mortgage-backed bond, the bank assumes the obligation and the responsibility in making the payments of principal and interest to the bondholder. In issuing the bond, the bank does not sell the mortgages in the portfolio. The mortgage-backed bonds do not constitute a sale of assets. The bank will receive the monthly payments from the property owner, use the money for a period of time, and mail the check to the bondholder every six months. This is called *pay-through* securities as opposed to *pass-through*. The bank earns additional income in investing the property owner's monthly payments until they are distributed to the bondholder. In a pass-through security, the principal and interest have to be paid to the security holder every month. In a pay-through, the principal does not have to be paid until the date of maturity. Here, again, the bank will invest the monthly principal amount, earning additional income until the bonds are retired.

Mortgage-backed bonds are usually callable by the issuing bank.

The tremendous popularity of mortgage-backed bonds has prompted the banks to issue different variations of these securities. One of them is a Euro-MBB and the other one is CARP (Certificates of Adjustable Rate Preferred).

The Euro-MBBs are mortgage-backed bonds issued by a domestic bank but sold overseas to foreign investors.

The CARP is a creative instrument in the form of an adjustable rate preferred stock. Unlike MBBs, CARPs are not debt obligations. They are equity securities issued by a bank based on a pool of mortgages, similar to a corporate preferred stock. CARPs offered attractive investment opportunities to corporate investors. The U.S. Tax Code allows the corporate investor purchasing a CARP to deduct 80 percent of the dividends received from the security. For tax purposes, therefore, the corporate investor will declare only 20 percent of the dividend received as part of its taxable income.

CARPs pay dividends. MBBs pay interest. This has its disadvantages to the bank issuing CARPs. For the issuing bank, the dividend on the CARP is not a deductible item for corporate tax purposes, whereas the interest on the MBB is.

PAY-THROUGH BONDS

Pay-through bonds are similar to mortgage-backed bonds. In both cases, the securities are pay-through. The difference between the two is the schedule of payment to the security holder. In a mortgage-backed bond, the bank pays interest every six months. In a pay-through bond, it pays the interest every month with the principal paid at maturity.

COLLATERALIZED MORTGAGE OBLIGATIONS (CMO)

The CMOs are pay-through securities introduced into the marketplace in June 1983 by Freddie Mac. Since then, the popularity of CMOs has increased tremendously. Today, CMOs are issued not only by Freddie Mac but also by banks, investment banking firms, mortgage bankers, homebuilders, and thrift institutions.

CMO is an especially designed multi-class pay-through security backed by the cash flow generated from a pool of mortgages. Unlike the regular pay-throughs where there is only one date of maturity, the CMOs are issued in several different classes. The payment of principal is not made to all bondholders on a pro-rata basis as in the case of a pass-through. Instead, payments of principal are prioritized according to different classes of CMO. This means that the bondholders of one class are paid off completely before the next class of bondholders receive their payments.

CMOs are generally issued in five different classes. Each class has its own rate of interest and maturity date. The classes are divided into Fast Pay/Slow Pay categories. The Slow Pay CMOs have a measure of protection. That means the Slow Pay bonds will not be retired until the owners of the Fast Pay class have been paid off. Maturities of CMOs range from three to 30 years in the following order:

Class	*Type*	*Maximum Maturity*	*Expected Maturity*
1	Fast pay	Up to 5 years	1 to 4 years
2	Short intermediary	5 to 10 years	1 to 8 years
3	Long intermediary	10 to 20 years	2 to 14 years
4	Slow pay	20 to 30 years	5 to 25 years
5	Zeros	Up to 30 years	5 to 22 years

Like regular pay-through securities, they are callable by the issuing entity at any time before maturity.

The different types of CMOs are:

1. *Zero Cash Flow CMO.* The Zero Cash Flow CMO has a stated rate of interest. The interest is not paid to the

CMO owner during the life of the CMO. The interest is added to the principal outstanding at each interest payment date. The bonds are then retired in sequence with all payments of principal (which includes the added interest) going to the holders of the earliest maturity class, then beginning with the next class.

2. *Interest bearing CMOs.* These CMOs pay interest during the life of the bond, either quarterly or every six months.

3. *CMO guaranteed by a letter of credit.* To induce the investor to buy the CMO, the issuing entity will have a letter of credit issued by a commercial bank. The issuer of the letter of credit will assume the obligation to pay the CMO holder the principal and interest in the event the issuing entity is in default. The letter of credit is important since the payments of principal and interest on the CMO are not guaranteed by the U.S. government.

The interest paid on the CMO is taxable to the CMO holder under the federal and state taxation codes, but it is a deductible item for the issuing entity. The only part that will be taxable to the issuing bank will be the spread between the mortgage rate on the underlying pool and the CMO interest that is always lower.

Pay-through securities and CMOs are generally issued with an Original Issue Discount. That means the securities are sold at original sale at a price lower than the face value. The difference in money between the proceeds of the sale and the face value is called the Original Issue Discount (OID). OID does not apply to pass-through securities, which may be sold at a discount price in the marketplace after the original issue date. The word *discount* refers to the two types of securities: one is the Original Issue Discount that is sold at a discount price to the public at the time of the original sale and during the primary offering, and the other is the Market Discount, which means the bonds are traded at a price below par in the secondary market.

For Original Issue Discount and bonds sold at a premium (at a price higher than par) during the primary offering, the bondholder must determine his tax basis by calculating the amount of the annual accretion for the OIDs and the amount of the annual amortization for bonds sold at a premium.

For OIDs the annual accretion amount is determined by:

$$\frac{\text{Amount of discount}}{\text{Number of years to maturity}}$$

Let us assume the investor buys a 5-year bond for \$800 with a face value of \$1,000 at the original issue. His annual accretion will be 200/5 = \$40. He must add this amount to his cost of \$800 to determine the tax basis for the first year. His cost for the first year, therefore, will be \$840. If subsequently he sells the security for \$1,000, the amount subject to income tax will be \$160 (1,000 – 840). If he holds the bond for two years, his total accretion will be \$80 (2 × 40). He will add \$80 to his original cost of \$800 to determine his tax basis.

For premium bonds, the amount of the annual amortization is determined by:

$$\frac{\text{Amount of premium}}{\text{Number of years to maturity}}$$

Let us assume the investor buys a 5-year bond for \$1,100 with a face value of \$1,000 at original issue. His annual amortization will be:

$$\frac{100}{5} = \$20$$

He must subtract the original cost of \$1,100 by \$20 to determine the tax basis for the first year. His cost for the first year, therefore, will be \$1,080 (1,100 – 20). If subsequently he sells the security for \$1,200, the amount subject to income tax will be \$120 (1,200 – 1,080). If he holds the bonds for two years, his total amortization will be \$40

(2 × 20). He will reduce his original cost of $1,100 by $40 to determine the tax basis.

For bonds sold in the secondary market, the tax basis is the actual purchase cost of the security. Accretion and amortization apply only to original issues sold during the primary offering.

RATING OF MORTGAGE-BACKED SECURITIES

The mortgage-backed securities are rated by Moody's and Standard & Poor's in the same way corporate and municipal bonds are rated. Because of their governmental guarantees, mortgage-backed securities guaranteed by GNMA, FNMA, and FHLMC are not rated by the rating agencies. There is no question as to the safety of these investments.

In rating the MBS securities, the agency will consider the credit-worthiness of the issuing entity and the quality of the mortgages in the pool. Some rating agencies require a legal opinion to be issued by the issuer's counsel.

DEFINITION OF TERMS

Adjustable-Rate Mortgage (ARM) A type of mortgage in which the interest is adjusted at different intervals as opposed to a fixed rate mortgage

Alternative Mortgage Instruments (AMI) New and innovative types of mortgages, other than fixed rate instruments

Amortization Payment The portion of the property owner's monthly check to the mortgage lending institution representing the principal of the mortgage

Cash-Flow Bond Another term for pay-through bond

Collateralized Mortgage Obligation (CMO) A multi-class pay-through bond issued by a financial institution based on a pool of mortgages

Conditional Prepayment Rate (CPR) A measuring device that will determine the amount of prepayment on a monthly basis

Due-On Sale Mortgage A provision in the mortgage agreement that requires the borrower to pay the mortgage balance upon the sale of the property

Federal Housing Administration (FHA) A division in the Department of Housing and Urban Development (HUD) that insures residential mortgages nationwide

Fully-Modified Pass-Through A type of pass-through security that guarantees the timely payment of principal and interest to the security holder. GNMA is a fully-modified pass-through security.

GNMA–Midgets A 15-year term pass-through GNMA security

Graduated-Payment Mortgage (GPM) A type of mortgage where payments start at a low level but rise later on

Homeowner's Equity The homeowner's equity in the property, which is the difference between the current market value of the property and the outstanding mortgage

Loan to Value Ratio (LTV) The ratio of the mortgage balance to the current market value of the property. It is determined by:

$$\text{LTV } \% = \frac{\text{Mortgage balance}}{\text{Current market value}} \times 100$$

Money Market Deposit Account (MMDA) An account at a bank used for money market funds

Mortgage The collateralization of a property to secure a loan

Mortgage Balance The amount of loan that is outstanding at a given time

Mortgage Banker Mortgage bankers create mortgages for resale to investors and financial institutions

Mortgage Delinquent The property owner who fails to make a mortgage payment

Mortgage Originators Institutions that originate or create mortgage loans. Mortgage originators are thrift institutions, commercial banks, mortgage bankers, and homebuilders

Mortgage Prepayment Excess payment of the principal before the mortgage maturity date

Mortgagee The lender of money

Mortgagor The person who borrows money to buy a property

Pledged-Account Mortgage (PAM) A type of mortgage where the property owner's downpayment is deposited in a savings account at a bank. The account becomes a collateral for the loan but the customer may withdraw funds to make his monthly payments.

Reverse Annuity Mortgage (RAM) A type of mortgage in which the property owner receives monthly payments from the bank based on the equity of the property. The bank will charge interest until the date of maturity.

Rollover Mortgage (ROM) A type of mortgage popular in Canada; sometimes referred to as Renegotiated Rate Mortgage (RRM). In this type of mortgage, the lender renegotiates the interest rate every three or five years.

Seasoning A term that refers to the age of the mortgage in a pool

Shared-Appreciation Mortgage (SAM) A type of mortgage in which the lender will reduce the interest rate; in return, the borrower agrees to share part of the increase in the value of the property

Trusts for Investments on Mortgages (TIM) A multi-class pass-through security, as opposed to CMO that is a pay-through bond. TIM represents the sale of an asset; CMO represents the obligation of the issuing institution.

CHAPTER FOURTEEN

THE FUNDAMENTALS OF CALCULATING INTEREST

Interest is the cost of borrowing somebody else's money. The borrower will pay interest to the lender, whether the borrowing is done for a car, a mortgage, credit cards, or issuance of bonds and notes. By purchasing a government bond, the investor makes a loan to the government; by purchasing a corporate bond, the bondholder makes a loan to the corporation. In agreeing to help the consumer buy a house, the bank makes a mortgage loan to him.

There are several methods of computing interest. The interest on a mortgage is calculated one way, on a car loan another way, and on a bond still another. There are various rules and regulations on the federal and state levels that make interest calculations less confusing to understand. The most important federal law is the Truth-in-Lending Act which passed Congress in 1968. On the state level, there are various usury laws that place a ceiling on interest rates charged by money lenders and creditors.

The Federal Reserve System has implemented Regulation Z to control the operation of the Truth-in-Lending Act. Under this regulation, creditors are required to disclose both the Annual Percentage Rate (APR) and the total dollar finance charge to the borrower.

HOW TO CALCULATE INTEREST

The calculation of interest takes the following factors into consideration:

1. The dollar amount
2. Length of time
3. The nominal annual interest rate
4. The repayment schedule

SIMPLE INTEREST CALCULATION METHOD

The Simple Interest Method is the easiest method to use and serves as a base for all other methods of calculation. The other methods are variations of the Simple Method. The following formula is used to determine the Simple Interest:

$$\text{Interest} = \text{Principal} \times \text{Rate of interest} \times \text{Time}$$

$$I = P \times \frac{R}{100} \times T$$

The customer borrows \$1,000 at 5 percent. The loan is repaid in a lump sum at the end of one year. The Simple Interest calculated will be \$50 (5% of \$1,000). The customer will pay \$1,050 to the lender.

To illustrate the above formula:

$$\text{Interest} = \$1{,}000 \times \frac{5}{100} \times 1 = \$50$$

The term "Year" has several meanings. For some people, it is 360 days. For others, 365 days and 366 for leap year. The 360-day method is generally used by broker–dealers and bankers.

At a 12 percent interest rate, the Simple Interest calculation will give \$120 in interest in one year:

$$I = \$1{,}000 \times \frac{12}{100} \times 1 = \$120$$

If the customer repays the loan in two years, the cost of interest will be \$240.

$$I = \$1{,}000 \times \frac{12}{100} \times 2 = \$240$$

By using the Simple Interest Method, the customer is paying interest only on the amount of money borrowed and not on any accumulated interest charge. At the end of the two-year period, the customer will pay the principal of \$1,000 plus the simple interest, which is \$240.

The amount of the total loan repayment under the Simple Interest Method may be determined through the use of the following formula:

$$\left(\begin{array}{c}\text{Total Loan}\\ \text{Repayment Amount}\end{array}\right) = P \times \left[\left(1 + \frac{R}{100}\right) \times T\right]$$

If the customer repays the \$1,000 loan in six months at 12 percent, the amount of the total loan repayment will be:

$$\$1{,}000 \times \left[\left(1 + \frac{12}{100}\right) \times \frac{1}{2}\right] = \$60$$

INTEREST ON DECLINING BALANCE

Let us assume that the customer does not make the repayment in one lump sum, but makes several payments to the lender. In this case, the interest will be calculated on the basis of interest on declining balance. The customer pays interest only on the *unpaid* portion of the original principal amount.

Using the Simple Interest Method on a declining balance basis, the $1,000 loan at 5 percent interest rate repaid in two installments—one at the end of the 6-month period and the other at the end of one year—will have a total interest charge of $37.50, instead of $50 when the customer repaid the loan in one lump sum at the end of the one-year period.

$37.50 is the result of the following calculation: $500 paid at the end of the one-half-year period. The interest charge will be $25:

$$\$1{,}000 \times \frac{5}{100} \times \frac{1}{2}$$

The customer will make a payment of $525.

The second payment will be calculated by taking the remaining $500 and adding the 5 percent interest cost for half a year.

$$500 \times \frac{5}{100} \times \frac{1}{2} = \$12.50$$

The interest cost for the second half, therefore, will be $12.50. The customer will make a payment of $512.50 at the end of the second half. Therefore, the interest cost will be $25 for the first half and $12.50 for the second half; combined, the interest charge for the year will be $37.50 (25 + 12.50).

ADD-ON INTEREST CALCULATION METHOD

The Add-On Interest Calculation Method determines the interest cost by:

1. Calculating the interest on the full amount of the original principal
2. Adding the interest to the original principal
3. Dividing the result by the number of payments to be made.

If the customer is repaying the loan in two or more installments, the interest cost through the Add-On Method will be higher than the nominal rate calculated through the Simple Interest Method.

Taking the previous example of $1,000 loan at 5 percent annual interest, the Add-On Calculation will give the following result:

Annual interest: 5% of $1,000 = $50

The customer wishes to repay the loan in two installments. Therefore, the total repayment amount will be: $1,000 + $50 = $1,050. Half of this amount will be paid at the end of the first six-month period, and the other half at the end of the second six-month period.

First payment = $525 (half of $1,050)

Second payment = $525

By using the Add-On Method, the effective rate is no longer 5 percent. It is higher than 5 percent because the customer does not have the use of $1,000 for the entire year. He uses $1,000 for the first six months but uses only $500 for the second six-month period. In this case, the effective interest rate will be 6.31 percent interest instead of 5 percent.

The interest charge will always be $50 in the above example, no matter how many payments the customer makes.

If the customer decides to repay the $1,050 in four quarterly payments of $262.50 for each quarter, the effective rate will be 7.92 percent. If he repays in 12 monthly payments, the effective rate will be 9.10 percent.

This method is generally used by finance companies in consumer loans.

BANK DISCOUNT CALCULATION METHOD

When using the bank discount calculation method, the interest is calculated on the amount to be paid back. The customer receives the difference between the amount to be paid back and the amount of interest.

Using the above example, this method will give the following result:

The amount of interest: 5% of $1,000 = $50 .

The bank will deduct the $50 from the principal amount of $1,000, leaving the customer $950 to use for one year. At the end of the year, the customer pays the bank $1,000. Here again, since the customer had the use of only $950 for a year and not $1,000, the effective rate of interest will be higher than 5 percent—it will be 5.26 percent ($50/$950).

COMPOUND INTEREST METHOD

Compound interest is the amount paid on the original principal plus all interest accrued to that point in time. The customer pays interest on interest. The method is generally used for bank deposits.

The customer deposits $1,000 at a bank that pays a 5 percent interest rate compounded twice a year.

At the end of the first half, the bank pays $25 in interest, which is 5 percent of $1,000 for six months. At the end of the year, the bank calculates the interest of 5 percent on $1,025 ($1,000 plus $25 interest received). This will bring the customer $25.63 for the second half (5% of $1,025). The interest amount for the entire year, therefore, will be $50.63 (25 + 25.63). In this case, the effective rate will be greater than 5 percent. It will be 5.063%. This effective rate is based on the frequency of the compounding schedule. The more often the interest is compounded, the higher the effective rate will be. For example, if the interest is compounded quarterly, the effective rate in the above example will be 5.09 percent. If it is compounded monthly, it will be 5.11 percent. If it is compounded daily on the basis of 365 days a year, the effective rate will be 5.12 percent.

MULTIPLE YEAR COMPOUNDING

Suppose a customer takes a two-year loan of $1,000 at 12 percent annual interest rate, compounded annually. In this case, the customer is required to pay the principal plus the accrued interest on interest.

1. Interest at the end of the first year: (12% of $1,000) $120.00
2. Interest at the end of the second year (12% of $1,000) $120.00.
3. Interest on the first year's interest of $120.00 for second year, $14.40. Total interest cost: $254.46.

The total amount of loan to be repaid at the end of the second year will be:

$$\$1{,}000 + \$254.40 = \$1{,}254.40 \ .$$

The Simple Interest Calculation Method would have given only $240 as the interest cost for two years ($1,000 ×

12/100 × 2). The annual compounding method has increased the interest cost by $14.40.

For compound interest calculation, the following formulas are used:

$$F = P\ (1 + R/100)T$$

F = the principal plus total compound interest

P = the principal

R = the annual interest rate

T = number of years

The amount of total compounded interest is

$$I = \left[P\left(1 + \frac{R}{100}\right)^{T}\right] - P$$

Let us assume the customer borrows $5,000 at 10 percent interest compounded annually. The customer repays the loan in five years. What will be the total amount of interest?

$$F = \$5{,}000\ \left(1 + \frac{10}{100}\right)^{5}$$

$$\text{Amount of interest} = F - P$$

The same formula may be used for multiple-period compounding. Instead of annual compounding, the interest may be compounded quarterly, monthly, or daily. The above formula may be used with certain modifications:

$$F = P\left[1 + \left(\frac{R}{100} \times \frac{1}{f}\right)^{T\times f}\right]$$

where

F = principal plus total compound interest

P = the principal

R = the annual interest rate

f = frequency of compounding during a year

For monthly compounding f will be 12, for quarterly compounding f will be 4, and so on.

T = the number of years

Let us assume the customer borrows $5,000 at 10 percent interest compounded monthly. The customer repays the loan in five years. What will be the total amount that must be repaid?

$$F = 5{,}000\left(1 + \frac{10}{100} \times \frac{1}{12}\right)^{T\times 12}$$

For interest compounded daily the above formula may be modified:

$$F = P\left[1 + \left(\frac{R}{100} \times \frac{1}{360}\right)\right]^{T\times 365}$$

The denominator 360 is the number of the daily compound periods each year. But T must be multiplied by the number of the actual calendar days of the year, 365 days or 366 for a leap year.

Let us assume the customer borrows $5,000 at 10 percent interest compounded daily. The customer repays the loan in five years. What will be the total amount that must be repaid?

$$F = \$5{,}000\left[1 + \left(\frac{10}{100} \times \frac{1}{360}\right)\right]^{5\times 365}$$

For quarterly compounding, the answer would have been:

$$F = \$5{,}000\left[1 + \left(\frac{10}{100} \times \frac{1}{4}\right)\right]^{5\times4}$$

INTEREST REBATE

If the customer decides to make a prepayment (paying the loan before it is due), the lender may give an interest rebate to the customer by applying "Rule 78." Rule 78 will determine the percentage of the total interest amount that will be returned to the customer. 78 is the sum of the digits from 1 to 12. The percent is determined by:

$$\frac{\text{Number of digits from 1 to the number of payments remaining}}{\text{Sum of the digits from 1 to the total number of payments specified in the loan contract}}$$

For example a five-month loan is repaid in three months

$$\frac{(1 + 2 + 3)}{(1 + 2 + 3 + 4 + 5)} = \frac{6}{15} = 4\%$$

The lender will rebate 40 percent of the interest to the customer.

Some savings banks pay interest from the first day of the month on deposits made up to the 10th calendar day of the month. In this case, the effective rate of interest will be greater than the nominal rate.

CALCULATION OF INTEREST ON U.S. TREASURY BILLS

The U.S. Treasury bills are issued with maturities in three months, six months, and one year. They are sold at a discount price from the face value. They pay no interest. The investor's dollar return is the difference between the discount price and the bill's face value at maturity.

For three-month bills the effective yield is calculated by:

$$\frac{(\$100 - \$P) \times 365}{\$P \times 91 \text{ days}}$$

use 366 days in the number for leap years.

$P is the purchase price .

Let us assume that the discount price of the three-month bill was $98.256, the effective annual yield or return will be:

$$\frac{(100 - 98.256) \times 365}{98.256 \times 91}$$

For six-month Treasury bills, the calculation of the yield is done by:

$$\frac{(\$100 - \$P) \times 365}{\$P \times 182}$$

CALCULATION OF INTEREST ON U.S. TREASURY NOTES AND BONDS

The U.S. Treasury notes and bonds pay a fixed rate of interest to the holder twice a year. They are sold at par, at a discount from the face value, or at a premium.

The yield to maturity is determined by using the following formulas:

For notes or bonds purchased at a discount:

$$\text{Yield to maturity} = \frac{\left(\begin{array}{c}\text{Annual interest}\\ \text{on one bond}\end{array}\right) + \left(\dfrac{\text{Amount of discount}}{\begin{array}{c}\text{Number of years}\\ \text{to maturity}\end{array}}\right)}{(\text{Purchase price} + \text{Face value}) \div 2}$$

EXAMPLE

A U.S. Treasury note with 8 percent interest rate sold at 95. Maturing in two years, the yield to maturity will be:

$$\frac{80 + \left(\dfrac{50}{2}\right)}{(950 + 1{,}000) \div 2}$$

For notes or bonds purchased at a premium:

$$\text{Yield to maturity} = \frac{\left(\begin{array}{c}\text{Annual interest}\\ \text{on one bond}\end{array}\right) - \left(\dfrac{\text{Amount of premium}}{\begin{array}{c}\text{Number of years}\\ \text{to maturity}\end{array}}\right)}{(\text{Purchase price} + \text{Face value}) \div 2}$$

CALCULATION OF MORTGAGES

Under a fixed-rate mortgage payment, the homeowner promises to pay a fixed monthly amount over the length of the loan. The monthly payment has two components: one is applied to paying the principal, and the other to paying the interest. During the initial year of the loan, most of the monthly payment is used to pay interest. The rest is applied to pay the principal. As the maturity date comes, more of the monthly payment is used to pay off the principal than to pay the interest.

The following formula is used to calculate the monthly payment of principal and interest on a conventional mortgage loan:

$$\text{Monthly payment} = \text{Loan} \times \frac{\begin{pmatrix}\text{Monthly}\\ \text{interest}\\ \text{rate}\end{pmatrix} \times \left[1 + \begin{pmatrix}\text{Monthly}\\ \text{interest}\\ \text{rate}\end{pmatrix}\right]^{T\times 12}}{(1 + \text{Monthly interest rate})^{T \times 12} - 1}$$

The monthly payment of a 25-year mortgage loan of \$50,000 at 11 percent annual rate of interest is:

$$\frac{50{,}000 \times \dfrac{0.11}{12} \times \left(1 + \dfrac{0.11}{12}\right)^{25\times 12}}{\left(1 + \dfrac{0.11}{12}\right)^{25\times 12} - 1}$$

CHAPTER FIFTEEN

THE FEDERAL RESERVE SYSTEM AND QUESTIONS OF ECONOMICS

The Federal Reserve System was established by an act of Congress in 1913 as the nation's central bank with fiscal responsibilities to the U.S. government. The Fed is charged by Congress to ensure a reasonably full employment, stable prices, and a high but sustainable rate of economic growth in the country. The Fed acts also as a *regulator*:

- It regulates credit policies for purchasing securities on margin or carrying equity securities in a margin account.
- It regulates the foreign activities of all U.S. banks and the U.S. activities of foreign banks.

Establishing a central banking institution was not unique to the United States. By 1913 many European banks had already established central banks in their respective countries. The Bank of England had been in existence since the 17th century and the Bank of France was established in 1800 by Napoleon Bonaparte. Today, the functions of Bundesbank in West Germany are similar to those of the Federal Reserve.

The principal components of the Federal Reserve are:

1. The Board of Governors
2. The Federal Open Market Committee
3. Twelve Federal Reserve District Banks

THE BOARD OF GOVERNORS

The System is governed by a board composed of seven governors, each appointed by the President with the advice and consent of the Senate. A governor's term is 14 years, and he cannot be reappointed after serving his term. The President also appoints the Chairman and the Vice Chairman, again with the advice and consent of the Senate, for a term of four years. The Board of Governors establishes the reserve requirements for banks and sets the discount rate as part of its monetary policy. It supervises and regulates member banks and oversees the district Federal Reserve Banks.

FEDERAL OPEN MARKET COMMITTEE

The Federal Open Market Committee (FOMC) is composed of 12 members. They are: seven governors; the President of the Federal Reserve Bank of New York, plus four presidents of the remaining 11 Federal Reserve Banks on an annual rotation basis. The Chairman of the Board of Governors is the Chairman of the FOMC and the President of the Federal Reserve Bank of New York is the Vice Chairman of the Committee. The Committee meets eight times a year in Washington, D.C. The minutes of the meetings are released to the press shortly after the next FOMC meeting is held.

The FOMC plays a major role in implementing the Fed's national monetary policies. The Committee instructs the Open Market Operations trading desk in New York to buy or sell U.S. government and federal agency securities to reduce or increase the money supply in the U.S. economy and directs operations in foreign exchange markets of foreign currencies.

FEDERAL RESERVE DISTRICT BANKS

There are 12 Federal Reserve Banks in the following cities: Boston, New York, Philadelphia, Cleveland, Richmond, Atlanta, Chicago, St. Louis, Minneapolis, Kansas City, Dallas, and San Francisco. In addition, the Banks have 25 branches in other cities.

Each Federal Reserve Bank has its own president and a board of directors. The district Federal Reserve Banks propose discount rates, hold reserve balances for member banks, lend them money at the discount rate, and collect and clear checks for participating institutions.

National banks, chartered by the Comptroller of the Currency, are required to be members of the Federal Reserve district bank. State chartered banks may elect to become members of the Fed.

THE ROLE OF THE FEDERAL RESERVE IN THE U.S. ECONOMY

The Federal Reserve plays a dominant role in the U.S. economy, particularly in the area of monetary policies.

To achieve its objectives, the Fed utilizes certain monetary tools to increase or reduce the money supply in the economy. To reduce the rate of inflation and maintain stable prices for goods and services, the Fed may decide to reduce the money supply. On the other hand, to promote the nation's economic growth, the Fed may decide to increase the money supply. The following monetary tools are used by the Fed to achieve its objectives:

1. Reserve requirements for banks
2. The Federal Open Market Committee Operations
3. The Fed's Discount Window

BANK RESERVE REQUIREMENTS

Regulations of the Federal Reserve require all depositary institutions in the U.S. to meet certain reserve requirements established by the Fed. The depositary institutions include commercial banks, savings and loan associations, credit unions, and branches of foreign banks. Reserves placed at the Federal Reserve District Bank in the form of cash or federal funds are held against customer deposits. The reserve requirements vary as to the type of account and the size of the institution.

The depositary institutions are required to maintain the required level of reserves over a 14-day period ending every other Wednesday.

The Fed uses the reserve requirement as a tool to implement its monetary policies. A rise in the reserve requirements will reduce the money supply and a reduction in reserve requirement will increase the money supply.

FEDERAL OPEN MARKET OPERATIONS

The day-to-day operation of increasing and reducing the money supply is conducted by the Federal Open Market Committee (FOMC). If the Fed wishes to reduce the money supply, the FOMC sells U.S. Treasury securities to primary government bond dealers. If the Fed wishes to increase the money supply, the FOMC buys U.S. Treasury securities from dealer organizations. By purchasing the securities, the Fed gives money to the dealers, thus increasing the availability of credit in the country.

Among the monetary tools used by the Fed to implement its policies, the most important is the Open Market trading operations. Through the process of buying and selling securities, the Fed influences the cost and the supply of money. The availability or the lack of credit will, in turn, influence the prices of goods and services, productivity, and employment.

The trading is done by telephone. On instructions from the FOMC, the manager of the Open Market trading operations will chart his trading day with senior members of his staff and the senior staff of the Board of Governors. All FOMC members will be informed of the actions the Manager expects to take during the course of the day. This action may be either to buy or sell a specific amount of securities from and to primary dealers. The staff members of the Trading Desk of the Federal Reserve Bank of New York will contact primary dealers and receive firm quotes of bids and offers of securities in their possession. The primary dealers are required to maintain regular markets in U.S. Treasury and federal agency securities and stand ready to trade these securities with the Fed at prices quoted.

These purchases and sales are conducted through an auction process. The primary dealers submit bids and offers to the Fed for securities that the Fed has decided to buy or sell on that particular day. After receiving all the bids and offers of the day, the Fed's Trading Manager will accept the highest price bid for sales and the lowest price offered for purchase, and execute the trades until the desired amount of securities is sold or purchased.

It may be necessary for the FOMC to increase the money supply on a temporary basis. In that case, the FOMC Manager will execute the securities transactions in short-term Repurchase Agreements (RPs) with the primary dealers. This means the FOMC will buy securities from the dealers with the agreement that it will sell the securities back to them by a specified date at a specific price. Through this arrangement, the Fed increases the money supply on a short-term basis. These RPs may be for one day and up to 15 business days.

If, on the other hand, the Fed wants to reduce the money supply, the FOMC will employ another procedure known as Reverse RPs, or matched sale–purchase transactions. Through this arrangement, the FOMC sells securities to the dealers with the agreement that it will purchase the securities back by a specified date at a specific price. This contract usually does not exceed seven days.

In making transactions with the FOMC, the primary dealers act as intermediaries between the Fed and their customers. In purchasing securities from the Fed, the dealers will sell them to their customers; and in selling securities to the Fed, the dealers will buy them from their customers. The Fed's buying and selling activities, therefore, affect the country's money supply.

THE DISCOUNT WINDOW

The discount rate is the official interest rate that the Fed charges its member banks when banks need to borrow money to meet their reserve requirements on a temporary basis.

This is yet another tool employed by the Fed to implement its monetary policies. To reduce the money supply, the Fed will raise the discount rate; and to increase the money supply, it will reduce the discount rate.

The Discount Window is available not only to member banks but also to nonmember institutions that maintain reserve deposits at the Fed. These nonmember institutions may include savings and loan associations, nonmember commercial banks, agencies of foreign banks, and credit unions.

The Discount Window is used, however, as the lender of last resort. The Fed places certain administrative constraints on participating institutions as to the use of funds borrowed from the Fed. The borrowing from the Window is usually done for very short periods. The borrowing bank must place certain securities, such as U.S. government and federal agency securities, as collateral with the Fed. In certain cases, the Fed allows the bank to hold the collateralized securities in its own vault, but they must be properly identified as collateral pledged to the Fed.

These activities of the Federal Reserve will influence

the rise and decline of interest rates in the U.S. economy. When the Fed reduces the money supply, the interest rates will rise and the market price of fixed-income securities will decline. When the Fed increases the money supply, the interest rates will decline and the market price of these securities will rise. Table 15.1 illustrates the Fed's activity and its impact on the market value of debt securities.

DEVICES OF MONETARY AGGREGATES

There are several devices employed by the Fed for its interpretation of the nation's monetary condition. These monetary measures are M1, M2, M3, and L.

M1 contains:

- Currency
- Traveler's Checks of non-bank issuers
- Demand deposits
- Other checkable deposits at all depositary institutions

M1 is issued weekly.

TABLE 15.1. FEDERAL RESERVE ACTIVITY AND ITS IMPACT ON MARKET VALUE OF DEBT SECURITIES

Fed Activity	*Money Supply*	*Interest Rates*	*Market Value of Debt Securities*
1. FOMC sells securities	decrease	rise	decline
2. FOMC buys securities	increase	decline	rise
3. Fed increases reserve requirement	decrease	rise	decline
4. Fed lowers reserve requirement	increase	decline	rise
5. Fed increases discount rate	decrease	rise	decline
6. Fed lowers discount rate	increase	decline	rise

M2 contains:

- M1
- Overnight Repurchase Agreements issued by commercial banks
- Overnight Eurodollars held by U.S. residents in overseas branches of U.S. banks
- Money market mutual fund shares
- Savings deposit at all depositary institutions
- Money market deposit accounts at all depositary institutions
- Small denomination time deposits at all depositary institutions

M2 is issued monthly.

M3 contains:

- M2
- Large time deposits at all depositary institutions
- Term Repurchase Agreements at all depositary institutions
- Term Eurodollars held by U.S. residents

M3 is issued monthly.

L contains:

- M3
- Bankers' Acceptances
- Commercial Paper
- Savings bonds
- Short-term Treasury obligations

L is issued monthly.

THE REGULATIONS OF THE FEDERAL RESERVE BOARD

The following is the subject matter of principal Regulations of the Federal Reserve Board of Governors:

Regulation A regulates advances and discounts of the Federal Reserve District Banks.

Regulation B regulates Open Market purchases of Bills of Exchanges and Bankers' Acceptances.

Regulation C regulates drafts and Bills of Exchanges issued by member banks.

Regulation D regulates the Reserve requirements by member banks.

Regulation E regulates the purchase of municipal warrants by the Fed.

Regulation F regulates the trust operation and procedures of member banks.

Regulation G regulates the extension of credit by nonbank and non-broker–dealer entities.

Regulation H regulates the membership requirements at the Fed by State banking institutions.

Regulation I regulates the increase and decrease of capital stock of Federal Reserve District Banks.

Regulation J regulates check clearing and collection procedures for member as well as nonmember clearing banks.

Regulation K regulates Edge Act banks. These are corporations conducting foreign banking operations.

Regulation L regulates interlocking bank directorates.

Regulation M regulates foreign branches of national banks.

Regulation N regulates activities with foreign banks and bankers.

Regulation O regulates loans to executive officers of member banks.

Regulation P regulates bank holding company affiliates.

Regulation Q regulates payment of interest on deposit by member and non-member banks.

Regulation R regulates the provisions of the Banking Act of 1933 that separates commercial banking activities from those of investment banking.

Regulation T regulates the extension of credit by broker–dealers.

Regulation U regulates the extension of credit by banks for the purpose of purchasing or carrying registered securities.

Regulation V regulates loan guarantees for defense production.

Regulation W regulates consumer credit.

Regulation X

Regulation Z covers the provisions of the Consumer Credit Production Act also known as the Truth-in-Lending Act.

ECONOMICS

The following is a discussion of some of the issues in economics.

How would one define the science of Economics?

Economics is a social science that deals with the study of goods, human desires, the creation and the explanation of wealth, value, price, and income. It is the study of development of resources, production, and distribution of goods. The word "economics" comes from the Greek word *Oeconomia*, which means household management.

What is "money" and what does "elasticity of money" mean?

Money is an instrument by which payment is made for the transfer of goods or values from one person or entity to another. For centuries, gold has been regarded as the basic monetary unit for the currency and the credit system around the world. For the last several decades, however, money is no longer secured by gold because nations, including the United States, have departed from the gold standard.

Governments issue money secured by various standards or collateral. They may also issue fiat money that is unsecured. In the United States, both paper and metallic currency are secured by U.S. government securities.

What is elasticity or elastic currency? Elasticity refers to the type of money that can be expanded or contracted according to the needs of commerce and business. In the United States, the Federal Reserve System provides for an elastic currency, which the United States did not have before the enactment of the Federal Reserve Act of 1913. The Federal Reserve, through its monetary policies, expands money in the banking system as business expands, and contracts money when business contracts. This expansion and contraction activity of the Fed is conducted mainly through its Open Market Operations. To expand money in the banking system, the Fed buys securities from primary government bond dealers. To reduce the money supply, the Fed sells securities to the dealers. When the Fed buys securities, the dealers have more money to lend to businesses and consumers. Conversely, when the Fed sells securities there is less money available to the public. The expansion of the money supply reduces the interest rate, and the contraction raises the interest rate.

What are "business cycles"?

Business cycles are periods in economic activity representing the expansion and contraction of businesses in the country. These cycles will affect the economic growth, inflation, and employment. The expansion is identified as recovery and contraction as recession.

What is the Consumer Price Index and how often is it issued?

The Consumer Price Index (CPI) is a measuring device that determines the change in the market value of goods and services—such as food, transportation, and utilities—that consumers buy or use. The CPI, also known as the Cost of Living Index is prepared monthly by the U.S. Bureau of Labor Statistics.

The Council of Economic Advisers: What does it do and how is it formed?

The Council of Economic Advisers is formed by the President and advises the President on economic policy and budget.

What is the meaning of "demonetization"?

Demonetization is the process of withdrawal of a specific form of money, such as gold, from circulation.

What is "depression"?

Depression is a condition in the country's economy caused by lack of economic growth, falling prices, and unemployment on a sustained duration.

What is the purpose of "devaluation" and "revaluation"? Why does a country devaluate or revaluate currency?

A country decides to lower the value of its currency relative to the currencies of other countries to stimulate the country's economic growth or adjust its balance of payments with other countries. Revaluation refers to an increase in the value of a country's currency as compared with the currency of another country.

What is the difference between "deflation," "disinflation," and "reflation"?

Deflation characterizes the decline in the market value of goods and services. It is the reverse of inflation. Disinflation is the process by which the rate of the increase in the market value of goods and service slows down. Reflation refers to the utilization of the government's power to stop deflation and to induce inflation.

What is the meaning of "disposable income"?

Disposable income is the amount of money at the disposal of the consumer to spend or to save. It is the amount after personal taxes have been paid.

What characterizes an "economic downturn"?

An economic downturn is a condition that characterizes the shifting of the economy from expansion to recession.

What is the meaning of "dumping" in domestic or international trade?

Dumping describes the sale of goods below cost. This is generally done to strengthen the company's competitive posture.

What is "econometrics"?

Econometrics is the science that analyzes major economic factors through the use of models and computer applications.

What is "fiscal policy"?

Fiscal policy is a combination of spending and taxation policies of a government. It is formulated to provide economic growth and price stability.

In "taxation" what is the meaning of "Flat Tax," "Progressive Tax," and "Regressive Tax"?

Flat Tax is tax applied at the same rate to all levels of income. Progressive Tax represents the system in which taxes go up as income level goes up. Progressive Tax is also referred to as Graduated Tax. Regressive Tax is the reverse of progressive tax. Here taxes decline as the level of income rises.

What is a "Floating Exchange Rate"?

Floating Exchange Rate is the reverse of Fixed Exchange Rate. Floating Exchange Rate describes the movement of currency exchange rate based on the forces of supply and demand. This flexibility in exchange rate will strengthen the country's economic growth. To promote international trade, the country's currency should not be too strong or too weak in relation to the currency of other nations. A strong currency will make goods manufactured in the country too expensive for foreigners to buy, and a weak currency characterizes weak economy with high inflation.

What is an "economic system with an open market"?

An open or free market describes a type of market where the forces of supply and demand are not dictated by any governmental regulations.

Gold standard. How is it applied?

Gold standard describes a monetary system in which the currency is exchangeable into a predetermined amount of gold.

What is "the Gross National Product" and how often is it computed?

The Gross National Product (GNP) is the combined value of all goods and services produced in the United States over a period of one year. GNP figures are published at the end of each calendar quarter. The GNP figure will characterize the condition of the economy.

When economists describe a country's currency as "hard money," what do they mean?

Hard money describes the currency of a financially stable country.

In labor negotiations what does "indexing" mean?

Indexing refers to the relationship of wages to an index, such as the Consumer Price Index, to ensure that wages are in proportion with the rising inflation rate.

What causes inflation?

Inflation describes the rise in the value of goods and services. There are two types of inflation: one is Cost–Push and the other is Demand–Pull. Cost–Push inflation is caused by a rising cost of producing or manufacturing the product. Demand–Pull inflation is caused by too much money chasing too few goods. The demand to purchase exceeds the supply.

Who was John Maynard Keynes and what is Keynesian Economics?

John Maynard Keynes was a British economist who became famous in 1935 with his landmark book entitled *The General Theory of Employment, Interest and Money*, which was published during the period of the Great Depression. Keynes advocated that government intervention in the marketplace was important and necessary for economic growth and stability. He believed that government should increase spending and increase the money supply to avoid depression. This government activity would result in higher employment and consumer spending, and, therefore, more economic growth.

The Keynesian theory has had great impact on the economic policies of industrial countries.

Who was Adam Smith and what did he believe in?

Adam Smith advocated an economic theory just the opposite of Keynesian economics. He believed that government intervention in business and economic activities should be minimal. His important book, *The Wealth of Nations*, was written in 1776 and established an economic doctrine called "Laissez-Faire." This doctrine stated that people running businesses should be free of government intervention to cultivate profitable opportunities. The Laissez-Faire economic doctrine was prevalent both in England and in America during the industrial and economic growth in the 19th century. It ended in the early part of the 20th century when depressions and economic downturns caused the government to intervene and regulate business activity. It was at this time that the Laissez-Faire doctrine was replaced by Keynesian economics.

And who is Arthur Laffer and what is the meaning of supply-side economics?

In the late 1970s, Professor Arthur Laffer advocated that if the government reduces the tax rates drastically, corporations and individuals will be encouraged to invest more in plants and equipment, and thus cause the economy to grow. This theory became the foundation of President Reagan's economic policy.

What does the monetarist say to all this?

The monetarist thinks that the money supply is the key to economic growth. One of the important champions of this theory was Professor Milton Freedman of the University of Chicago. The monetarist believes that if the money supply in the country grows slowly and at a steady level, it will encourage economic growth much more effectively than through the Keynesian route.

Adam Smith, John Maynard Keynes, Milton Freedman, and Arthur Laffer are all representatives of the capitalist system. Did the Soviet Union have any economic advocates?

One of the most prominent Soviet economists was Nikolai Kondratieff who developed an economic theory in the 1920s known as the Kondratieff Wave. The Kondratieff Wave advocates supercycles in the Western capitalist world that last between 50 and 60 years. According to the Kondratieff theory, the Western world will experience an economic crash every 50 or 60 years.

What are the leading economic indicators?

The leading economic indicators are released by the U.S. Department of Commerce Bureau of Economic Analysis on a monthly basis in the form of an index. There are 12 leading economic indicators:

1. Average workweek of production workers
2. Average weekly claims for state unemployment insurance
3. New orders for consumer goods and materials
4. The performance of vendors
5. Net business formation
6. Contracts for plant and equipment
7. New building permits
8. Changes in the inventory
9. Prices of sensitive materials
10. Stock market prices
11. M2 money supply
12. Business and consumer borrowing

What is the difference between macroeconomics and microeconomics?

Macroeconomics considers price levels, inflation, unemployment, and industrial production in analyzing the nation's economy as a whole. Microeconomics, on the other hand, studies the behavior of important economic units, such as industries and companies.

What is the meaning of "nationalization"?

Nationalization is the process in which the government acquires the assets of a private corporation. This is generally done by Socialist governments.

What is "Par Value of Currency"?

The Par Value of Currency is the ratio of one country's currency to that of another country.

What is the Producer Price Index?

The Producer Price Index is a device that measures the rate of inflation or deflation of products wholesalers produce. It is issued monthly by the Bureau of Labor Statistics in Washington, D.C.

What is the meaning of the "purchasing power of the dollar" and "real income"?

The purchasing power of the dollar is a device that is used to measure the amount of goods one dollar can buy compared with periods in the past. Real Income refers to the income of a country or a person adjusted for changes in the purchasing power of the dollar. These changes are caused by inflation or deflation.

At what point does a country's economy fall into a recession?

Recession refers to an economic downturn. When the Gross National Product declines during two consecutive quarters, the country is considered to be in a recession.

Is economic recovery the reverse of recession?

Recovery refers to the expansion period of the business cycle. This will be manifested in the growth of the Gross National Product.

What is "soft currency"?

Soft currency refers to the currency of a country not acceptable for international trade. Example: Soviet Union's ruble.

In currency what is the meaning of "pegging" and "stabilization"?

They are synonyms. A country stabilizes or pegs its currency when it buys and sells its own currency to protect its exchange rate in the international market.

What is "stagflation"?

Stagflation is a word created by some economists by combining the words *stagnation* and *inflation*. Stagflation refers to the period when the country's economy is growing slowly with a rising rate of inflation. Stagnation is the period in which the economic growth is declining.

What is "trade deficit" and "trade surplus"?

The trade deficit is the excess of the country's import over export, and the trade surplus is the reverse. A trade deficit adversely affects the country's economy.

Trickle Down Economy. What does it mean?

The trickle down theorist advocates that if the government helps businesses to flourish, their prosperity ultimately will trickle down to lower income people. This is a phase of supply-side economics.

What is the Bretton Woods Agreement and when was it signed?

Bretton Woods, a town located in New Hampshire, was the site of an international monetary conference held in July of 1944. The conference was held to lay down the foundation for international economic and monetary policies. The conference established two institutions: the International Monetary Fund (IMF) and the International Bank for Reconstruction and Development, popularly known as the World Bank. The Bretton Woods Agreement was signed by representatives of member nations on December 27, 1945, in Washington, D.C.

IMF is organized to promote international monetary cooperation and the expansion of trade among nations. Its specific purposes are:

- To make orderly adjustments of foreign exchange rates
- To furnish expert technicians to advise member nations in solving their financial and monetary problems
- To help member nations to meet their short-term obligations
- To find practical solutions to help member nations in their exchange problems

The International Bank for Reconstruction and Development is organized as a cooperative organization associated with the United Nations. The Bank makes loans to member countries to establish a sound foundation for economic growth. The member country may apply the loans to promote its industrial production, to generate electricity, to build highways, railways, waterways, to strengthen its agriculture, or to use the funds for general development purposes.

What is the meaning of the National Debt and when did it start?

The National Debt started in September 1917, when Congress authorized the issuance of Second Liberty Bonds in the amount of $7.5 billion. The National Debt represents the total face value of all outstanding securities issued by the U.S. Treasury Department. Through the issuance of securities, the Treasury borrows money to ostensibly finance the deficit condition of the U.S. budget. Deficit is the excess of expenditures over revenue. The Federal Debt Limit has been raised progressively since 1917. Currently, it is in excess of $3,000 billion.

The three major political systems in the world exert tremendous impact on economics. How would you define capitalism, communism, and socialism?

Capitalism is a free enterprise system in which individuals work and compete with each other for their own benefit and well-being. It is a system in which there is private ownership of property.

Communism, on the other hand, abolishes private ownership of property, individual initiative, and profits. It advocates collective or governmental ownership of properties and governmental utilization of resources.

Socialism removes individual capitalism and advocates a system in which a democratically run government manages and controls land, natural resources, production, and distribution for the well-being of the society in general.

GLOSSARY

Above Par The market price of the security is above its face value.

Absolute Title Absolute ownership of property by the owner and his heirs.

Absorbed Security A security that has been distributed and sold to the public.

Abstract of Title A legal document prepared to establish the present title to property.

Accommodation Paper A note signed by a person to help another person with a weak credit rating to borrow money. The signer of the note is also called the maker, the endorser, or the acceptor. He assumes full responsibility in the event the borrower does not honor his obligation to pay off the loan.

Accredited Investor As defined by Regulation D of the SEC, a wealthy person qualified to purchase a security in a private placement under Rule 506 of Regulation D. To be qualified, the person must have a minimum net worth of $1 million and a minimum annual income of $200,000, or must invest at least $150,000 in buying the security. This investment must not exceed 20 percent of the investor's net worth.

Accretion of a Discount A procedure by which the book value of a bond purchased at a discount is increased during the period of time in which the investor holds the security. There are two types of methods in calculating the amount of accretion: one is "straight line" method and the other, "constant interest" method. Under the straight line method, the amount of the annual accretion is the same for all years. It is calculated by dividing the amount of the discount by the number of years to maturity. This will then be added to the cost of purchasing the bond to determine the cost basis of the security. Under the constant interest method, the amount of accretion increases as the bond approaches its maturity date. It is calculated by:

$$\begin{pmatrix}\text{Semi-annual}\\ \text{yield to}\\ \text{maturity}\end{pmatrix} \times \begin{pmatrix}\text{Current}\\ \text{book}\\ \text{value}\end{pmatrix} - \begin{pmatrix}\text{Currrent}\\ \text{interest}\\ \text{payment}\end{pmatrix}$$

Accrual Basis A method of accounting. Through this method, the accountant will record all income and expenses in the books of the corporation for the fiscal year, regardless of whether the income was actually received or expenses paid during the fiscal year.

Accrued Interest The amount of interest covering a period in which the seller of the bond held the security. The buyer pays accrued interest to the seller. Accrued interest is calculated on the basis of 30 days each month for most of municipal and corporate securities. The buyer pays interest calculated from the last interest payment date until the day of the settlement of the trade, but not including the day of settlement.

Accumulation Account An account generally used by unit investment trusts. The trust purchases the securities and places them in an accumulation account.

Across the Board Market A market in which all stocks move generally in the same direction.

Active Market Large volume of trading in the securities market, regardless of whether the prices move upward or downward.

Active Trust A trust in which the trustees perform an active duty or function.

Actuals A term referring to the actual physical product or a commodity, such as gold, wheat, corn, or silver.

Ad Valorem Tax Latin term that means "according to value." Property tax based on the assessed valuation of the property.

Additional Bonds Test The earnings test that must be conducted before another municipal revenue bond on the same revenue source can be issued.

Adjustable Rate Mortgage A mortgage with an adjustable rate. The lender will adjust the mortgage interest rate at specific intervals.

Adjusted Gross Income Known as the AGI. The gross income of an individual reduced by certain qualified deductions, such as moving expenses, alimony payments, contributions to IRA and Keogh accounts. After such deductions are made from the taxpayer's gross income, the result is called the Adjusted Gross Income (AGI). From this amount, the taxpayer will then deduct other allowable expenses, such as cost of interest, medical expenses, property taxes, and so on.

Adjustment Bonds Also known as Income bonds. These are bonds issued by a corporation in financial straits. A corporation, in its effort to reorganize the company, will issue an adjustment bond in exchange of an existing debenture. Adjustment bonds pay interest only when or if the corporation earns income.

Advance Refunding Also known as pre-refunding. The issuer will issue a new security in advance of the maturity date of the old issue. The proceeds of the sale of the new issue will be used to redeem the old security. The advance refunding may be done in one of three methods 1) *Net Cash Refunding:* Through this method, the issuer will issue a new bond with a face amount plus the interest earnings that will be sufficient to redeem the old bond. 2) *Full Cash or Gross Refunding:* Through this method, the issuer will issue a new bond with a face amount that is enough to redeem the old bond. 3) *Crossover Refunding:* Through this method, the revenue pledged to secure the old bond continues to be used to pay the interest on the refunded security until it matures.

Affiliated Person Also known as an insider or a control person. A decision-making person or a major stockholder (owning over 10 percent of the outstanding shares) of a corporation.

After Acquired Clause A provision in a mortgage agreement which states that any additional property purchased by the mortgage borrower after the mortgage is extended will be used as collateral for the same mortgage.

After Tax Basis A basis that will compare the yield of a taxable corporate bond with a tax exempt municipal bond. Also known as Tax Equivalency Basis.

After Tax Real Return The yield on a security adjusted for inflation.

Agency Security Securities of the agencies of the U.S. government.

Aggregate Supply The total amount of goods and services in the marketplace. A term used in economics to determine total output.

A.I.D. Call Any Interest Date Call. Through this call feature, the issuer may call the bonds at any date on which there is an interest payment due.

Alien Corporation A corporation organized under a foreign jurisdiction.

Alloy A metal used in gold or silver currency to make it more durable.

Alternative Minimum Tax Federal tax that will ensure everybody pays at least some amount of tax.

American Institute of Banking An educational facility to train and educate bank personnel in the theory and practice of banking.

Amortization The procedure of reducing the price of a bond purchased at a premium in an attempt to bring its basis value to the par value or the face value.

Amortized Loans A long-term loan in which the principal is paid or amortized during the life of the loan. The borrower makes a monthly payment that includes both the principal and the interest on the loan.

Annuity A payment made by an insurance company in consideration of payments made to the insurance company. The annuity payments start after the customer has completed his payment program.

Antitrust Laws Federal legislation enacted to prevent monopolies in businesses and commerce.

Approved Bonds Bonds eligible for investment by commercial banks as approved by the U.S. Comptroller of the Currency.

Arbitrage Simultaneous purchase and sell of the same security in two different markets. In the case of municipal bonds, arbitrage means the difference between interest paid on tax exempt securities and interest earned on taxable securities.

Arbitration A procedure established by a self regulatory organization to resolve disputes and controversies among broker-dealers or between broker-dealers and customers.

Arm's Length Deal A business arrangement made with no conflict of interest among the parties involved.

Arrears An obligation due but unpaid, such as an outstanding loan or interest on a bond that the issuer has not paid yet.

A.S.C.A. All Subsequent Coupons Attached. Generally used for bonds with coupons attached.

Assay A measuring device used to determine a metal's purity before the metal is traded at a commodity exchange.

Assessed Valuation Assessed Valuation of a property determined by a taxing authority.

Assessment A levy on the security holder to raise additional funds. This type of assessment is made by corporations in financial straits.

Assignats Paper money issued by the French government during the Revolution in 1789.

Associated Person A partner, officer, director, or a decision-making person of a financial institution.

Assumed Bonds Bonds of one corporation acquired by another corporation. When corporation A acquires corporation B, it assumes the bonds of corporation B. These bonds will then be called *Assumed Bonds*.

Attachment A legal document issued by an officer of the law, authorizing the seizure of a defendant's property to satisfy the claims of a plaintiff.

Autarchy A political system in which a nation relies entirely upon its own resources to satisfy its own needs. The nation neither exports nor imports products.

Authority An agency of a government.

Authority Bond Bond issued by a governmental agency.

Authorized Bonds Amount of bonds authorized to be issued by a corporation or a municipality.

Average Maturity The period during which half of a bond issue would have been redeemed. It is usually determined by:

$$\frac{\text{Number of bond years}}{\text{Number of bonds}}$$

Baby Bonds Bonds with a face value of less than $1,000.

Back Spread A technique used in an arbitrage transaction when the price of the security is less than the normal difference. Example: the price of Bee Corp. at the NYSE is $50 a share and at the London Stock Exchange, $52. There is no benefit in making an arbitrage here if the difference of $2 will be used to cover expenses of making the transaction in London; expenses such as transportation of the security, loss of interest, etc. But if the price of Bee Corp. at the London Stock Exchange was $51 a share, the arbitrageur will do a *back spread*. That means he buys the security at the London Stock Exchange and simultaneously sells it at the NYSE.

Backing Away A market maker's failure to honor his quote in a securities transaction.

Backup Line A line of credit by a bank extended to an issuer of a commercial paper.

Backwardation A delayed settlement procedure at the London Stock Exchange.

Bad Debt A loan that has been written off.

Bailee A person or an entity who has temporary possession of some property to be returned eventually to the true owner.

Bailment The procedure of depositing the personal property with the bailee.

Balloon Maturity Maturity of a serial bond.

BAN Bond Anticipation Note. A short-term municipal note issued in anticipation of underwriting a long-term bond.

Bank An entity authorized to receive deposits of money and lend, discount and negotiate promissory notes, drafts, and bills of exchange. The word has a Latin origin. It is derived from the word *Bancus*, which means bench in Latin.

Bank Examiners Authorized personnel of regulatory agencies assigned to examine bank records and operation. All national banks are examined by examiners of the Comptroller of the Currency, by the Federal Reserve Board and by the Federal Deposit Insurance Corporation. The Comptroller's examiners have the power to examine the activities of the national banks and their officers and employees. At the conclusion of the examination, they are required to make a detailed report of the condition of the bank to the Comptroller of the Currency.

Bank Line A moral but not a contractional commitment of a bank to extend a loan to a customer.

Bank Money Order A form of a cashier's check issued and sold by a bank.

Bank Note A form of money issued by a bank. Prior to the enactment of the Federal Reserve System, banks were authorized to issue money as bank notes.

Bank of Issue A bank authorized to issue notes or money, such as the Federal Reserve.

Bank Reserve An amount of money deposited by a bank with the Federal Reserve Bank to comply with the reserve requirements of the Federal Reserve Board of Governors.

Bankers' Acceptances Money market instruments issued by a bank to finance the purchase or shipment of goods from foreign countries.

Bankrupt A person or entity unable to meet financial obligations and has been declared as bankrupt by a court. The person will seek protection under various bankruptcy laws to liquidate his assets in an orderly fashion to satisfy the claims of creditors. The word is Latin in origin. It is a combination of two words, *Bancus*, meaning bench in Latin, and *Rupt*, which means broken. The early bankers in Venice used to sit on a bench to conduct banking. When someone was in financial difficulty, they would say that his *bench was broken*.

Barron's Confidence Index A weekly index of corporate bond yields. The index determines the ratio of the average yield of 10 top corporate bonds against the average yield of 40 corporate bonds in the Dow Jones Average.

Barter An exchange of one commodity with another, without the use of money.

Base Coins Minor coins or counterfeit coins. Coins made of such metals as nickel or copper.

Basis The annual rate of yield on a bond if held to maturity. For example: the price of a bond is 95, basis 8½ percent. This means it will cost the customer $950 to buy a bond with a face value of $1,000, and the yield to maturity is 8½ percent.

Basis Book A book of tables used to convert basis prices to dollar prices.

Basis Point 1 Basis Point is equal to 1/100th of 1 percent.

Basis Price The price of the security as expressed in terms of yield.

Basis Value Value of a bond as determined by the effective interest rate. Bonds are purchased on a certain "basis" or to yield a certain percentage until the date of maturity.

Bear Raid A term used to describe the heavy short selling activity by traders in the stock market.

Bearer Bond A bond without any indication as to the name of the owner. The holder of the certificate is the owner.

Bearish Market A market with declining security or commodity prices.

Below Par A price below the face value of the security. Example: The bond price is $95. This is $5 below par.

Bequest A property left by a deceased person in his last will and testament.

Beta Coefficient A measuring device used to indicate the price movement of a security in relation to the stock market in general.

Bid The proposal to buy a security.

Bid Form A form used by underwriters in submitting their bids to municipal issuers.

Bid Wanted A procedure in which a dealer solicits bids from other dealers interested in purchasing a security.

Bidding Limitation Restrictions published by the municipal issuer for the terms of bids submitted by interested parties.

Bidding Syndicate A syndicate that is making the proposal to underwrite a security.

BIGI Bond Investors Guaranty Insurance Company. An insurance company that guarantees payment of principal and interest of municipal bonds and notes.

Bill of Lading A receipt issued by a carrier certifying that it has received goods from a person for transportation to another person located at a specified destination.

Billing Cycle Periods in which bills are submitted for payment of goods sold or services rendered.

Blanket Mortgage A mortgage covering all the properties of a corporation.

Blind Pool A form of limited partnership with no indication as to the type of properties the general partner intends to buy.

Blocked Currency A specific currency for a specific use; generally used during times of war.

Blowout Immediate sale of all securities in a public underwriting.

Blue List A daily listing of municipal securities offered by broker–dealers.

Blue List Total The aggregate par value of all municipal bonds listed in the Blue List. This is a measure to determine the supply of municipal bonds available in the secondary market.

Blue Sky Law A term referring to the state securities laws.

Bond A certificate of debt. An obligation of a government or a corporation to pay to the holder of the certificate a certain sum of money at a predetermined date.

Bond Amortization Fund Also known as Mandatory Redemption Account. An account used for a sinking fund in which the issuer makes deposits used to call or purchase a bond bearing a mandatory redemption schedule.

Bond Anticipation Note (BAN) A short-term municipal security issued in anticipation of the issuance of a long-term bond. The note will be paid off with the proceeds of the bond after the process of the underwriting is concluded.

Bond Broker A broker assigned to execute bond trades in the marketplace.

Bond Buyer A daily publication for municipal securities, containing advertisements of new offerings, notices of bond redemptions, and market analysis.

Bond Buyer's Index A daily index published by the Bond Buyer. The index will show the yield of a group of municipal bonds.

Bond Circular An advertisement issued by a bank or an underwriting firm offering bonds for sale.

Bond Contract A contract under which a bond is issued. The contract will state the terms and the obligation of the issuer.

Bond Counsel An attorney retained by the issuer to determine whether the issuer has the statutory or constitutional authority to issue the bond.

Bond Covenants The issuer's obligation and promise to perform certain actions.

Bond Crowd Members of the New York Stock Exchange assigned to execute, buy, and sell orders of bonds.

Bond Equivalency Yield The yield on a tax exempt bond in comparison with interest bearing corporate bonds.

Bond Fund Investment company holding municipal bonds in its portfolio.

Bond House A firm engaged in underwriting and dealing in bonds.

Bond of Indemnity A document signed by a person guaranteeing to protect another person against any loss, liability, or damages.

Bond Ordinance Resolution authorizing the issuance of bonds.

Bond Power An instrument separate from the bond certificate. The bond power, when signed, will enable the bondholder to transfer or sell the bond certificate.

Bond Ratings Measuring device to determine the creditworthiness of entities that issue bonds.

Bond Referendum Voting procedure through which voters approve the issuance of a municipal security.

Bond Register Records of the bond registrars.

Bond Transcript All documents concerning the offering of a new municipal bond.

Bond Year $1,000 of bond outstanding in one year. Bond years = Number of bonds × number of years to maturity.

Bonded Debt The fixed obligation of a government or a corporation. Also called Funded Debt.

Bondholder An owner or a holder of a bond.

Bonus Bonds Bonds issued by a municipality to induce a corporation to build its facility in the municipal district. A form of industrial revenue bond.

Book-Entry Security Ownership of the security is evidenced by a statement rather than a certificate of ownership.

Borrowed Reserve Money borrowed by a bank from the Federal Reserve to meet the required reserve of the Fed.

Bottom The lowest level of a business or economic cycle.

Bottom Dropped Out A sharp and sudden drop in security prices in the stock or the bond market.

Bought Deal Firm commitment underwriting.

Bourse The French word for stock exchange.

Boursiers Members of the French Bourse.

Boutique Brokerage House A brokerage house specializing in certain products.

Break-Up Point The liquidating value representing the actual market value of the assets of a corporation.

Bretton Woods Agreement An agreement adopted by the international monetary conference of 44 nations held at Bretton Woods, New Hampshire, in July of 1944. The agreement established the International Monetary Fund to maintain orderly currency practices in international trade, and the International Bank for Reconstruction and Development.

Bridge Bonds Bonds issued to finance the construction of bridges.

Brokers' Loans Loans made by banks to broker–dealers.

Bubble Act An act passed in England in the early 18th century to restrain promoters from selling securities of questionable value to the public.

Budget An estimate of an anticipated income and expense for a certain period. The term is Latin in origin. It comes from the Latin word *bulga*, meaning leather bag. Seagoing merchants used to place enough money in the bag to cover their expenses during the journey to a foreign land.

Building and Loan Association An old name for the Savings and Loan Associations.

Bulge A sudden rise in prices of securities or commodities.

Bullion Gold or silver in the form of bars or ingots.

Bullish Market A market with rising security or commodity prices.

Business Cycle A phenomenon in a capitalistic system indicating periods of prosperity, recession, depression, inflation, deflation.

Buy Minus A type of order to buy a security at a price lower than the prevailing price.

Buyback A procedure in which a corporation purchases its own bonds at a discount price in the bond market.

Buy-In Closing-out the transaction.

Bypass Trust A trust established by parents to transfer assets to their children to avoid or reduce inheritance taxes.

Cabinet Crowd The crowd at the New York Stock Exchange Bond Room specialized to trade inactive or cabinet bonds listed at the NYSE.

Calamity Call Also known as Catastrophy Call. The issuer is required to call all or part of an issue when the project is destroyed during construction due to an accident.

Call Redemption of bond.

Call Loan Loan payable on demand.

Call Loan Rate The rate of a loan that banks have lent to broker–dealers.

Call Money A bank loan that may be called at any time.

Call Option Bond A bond that gives the bondholder the privilege to redeem the bond prior to maturity date.

Call Premium For bonds, the amount of money paid in excess of the face value of the bond.

Call Price Price at which the issuer will call the bonds.

Call Protection A provision in the call feature of a bond that will protect the bondholder. For example, the issuer may agree not to call the bond for a period of 10 years after issuance.

Callable Bond A bond allowing the issuer to call the bond before maturity.

Called Away A bond called before maturity.

Called Bonds Bonds that have been called.

Cambist A person specialized to exchange foreign currencies.

Cambistry The art of exchanging foreign currencies.

Capital Appreciation Bond CAB. A compounded interest bond or multiplier bond.

Capital Budget Amount of money used to finance corporate plant expansion or research and development.

Capital Flight Removal of a large amount of money from one country to another to seek safer havens.

Capital Intensive Industry An industry that requires large sums of money to operate.

Capital Outlay Capital expenses.

Capital Structure The capitalization of a corporation including long-term bonds and the stockholder's equity.

Capitalized Interest Also known as Funded Interest. A portion of the proceeds of an issue is put aside to pay interest on the securities for a period of time.

Captive Finance Company A finance subsidiary of a corporation established to finance the consumer purchases of products made by the parent corporation.

Carrying Cost The interest cost to carry a security in an inventory.

Cartel An industrial combination of various corporations in the same industry or group.

Cash Money, derived from the Latin word *Casa*, meaning box, the container used to place money.

Cashier's Check A check drawn on a bank, signed by the cashier of the bank.

Casualty Loss A financial loss caused by damage, flood, or destruction.

Catastrophy Call Calamity call.

Caveat Emptor Buyer beware. A Latin phrase warning the buyer to protect himself before making a purchase.

Caveat Venditor Seller Beware. A Latin phrase warning the seller to protect himself before making a sale.

Central Bank A bank empowered to issue currency, formulate monetary policies, and act as the fiscal agent of the government. Examples: the Federal Reserve Bank in the U.S., the Bundesbank in West Germany, and the Bank of England in Great Britain.

Certificate of Accrual on Treasury Securities (CATS) A certificate issued by an investment banking firm representing the principal and interest of a U.S. Treasury bond. CATS are sold at a discount. They pay no interest. At maturity, the certificate holder will receive the full face value.

Certificate of Deposit (CD) A debt instrument issued by a bank.

Certificateless Bonds Bonds that have no certificates. Bonds that are sold in book-entry form.

Certified Check A check that guarantees that there is sufficient funds on deposit to honor the check.

Certified Financial Planner (CFP) A person licensed to help the customer plan his banking, insurance, and tax affairs.

Certified Public Accountant (CPA) A person licensed to prepare tax returns, conduct audits, and perform general accounting functions for individuals, corporations and incorporated entities.

Chattel Movable tangible property, such as equipment and furniture.

Chattel Mortgage A mortgage with chattels as collateral.

Cheap Money Loans made at a low interest rate.

Check A draft drawn on a bank against funds deposited at the bank.

Citizen Bonds Certain municipal bonds issued in book-entry form.

Civil Bonds Bonds issued by a political entity.

Clean Orders Orders for securities transactions that have corresponding buy and sell orders.

Clearing House An association or a company formed to facilitate the exchange and clearance of checks or securities.

Clearing House Funds Funds in the process of collection. Clearing house funds mature into federal funds usually on an overnight basis.

Closed Lien A provision for revenue bonds. The issuer may not issue additional bonds that have an equal claim on the pledged revenue.

Closed-End Mortgage A type of mortgage that forbids payment before maturity.

Closed-Out A security position that has been liquidated by the broker–dealer due to a margin call.

Closing The meeting between the issuer and the underwriter during which the issuer surrenders certificates in exchange for payment.

Coinage The process of preparing a piece of metal to be used as currency.

Coins Money represented by a metal.

Coinsurance An insurance policy that assumes a joint risk with another insurance coverage.

Collateral A security or an asset pledged for a loan.

Collateral Loan A loan secured by a collateral.

Collateral Mortgage Bonds Bonds secured by mortgage bonds.

Collateral Trust Bond A corporate bond secured and supported by the value of another security held at a bank.

Collateralized Mortgage Obligation (CMO) A mortgage-backed security representing a certain mortgage pool. CMOs are similar to Ginny Maes. They represent pools for short-, medium-, or long-term mortgages.

Collectibles Objects that may be collected by investors as a hobby or for purposes of investment.

Collection The process of presenting a check for payment.

Combination Bond A type of revenue bond issued by the revenue of a particular project and also by the issuing government.

Commercial Loan Short-term funds borrowed to finance the working capital of a corporation.

Commercial Paper A short-term negotiable instrument issued by a corporation with a maximum life of 270 days.

Commitment Fee A fee charged by a lender for a commitment of a bank to make funds available for a loan.

Commodity-Backed Bonds A bond supported by the value of a certain commodity.

Competitive Bid A bid presented by an underwriter to an issuer. The issuer will award the underwriter who had presented the most favorable bid.

Composition A process in bankruptcy in which creditors accept partial payment to settle their claims.

Compound Accrued Value The method used to determine the value of zero bonds and other original issue discount bonds that pay no interest. The compound accrued value is the current value of the sum of money invested to yield compounded interest.

Compound Coupon Bond A long-term bond in which the interest is reinvested at a stated rate. The bondholder will receive the face amount and compounded interest at maturity.

Comptroller of the Currency An official of the U.S. government charged with the responsibility to regulate the operation and the organization of national banks.

Consolidated Loans Loans covering combinations of other loans.

Consolidated Mortgage Bonds Bonds secured by a group of mortgages consolidated into one.

Consols A term used to describe British government bonds.

Construction Loan Funds borrowed to construct a building.

Construction Loan Notes (CLN) Notes issued to finance housing projects.

Consumer Bond A bond issued by a financial institution and sold directly to the public.

Consumer Credit Credit extended to consumers.

Consumer Price Index A measuring device used to determine changes in prices of goods and services purchased and used by consumers. The Index is issued on a monthly basis by the U.S. Bureau of Labor Statistics.

Continued Bonds Bonds with a maturity date extended beyond the original maturity date. Also known as Extended Bonds.

Contract An arrangement between two persons or entities enforceable by law.

Contract Clause Constitutional provision preventing state governments from enacting laws that jeopardize the obligation of a contract.

Conventional Mortgage A mortgage with a fixed rate and term.

Conversion Price Price at which convertible securities may be converted into common stock.

Conversion Ratio The ratio that determines the number of shares of common stock that will be received in exchange for each convertible bond.

Convertible Bonds Bonds that may be converted into another class of security of the same corporation.

Correspondent A financial institution that performs services for another institution.

Cost-of-Living-Adjustment (COLA) An arrangement in which wages are adjusted to the cost of living as measured by the Consumer Price Index.

Cost–Push Inflation Inflation caused by the rising cost of products and services.

Council of Economic Advisers A council of economists appointed by the President. The economists counsel the President on economic policy.

Counter Check A convenience check prepared by a bank for use by a customer on an emergency basis.

Coupon Interest rate on a bond or a detachable certificate evidencing interest due.

Coupon Bond A bearer bond issued with coupons attached. The bondholder must clip the coupon when due and present it to the bank for payment.

Coupon Rate Nominal interest rate.

Covenant A provision in a trust agreement that commits the issuer to perform certain acts.

Cover The difference between the winning bid on a new security and the next best bid.

Credit A term that describes someone's ability to buy in advance of payment. It comes from the Latin word *Credo*, which means "I believe."

Credit Balance Uninvested proceeds of sale of securities held by a broker–dealer.

Credit Card A card used to extend credit to the consumer.

Credit Market A weekly publication for municipal securities.

Credit Rating A rating that determines the creditworthiness of a company or a municipality with regard to payment of an obligation.

Creditor A person or an organization to whom money is due.

Currency Bonds Bonds payable in U.S. dollars as opposed to bonds payable in gold coins.

Current Coupon Bond A bond bearing an interest rate based on current market rates.

Current Maturity The period between the present time and the maturity date of a bond.

Current Production Rate Interest rate on a Ginnie Mae bond. The interest rate is one-half percent less than the mortgage rate in the same unit.

Current Yield The yield determined by the annual dollar amount of interest paid, divided by the market value of the bond.

Cushion The period between the date of the issuance of a callable bond and the call date.

Cushion Bond Callable bond.

Dated Date The date printed on a new security from which interest starts to accrue.

Day Loan A one-day loan to a broker without any securities pledged as collateral.

DBA Dealer Bank Association. A trade organization.

Dealer Bank A bank engaged in municipal and government securities activities.

Dealer Book The Directory of Municipal Bond Dealers of the United States (the Red Book). The semi-annual publication directed to the bond buyer, listing municipal bond dealers, municipal finance consultants, and bond attorneys.

Dealer's Concession The amount of money that the syndicate gives to a selling group member for the sale of a new security at the public offering price.

Debenture Unsecured bond supported only by the good faith of the issuer.

Debt An obligation to pay.

Debt Limit The maximum amount of money that the U.S. government is authorized by Congress to borrow.

Debt Ratios Ratios between the issuers' total debt and their tax base, income, or population.

Debt Service An arrangement in which the issuer is obligated to pay the interest and the principal on a bond when due.

Debt Service Coverage The ratio of pledged revenues to pay the debt service to the annual debt service requirement.

Debt Service Reserve Fund The fund used to pay the debt service when the pledged revenues are not enough to satisfy the debt service.

Debt-to-Equity Ratio Ratio determined by dividing the total liability of a corporation by the stockholders' equity.

Debtor Borrower of funds.

Decimal Coinage Coins issued in a denomination of a monetary unit. A dime is a decimal coinage of one dollar, which is the monetary unit in the U.S.

Deep Discount Bond A bond sold at a discount price in excess of 25 percent of the face value.

Defalcation Theft or embezzlement.

Default Failure to pay principal and interest when due.

Defeasance Termination of the right of the bondholder in accordance with the terms of the bond contract.

Deferred Bonds Bonds in which interest or the principal payment has been deferred to a future date.

Deferred Interest Bond A zero-coupon bond that pays both interest and principal at the time of maturity.

Deficit Excess of expenditures over revenue.

Deficit Financing A procedure in which bonds are issued to finance the deficit of a government.

Definitive Bond An engraved bond certificate.

Deflation Process in which prices of goods and services decline.

Deflator A device used to adjust the difference between the real value and the value impacted by inflation.

Delinquency Failure to make payment of an obligation when due.

Demand Bond Long-term bond. The bondholder will have the option to redeem the bond at a set schedule before maturity.

Demand Deposit A type of account from which funds may be withdrawn by the customer at any time without receiving approval from the bank.

Demand Loan A loan that can be called at any time by the lender.

Demand-Pull Inflation Inflation caused when demand to purchase goods exceeds the supply.

Demonetization The process in which a specific currency is withdrawn from circulation.

Depository An organization charged with the responsibility of holding assets for the account of other organizations or customers.

Depression A period representing a severe economic downturn with falling prices, rising unemployment, and reduced business activity.

Deregulation The process in which governmental regulations are reduced to create a free marketplace.

Designated Order An order for securities held by a syndicate. The buyer will designate the portion of the take-down to be credited to the account of a syndicate member.

Devaluation The process in which the value of a country's currency is lowered in relation to the currencies of other countries.

Direct Bonded Debt Also known as Gross Bonded Debt. The sum of the issuer's total bonded debt.

Direct Placement Private placement of securities as opposed to public offering.

Disbursement The process in which funds are paid to satisfy an obligation.

Discharge of Lien The process in which a lien on a property is removed.

Discount The difference in money between the current market value of the bond and its face value.

Discount Bond A bond sold at a price lower than its face value.

Discount Rate The official interest rate that the Federal Reserve charges member banks for funds borrowed from the Fed.

Discount Window The window at the Federal Reserve where member banks borrow money.

Discount Yield The yield of a discount bond.

Discounted Security A security sold at a discount price from the face value.

Disinflation The process in which the pace of the rise in value of goods and services is on a decline.

Disintermediation The process in which funds are removed from banks to be invested in higher-yielding instruments.

Disinvestment The process in which capital investment in a certain project is reduced.

Disposable Income Funds at the disposal of the consumer after personal taxes have been paid.

Divestiture The process in which assets or investments are sold or liquidated.

Divisional Bonds Bonds issued by a division or a subsidiary of a company.

Dollar Bond A bond quoted in terms of dollar price.

Double-Barreled Bond A municipal bond insured by the revenue of a particular project and also by the taxing power of the municipality.

Downgrade The lowering of the bond rating.

Draft A document by which the drawer instructs the drawee to pay a certain sum of money to a payee. The drawer is the person signing the draft, the drawee is the bank, and the payee is the person who will receive the funds.

Drawn Bonds Bonds that have been called for redemption.

Dumping Selling products below their manufacturing cost.

Early Withdrawal Penalty Penalty charged to customers for withdrawal of funds before maturity.

Easy Money An increase in the money supply at the banking system by the Fed.

Economic Indicators Indicators, such as inflation and the unemployment rate, used to determine the condition of the economy.

Econometrics A technique that uses computer analysis to describe and interpret key economic indicators.

Edge Act Legislation enacted in 1919, allowing national banks to conduct foreign banking activities.

Effective Debt The total debt of an organization.

Effective Interest Rate The actual rate of interest.

Effective Yield The yield on a bond as determined by the purchase price, the coupon rate, and the period until maturity.

Elastic Money Money that can be increased or reduced to accommodate business needs.

Eligible Paper Negotiable securities that may be accepted by the Federal Reserve as collateral when a member bank borrows money from the Fed's Discount Window.

Emancipation of a Minor The process in which a minor assumes full responsibility of his action as an adult.

Embargo The procedure in which the government prohibits shipment of certain goods to another country or another region of the same country.

Enterprise Activity Project that provides funds to pay interest on securities issued to finance the project.

Equal Credit Opportunity Act A U.S. law that prohibits discrimination in extending credit to individuals based on sex, race, religion, or ethnicity.

Equity Funding A type of mutual fund that is a combination of a life insurance policy and a mutual fund.

Equity Kicker The procedure in which a lender charges a low interest rate on a loan in return for an equity ownership in the project for which the loan is being used.

Equivalent Bond Yield The yield that compares the discount yield with yield on interest bearing bond.

ERISA Acronym for Employee Retirement Income Security Act. A U.S. law that governs the operation of pension and profit sharing plans.

Escrow Account An account for monies used to pay interest on a bond issue.

ESOP Acronym for Employee Stock Ownership Plan. A procedure in which employees purchase their own company stock.

Euro CD Certificate of deposit issued on Eurodollars.

Eurocurrency Funds deposited in banks located in countries other than the country of the depositor.

European Economic Community (EEC) Popularly known as the "Common Market." The EEC was established in 1957 by the Treaty of Rome to provide and facilitate commerce among the major European nations.

Exact Interest Interest calculated on a 365-day basis as opposed to 360-day basis.

Exchequer Bonds Bonds issued by the British government.

Excise Tax Tax on manufacture or sale of certain commodities. Example: cigarette tax.

Exempt Security A security not subject to the registration requirements of the Securities Act of 1933.

Ex-Legal A municipal trade to be consummated without the delivery of the legal opinion.

Export–Import Bank An independent agency of the U.S. government established to facilitate the financing of imports and exports for the U.S.

External Bond A government bond issued in a foreign country.

Face Amount Par value or principal value of a bond.

Factoring A procedure in which a company sells its accounts receivable to a factoring company that will then assume the responsibility of collecting the money as a dealer.

Fannie Mae Federal National Mortgage Association. A quasi-governmental corporation authorized to purchase and sell existing home mortgages in the secondary market.

Farmers Home Administration (FAHA) A division in the U.S. Department of Agriculture. FAHA extends credit to farmers at a reasonable rate.

Federal Agency An agency of the U.S. government, such as Government National Mortgage Association.

Federal Deposit Insurance Corporation An agency that insures customers' funds at a commercial bank.

Federal Funds Immediately available funds deposited in a bank's reserve account at a Federal Reserve district bank.

Federal Home Loan Bank An agency established in 1932 to supervise federal savings and loan associations; similar to the Federal Reserve System for commercial banks.

Federal Home Loan Mortgage Corporation Popularly known as Freddie Mac. An agency of the U.S. government that buys residential mortgages from lenders, consolidates them into a package, and sells securities based on the pool of these mortgages. Freddie Mac has played an important role in the secondary market of residential mortgages since its inception in 1970.

Federal Housing Administration (FHA) A U.S. agency established to provide home financing at a reasonable rate.

Federal Intermediate Credit Bank An agency that helps the farmer to finance his seasonal needs.

Federal Land Bank An agency that provides long-term mortgage loans to farmers.

Federal National Mortgage Association Popularly known as Fannie Mae. A quasi-governmental agency that provides a secondary market for mortgages on real estate properties.

Federal Reserve Bank One of the 12 Federal Reserve district banks.

Federal Reserve Notes Notes issued by the Federal Reserve.

Federal Reserve System The central banking institution in the U.S., established in 1913 by an act of Congress.

Federal Savings and Loan Association Federally chartered organization engaged primarily in home mortgage financing. Created in 1933, the organization is under the jurisdiction of the Federal Home Loan Bank.

FGIC Financial Guaranty Insurance Company. A corporation that offers insurance guaranteeing payment of principal and interest due on securities on stated maturity and interest payment dates.

Fiat Money Money decreed by government to be a legal tender not supported by any specie, such as gold or other governmental obligations.

Fidelity Insurance Insurance policy that provides coverage against losses due to employee dishonesty.

Fiduciary Currency Paper money not supported by gold.

Finance Charge Cost of using credit extended by someone else.

Financial Accounting Standards Board (FASB) A board that establishes generally accepted accounting principles.

Financial Intermediary A financial institution, such as a bank or a savings and loan association, that acts as an intermediary.

First Call Date The first date on a callable bond when the bond may be called by the issuing corporation or the municipality.

First Leasehold Bonds Bonds secured by a property under a lease, rather than by the property directly.

First Lien The first claim on a property.

First Mortgage A loan on a property that allows the lender to have the first lien on the property.

First Mortgage Bonds Bonds secured by a first mortgage.

Fitch Investor's Service A financial service company that provides ratings for municipal bonds.

Fitch Sheets Sheets published by Fitch Investor's Services that report quotations of securities listed on stock exchanges.

Fixed Exchange Rate A preestablished rate of exchange for foreign currencies.

Fixed Income Security A security, such as a bond, that pays a fixed rate of interest.

Fixed Loan A loan with a fixed rate of interest.

Flat Bond A bond that is traded without accrued interest. Bonds in default and Income bonds are traded flat.

Flat Yield Curve A graphic illustration showing short-term rates are the same as long-term rates.

Float Float is the value of checks in the process of collection. The term also describes the amount of time it takes to receive settlement for checks cleared through the clearing house or the Federal Reserve. Float can be expressed in terms of dollars or number of days.

Floater A bond with no fixed rate of interest. The interest rate is adjusted periodically based on a major interest rate determinant, such as a U.S. Treasury bill.

Floating Rate Bond A bond whose interest rate changes at various intervals.

Floating Supply of Bonds Total outstanding bonds in the hands of the public.

Flotation Cost The cost of issuing and underwriting new securities.

Foreclosure The process in which property is sold by the lender when the borrower fails to make payment of interest and principal.

Foreign Currency Bonds Bonds issued by a foreign country payable in the currency of the country.

Forfeiture The loss or seizure of funds to secure a contractual obligation.

Free Market A market in which there is competition between buyers and sellers.

FSLIC/FDIC Bonds Bonds secured by Federal Savings and Loan Insurance Corporation or Federal Deposit Insurance Corporation certificates of deposit.

Full Coupon Bond A bond bearing an interest rate close to the current interest rates in the market.

Fully Registered A security registered as to both the principal and interest.

GAN An acronym for grant anticipation notes, issued to cover cash flow deficit before the grant is received.

Garnishment A legal process in which a third party will be ordered not to pay money to a defendant if the plaintiff has sued the defendant for non-payment of funds.

GASB Governmental Accounting Standards Board. A body that prescribes standard accounting practices for governmental entities.

General Loan and Collateral Agreement An agreement between a broker–dealer and a bank that will allow the broker–dealer to borrow from the bank on a continuous basis.

General Obligation Bonds Municipal bonds secured by the full faith and credit of the issuer.

GFOA Government Finance Officers Association. Formerly known as Municipal Finance Officers Association

Global Certificate A single certificate representing the entire issue of a security.

Go-Around The process in which the trading desk of the Federal Reserve Bank of New York contacts primary government bond dealers to receive bids and offers for securities to be purchased or sold by the Federal Open Market Committee of the Fed.

Gold Bonds Bonds payable in gold.

Gold Reserve Gold held by governments or central banks.

Good Faith Deposit A check presented to a municipal issuer by a dealer bidding to underwrite the issue.

Good Money Money that is good on the same day.

Government National Mortgage Association Popularly known as Ginnie Mae. A U.S. agency that buys residential mortgages from lenders, consolidates them into a pool, issues securities based on the pool, and sells securities to the public.

Graduated Payment Mortgage (GPM) Popularly known as "Jeeps." A type of mortgage that initially will have a lower monthly payment, but in time the monthly payments will increase and then level off after a period of years.

Greenbacks Legal tender issued by the U.S. government immediately after the Civil War.

Gresham's Law A monetary policy that states "bad money drives good money out of circulation." Named after Sir Thomas Gresham, a British economist under Queen Elizabeth I.

Gross Debt The total sum of a debtor's obligations.

Group Net Order An order submitted to a syndicate for a new municipal bond allocated at the public offering price without deducting the concession or takedown.

Guaranteed Bonds Bonds secured by a party other than the issuing entity.

Guaranteed Income Contract An insurance contract that guarantees a fixed rate of return on investments in a pension or profit sharing plan.

Half-Life Ginnie Mae A Government National Mortgage Association bond on which half of the principal has already been paid. The same term may apply to other mortgage-backed securities, such as Fannie Mae and Freddie Mac.

HIBI Health Industry Bond Insurance. A company that provides insurance for payment of principal and interest to health-care institutions.

High Grade Bond A highly rated bond, triple A or a double A.

Home Equity Financing The process by which a homeowner applies for a second mortgage based on the current appreciated value of his house.

Humpbacked Yield Curve or Bell-Shaped Yield Curve A graphic illustration showing that rates are low in the early years, peak in the middle years, and decline in the later years.

IDB Industrial Development Bond. Securities issued by a local government to finance the construction of industrial or commercial projects.

IDBI IDBI Managers, Inc. A company that offers insurance for payment of principal and interest on industrial development bonds.

Illiquid An asset that cannot be easily convertible into cash.

Indenture A contract or a trust between the bond issuer and the bondholder.

Indeterminate Bonds Bonds with no fixed maturity date.

Indorsed Bonds Bonds secured by a party other than the issuing entity.

Insolvent A person or entity unable to meet his debts.

Instrumentality An agency of the U.S. government.

Inter-American Development Bank A bank organized in 1959 to promote economic growth in Central and South American countries.

Interest The cost of using someone else's money.

Interest Coverage Margin of safety for payment of debt service.

International Bank for Reconstruction and Development A bank founded in July of 1944 in Bretton Woods, New Hampshire, to encourage and promote economic and industrial development in member countries.

International Monetary Fund An institution established in 1944 in Bretton Woods, New Hampshire, to promote international trade and to provide an orderly adjustment of foreign exchange rates.

Interpolation A procedure to determine the intermediate yields or prices of bonds on a bond yield table.

Inverted Yield Curve A graphic illustration showing short-term rates exceeding long-term rates.

Invested Sinker A sinking fund for a term bond in which the deposited money is invested in U.S. Treasury obligations rather than used to redeem the securities.

Investment Grade Bonds rated AAA to BBB.

Irredeemable Bonds Bonds that cannot be redeemed before the maturity date.

Joint Account Syndicate An account formed by two or more dealers to underwrite a security.

Joint Bonds Bonds secured jointly by two or more entities.

Junior Lien Bonds Bonds with subordinated claims against revenues.

Junk Bonds Bonds rated BB or lower.

Kiting Checks The method in which checks are drawn against insufficient funds.

Lead Manager Managing underwriter.

Lease–Purchase Agreement An agreement that allows the leaseholder to apply the lease payment toward the purchase of the property.

Lease Rental Bond A bond secured by lease payments made by the entity leasing the facility financed by the bond.

Lease Revenue Debt Debt secured by an obligation to make annual lease payments.

Legal Bonds Bonds that are legal investments for certain financial institutions, such as banks and savings and loan associations.

Legal Interest Rate The maximum interest rate allowed by law. Any interest in excess of the legal interest rate is called usury.

Legal Opinion A document signed by bond counsel certifying that the bonds comply with applicable laws.

Lessee The party that uses the facility under a lease arrangement.

Lessor The party that owns the property being leased.

Letter of Credit A commitment made by a commercial bank to make payments of a debt upon compliance with certain conditions.

Level Debt Service Interest and principal on a mortgage is paid in equal amounts during the life of the mortgage vs. unequal payments, such as the one shown on the chart.

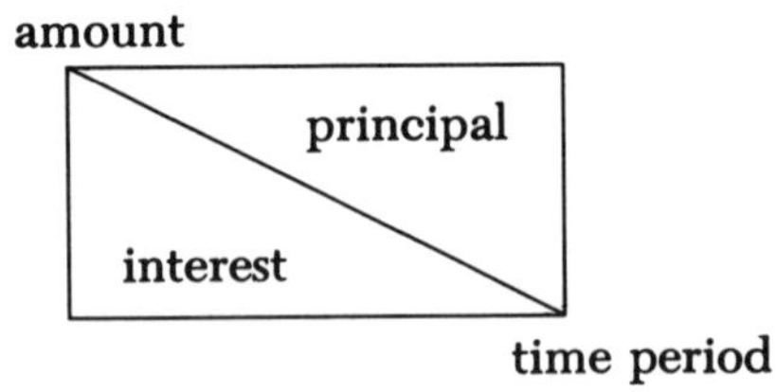

LIBOR London Interbank Offered Rate. The official rate for Eurodollars and Euro CDs.

Limited Tax Bond A bond secured by a tax limited as to the rate and the principal amount of the bond.

Line of Credit An amount of money that a person or an entity is allowed to borrow from a bank.

Loan Value The amount of money a lending institution will loan based on the value of collateral securities.

Locked Market A market condition in which the highest bid and the lowest offer for a security are the same.

Lower Floater A variable rate bond with a put option feature.

Maturity The date on which a loan or a bond comes due.

Maturity Date The date on which the principal on a security becomes due.

MBIA Municipal Bond Insurance Association.

Mechanic's Lien An attachment on a land or a property for the benefit of a person who has performed work for the building or the property.

Medium Term Bond A bond with a maturity between two and 10 years.

Member Order An order for a new municipal bond placed with the syndicate by the syndicate member.

MFOA Municipal Finance Officers Association.

MIG Moody's designation of ratings for short-term municipal notes.

Mill $.001 or one-tenth of one cent.

Millage The rate used to calculate the ad valorem tax on a property.

Money Broker A person acting as agent between a borrower and a lender.

Money Market An open market where money market instruments, such as U.S. Treasury bills, commercial papers and CDs, are traded.

Money Order An instrument calling for the payment of money to the payee.

Money Rates Key money market rates, such as the prime rate and the federal funds rate.

Money Supply The following devices are used to monitor the country's money supply.

M1 = Currency + demand deposits + monies in customers' checking accounts.

M2 = M1 + { Savings accounts, Time deposits, Overnight REPO's, Overnight Eurodollars, Money market mutual fund shares }

M3 = M2 + { Large CDs, Term REPO's }

L = M3 + Other liquid assets, such as term Eurodollars, BAs, commercial papers, U.S. Treasury bills.

Moody's Investor's Service A financial service subsidiary of Dun & Bradstreet that provides rating for corporate and municipal securities.

Moral Obligation Bond A municipal bond secured by the moral obligation of the issuing government.

Mortgage Bonds Bonds secured by mortgages on a property.

Mortgage Loans Loans made to purchase or finance real estate properties.

MSRB Municipal Securities Rulemaking Board. A self-regulatory organization responsible for developing rules for municipal security business.

Multiplier Bond A long-term municipal security on which the investment return accretes at a compounded rate to maturity.

Municipal Notes Short-term municipal obligations.

Munifact A teletype service provided by the Bond Buyer. The service transmits bond market information.

Muniment of Title A document by which right to possess a property is maintained.

Mutual Reciprocity Doctrine Ruled by the U.S. Supreme Court, the doctrine states federal income tax exemption for interest on municipal bonds.

NABL National Association of Bond Lawyers.

National Bank A bank chartered under the National Bank Act.

National Debt The total indebtedness of the U.S. government.

Negative Covenants Covenants in the bond contract in which the issuer is obligated to refrain from performing certain actions.

Negotiable Securities Securities in good deliverable form.

Net Debt Gross debt minus the self-supporting debt.

Net Direct Bonded Debt The issuer's direct debt minus the sinking fund and self-supporting debt.

Net Interest Cost (NIC) A method of calculating the interest expense to the issuer in an underwriting. It is calculated by:

$$\frac{\text{Total Interest Payments} + \text{Discount (or} - \text{Premium)}}{\text{Bond Years}} = \text{NIC}$$

Net Overall Bonded Debt Also known as Net Direct and Overlapping Debt. The issuer's net direct debt plus the applicable share of the net debt of all overlapping jurisdictions.

Nominal Interest Rate The annual rate of interest determined at the creation of the security.

Non-Callable Bond Irredeemable bond.

Normal Yield Curve A graph indicating that a short-term bond has a lower interest rate than a long-term bond.

Note A short-term promissory security.

Notice of Sale A notice by the municipal issuer describing the terms of sale of a new municipal offering.

Novation The process in which an older bond is replaced by a new one.

Obligor An issuer of a bond obligation to pay the interest and principal when due.

Odd Coupon An interest payment made not on a semi-annual basis.

Offering Circular A document prepared by the underwriter about a new issue.

Offering Scale Prices or yields at which different maturities of a serial bond are sold to the public.

Official Notice of Sale A formal notice issued by a municipality for underwriters interested in underwriting a new municipal security.

Official Statement A document issued by a municipal issuer disclosing all material information on a new issue.

O.I.D. Original Issue Discount. The difference in money between the cost of purchasing a zero bond and its face value.

Open-End Lien A feature of a revenue bond that allows the issuer to issue additional bonds that will have equal claims on pledged revenues.

Order Period The period following the competitive sale of a municipal bond. During this period non-priority orders submitted by a syndicate member are allocated without any consideration of time of submission.

Original Issue Discount Bonds Bonds sold at a discount from the face value at the time of the original sale.

Originator An investment banking firm that promotes the distribution of a new security.

Overcertification The procedure in which a bank certifies a check for an amount in excess of the amount of funds in the customer's account.

Overdraft A situation in which the customer writes a check in excess of funds in his account.

Overlapping Bonded Debt The issuer's share of the debt of other jurisdictions that overlap the issuer's geographic area.

Overnight Loan A short-term loan extended by a bank to a broker–dealer.

Par Bond Bonds selling at face value.

Par Option The issuer has the privilege to redeem the bonds at par.

Par Value The principal value or the face value of the bond.

Parity Bonds Issues of bonds having the same priority of claims against pledged revenues.

Parking A manipulative trading device. Selling securities to a customer and repurchasing the security in an unbooked account.

Paying Agent The bank pays interest and principal on a bond acting on behalf of the issuer.

Per Capita Debt Government's debt divided by the number of residents.

Per Pro Short for Per Procuration. The signature of a person authorized to sign on behalf of the firm.

Perpetual Bond Bond with no maturity date.

PHA Bonds Public Housing Authority Bond. A bond issued by a housing authority to finance public housing. PHA bonds are guaranteed by the Department of Housing and Urban Development (HUD) under the U.S. Housing Act of 1937 in the event the revenues are not sufficient to pay off the bondholder.

Philadelphia Plan Equipment Trust Bond.

Pickup Bond A high interest paying bond close to the maturity or the call date.

Placement Ratio A weekly ratio published by the Bond Buyer. It is determined by the number of bonds sold divided by the number of bonds issued during a week.

Position Trading The dealer buys the securities and holds them in his inventory.

Premiums The amount by which the market value of the bond exceeds the face value.

Pre-sale Order An order given to the syndicate before the securities are purchased from the issuer.

Prime Rate Bank interest rate charged to preferential customers.

Prior Issue An outstanding security of a municipal entity.

Protective Covenant The issuer's obligations to protect the interest of the bondholder.

Public Securities Association (PSA) A trade organization for municipal broker–dealers.

Put Bond Option bond. A bond granting the privilege to the bondholder to redeem the bond at set schedules before maturity.

Put Option Bond A bond that gives the bondholder the right to demand the repayment of the principal prior to maturity. For short-term bonds, this is known as *demand option*.

Qualified Legal Opinion A legal opinion stating that there are certain legal constraints for the municipality issuing the bond.

RAN Revenue Anticipation Notes.

Real Money Metallic money.

Redeemable Bonds Callable bonds.

Redemption Procedure in which the issuer pays the face value of the bond at the time of maturity.

Refinancing The procedure of issuing equity securities for the purposes of redeeming an old bond.

Refunding The procedure of issuing a new bond for the purposes of redeeming or calling an old bond.

Registered Bond Bond registered in the name of the bondholder.

Repurchase Agreement (REPO) An agreement in which a party agrees to purchase a security from a second party and the second party agrees to repurchase the security at a pre-determined price in the future.

Revenue Bond Municipal bond secured by the revenue on a particular project.

Reverse Repurchase Agreement (Reverse REPO) An agreement in which a party purchases security from a second party with the agreement that he will sell it to the second party at a predetermined price in the future.

Revolving Assets Current assets of a corporation.

Robert Morris Associates An organization of bank credit personnel.

Rollover Similar to refunding. A process in which a new security is issued, such as a U.S. Treasury bill to call or redeem another U.S. Treasury bill.

Sallie Mae Student Loan Marketing Association. A private corporation engaged in student loan programs.

Secured Creditor A creditor who holds adequate collateral against a loan.

Securities Dealer A dealer who acts as a principal in a securities transaction with a customer.

Self-Supporting Bond A bond secured by a project that will receive sufficient revenue to satisfy the payment of interest and payment to the bondholder.

Senior Bonds Bonds that have prior claim upon properties or assets of a corporation.

Senior Lien Bonds Bonds having a prior claim.

Serial Bonds Bonds having several dates of maturity.

Series Bonds Bonds having several dates of issuance.

Sight Draft A draft payable on presentation.

Sinking Fund A fund established under the bond contract. The issuer will make scheduled deposits at a bank in such a way that at the time of maturity the bank will have sufficient money to redeem the bond.

Slump Economic downturn.

Special Assessment Bonds Bonds payable from special assessment of a municipal entity.

Special Tax Bond Bond secured by special tax other than property taxes.

Specie Metallic money such as gold or silver.

Standard & Poor's Corporation A financial service corporation engaged to determine the rating of entities.

Stepped Coupon A serial bond on which the interest rate is changed annually for all outstanding bonds.

Stickering The procedure of changing the information in the official statement of a new issue.

Strip Call Partial redemption of bonds.

Subrogation The process in which a creditor is substituted by another person.

Surety Bond A bond from a surety company by which the replacement of a lost or stolen security is made possible.

Swap A sale of a security and a simultaneous purchase of another.

Syndicate A group of underwriters formed to underwrite a new security.

Syndicate Account Letter The syndicate agreement signed by underwriters for municipal bond underwriting.

Syndicate Is Broken A phrase to indicate the termination of the syndicate group that was formed to underwrite a security.

Takedown The spread between the cost of purchasing the bond from the managing underwriter by the counderwriter and the public offering price.

TAN Tax Anticipation Notes.

Tax Equivalency Yield The interest rate which would be received on a taxable security. It is determined by

$$\frac{\text{Tax exempt rate}}{100 - \text{Tax bracket}}$$

Tax Exempt Bond Municipal bond. Interest is tax exempt under Internal Revenue Code.

Tax Swap The sale of a security at a loss and simultaneous purchase of a similar security.

Term Bond A bond with one date of maturity.

30-Day Visible Supply The total dollar volume of bonds expected to be offered during the next 30 days.

Tombstone Advertisement placed by the underwriters announcing the issuance of a new security.

Total Overall Bonded Debt Also known as Total Direct and Overlapping Debt. The issuer's total direct debt plus the applicable share of the debt of overlapping jurisdictions.

Transit Department The department of a bank where out-of-town bank checks are processed.

Triple-Exempt Bond Bonds issued by U.S. possessions (Guam, Puerto Rico, and the Virgin Islands). These bonds are exempt from federal, state, and local income tax.

True Interest Cost (TIC) The average interest cost in present value terms.

True Lease An operating lease.

Trustee Bank A bank acting on behalf of bondholders.

Underwriting Agreement Syndicate agreement.

Unit Investment Trust An investment company created under a trust agreement. The company sells unit of fixed portfolio of municipal securities to investors.

Unlimited Tax Bond A bond secured by taxes that may be levied in an unlimited rate or amount.

Validation A procedure whereby a mutilated coupon or certificate is validated by the issuer or the trustee.

Variable Rate Bonds Floating Rate Bonds.

Voucher Check The combination of a check representing formal receipt and a check.

Wooden Ticket A confirmation of a fictitious transaction in a customer account.

Yield Curve A graphic illustration of market yields on securities of similar quality but different maturities.

Yield to Call The rate of return on a bond held until called before the maturity date.

Yield-to-Maturity The percentage rate of return on a bond taking into account the market price, the coupon rate, the date of purchase and the date of maturity.

Yield to Option A yield to a call at par.

Yield to Put Option The rate of return on a bond on the assumption that the bondholder will redeem the bond before maturity.

Zero Coupon Bond Bond that pays zero interest to the bondholder but sold at discount from the face value.

INDEX